❖

The Victorian Clown

❖

Jacky Bratton
and Ann Featherstone

❖

CAMBRIDGE
UNIVERSITY PRESS

CAMBRIDGE UNIVERSITY PRESS

Cambridge, New York, Melbourne, Madrid, Cape Town, Singapore, São Paulo

Cambridge University Press
The Edinburgh Building, Cambridge CB2 2RU, UK

Published in the United States of America by Cambridge University Press, New York

www.cambridge.org
Information on this title: www.cambridge.org/9780521816663

First published 2006

Printed in the United Kingdom at the University Press, Cambridge

A catalogue record for this book is available from the British Library

ISBN-13 978-0-521-81666-3 hardback
ISBN-10 0-521-81666-1 hardback

❖

Illustrations

❖

Contents

✣

Dedicated to the memory of Paul Newman, who was sadly killed in a road accident before he could see this book, inspired by the work of his ancestor Tom Lawrence.

The Victorian Clown

The Victorian Clown is a microhistory of mid-Victorian comedy, spun out of the life and work of two professional clowns. Their previously unpublished manuscripts – James Frowde's account of his young life with the famous Hengler's Circus in the 1850s and Thomas Lawrence's 1871 gagbook – offer unique, unmediated access to the grass roots of popular entertainment. Through them this book explores the role of the circus clown at the height of equestrian entertainment in Britain, when the comic managed audience attention for the riders and acrobats, parodying their skills in his own tumbling and contortionism, and also offered a running commentary on the times through his own 'wheezes' – stand-up comedy sets. Plays in the ring connect the circus to the stage, and since both these men were also comic singers, their careers give a sharp insight into popular music just as it was being transformed by the new institution of music hall.

JACKY BRATTON is Professor of Theatre and Cultural History in the Department of Drama and Theatre, Royal Holloway, University of London. She is the author of a number of books and many articles on nineteenth-century culture. Her latest monograph is *New Readings in Theatre History* (Cambridge, 2003), and, with Julie Hankey, she is Joint Series Editor of the Shakespeare in Production series published by Cambridge University Press. She is also a frequent contributor to BBC radio documentaries.

ANN FEATHERSTONE is a Lecturer in the Department of Drama at the University of Manchester and Research Assistant in the Department of Drama and Theatre, Royal Holloway, University of London. Her interests encompass popular entertainment and culture, and she has published on subjects such as pub entertainments, the diary of a Victorian theatregoer in Nottingham, and the portable theatres in *Nineteenth Century Theatre and Film* and *Early Popular Visual Culture.*

✤

Preface

✤

The project on which we are engaged, under the auspices of the Arts and Humanities Research Council, is to map 'an alternative history of the Victorian theatre'. An alternative vision depends not only on new methods and new approaches, but also on new materials for study. The perennial problem that faces commentators, theorists and historians working with texts that are outside the canon is how to share those materials fully and fairly with their readers. Voluminous records survive from the artistic life of the nineteenth century, but only a small proportion of the material that might be utilised in creating our working understanding of that past has been published, even less kept in print. In challenging that selection, and the wisdom based upon it, we have somehow to juggle new suggestions and perceptions against the imperative need to show readers the texts on which we have based our fresh ideas. This volume is primarily intended to share with future readers and analysts some of the materials we are using in our attempt to frame a new approach to the performance culture of the mid-Victorian period. The major part of this book consists of two lengthy manuscripts by two men who worked as clowns; they have never been printed before, and were not written for publication, so they have not so far passed through the process of assimilation to the conventional narrative of Victorian performance history. We have tried to provide enough editorial explication, and prefatory discussion, to suggest their significance as a microhistory of Victorian comic performance; but our efforts are tentative and by no means exhaustive, and we hope that some readers will find their own ways, whether as students and scholars or performers and entertainers, to explore the Victorian clown much further than we have done so far.

❖

Acknowledgements and note on authorship

❖

As is wholly appropriate for a microhistory of an entertainment form in which collaboration is vital, this book is the creation of many hands. Its point of origin is a text by Thomas Lawrence, clown and proprietor of a portable theatre, the manuscript of which was most generously donated to Royal Holloway, University of London by Lawrence's descendant Paul Newman. This unique Victorian clown's gagbook is transcribed here by Jacky Bratton and Ann Featherstone, as are James Frowde's circus recollections. John Turner had pre-viously lodged a photocopy and an initial transcription of this second manuscript at the Theatre Museum in London, and he kindly put us in touch with David Stabb, Frowde's descendant, who lent us the original notebooks and also the sketches of Frowde that we repro-duce. We are very grateful to both of these descendants for permission to reproduce their invaluable materials here. John Turner has written a full account of the Henglers and their circuses, and published two volumes of circus biographies, and we have drawn extensively on his published and unpublished expertise. The introductory materials and many annotations are our joint creation. We have evolved a mode of writing, checking, editing and rewriting that eventually blends the work of our two hands together; and we take joint responsibility for the opinions and decisions it embodies, as well as for all our errors and shortcomings.

Many local librarians and archivists have lent their unstinting assistance: we would like to thank Roger Beacham, Central Library, Cheltenham; the Staff of the Local Studies Library, Central Library, Birmingham; Peter Blake and Paul Jordan, Brighton History Centre,

Brighton; Dr Steven Blake, Museum and Collections Manager, Cheltenham Art Gallery and Museum; Joyce Brown, Local and Naval Studies Librarian, Plymouth; Frances Carlyon, Assistant Keeper, University of Bristol Theatre Collection; Tony Carr, Local Studies Library, Shrewsbury; Heather Coleman; Lucy Cook, Norfolk and Norwich Millennium Library, Norwich; the Staff of the Local Studies Library, Derby; Trish Godfrey, Local Studies Librarian, Dover; Katy Goodrum, Senior Archivist, Cheshire Record Office; Graham Gower, Archivist, Local Studies Library, Lambeth; Eric Hollerton, Local Studies Centre, Central Library, North Shields; Aidan Jones, Area Archivist, Cumbria Record Office and Local Studies Library, Barrow; Hilary Jones, Kidderminster Library Reference Team; Alan King, BA, Dip.Lib., MCLIP, AIL, Historical Collections Librarian, Portsmouth; Mark Lawrence, Senior Librarian, Centre for Oxfordshire Studies, Oxford; Lorraine Mackenzie, Archive Assistant, West Yorkshire Archive Service, Bradford; Eileen Moran, Library and Information Worker, Dundee Library; the Reference Library Staff, Newark Library, Nottinghamshire; the Staff of the Nottinghamshire Archives; Colleen Powell, Local Studies Library, Gloucester; Sue Raistrick, Senior Information Manager, Local Studies Library, Bradford; Sue Rigby, Information Services Librarian, Local Studies, City of York Council; the Staff of the Shropshire Archives, Shrewsbury; the Staff of the Theatre Museum, London; Dr Vanessa Toulmin, Director, National Fairground Archive, Sheffield; Anna Wheeler, York City Archives.

Even more than most writers, we must thank our families and friends, who have exercised great forbearance with our immersion in sometimes rather dubious Victorian jokes; moreover, we have had careful and insightful readers in Jane Traies, Gilli Bush-Bailey and Dennis Featherstone. Vicki Cooper of Cambridge University Press has been extremely generous with editorial help and advice. Finally, we would like gratefully to acknowledge the very substantial financial support of the AHRC, without which this project could not have been carried out.

❖

Editorial practice

❖

James Frowde began to write his memoirs on 21 June 1894, using a foolscap account-book (13 × 8 inches) with 45 leaves (of which 39 are used for the memoirs) that already contained some lists and figures connected with his local concerns and societies ('no. 8 battery 1st Gloucester Artillery Volunteer Corps', among other things) in the back and front. He continued in four other notebooks, the next two similar to each other, both black, measuring 8 × 6½ inches and with 80 leaves; the fourth is covered in red marbled paper and measures 9 × 7 inches with 60 leaves; the fifth is again black, 9 × 7 inches with 60 leaves (of which the final 23 are unused). He wrote in indelible pencil, a faint purple, and in some patches went over his work in black or red ink. He tended to write on the verso, left-hand pages and then sometimes to double back and fill in the rectos, either with additions or with the continuation of the narrative. These practices make it extremely difficult to disentangle a story which is in any case not particularly consecutive. He numbered the pages straight through all the volumes, but the numbers are as often as not confusing rather than helpful, and we have omitted them, sorting the story into chronological order as far as possible and noting our deductions about its dating.

Our selection from the manuscript is intended to include everything that bears in any way upon Frowde's experience as a performer: accounts of his travels, his appearances, his relations with his family (his mother was a Hengler) and fellow-workers, and any incidental comment about theatre or circus life. We have amended the punctuation where this was essential, since there is often none in the original, but have otherwise left the text as Frowde punctuated it as far as possible, however strange it may seem to modern eyes. We have silently corrected the (relatively very few) spelling errors he made, except where there seems some significance in the way he chose to write a word, which we have retained and noted. Large parts of the manuscript, notably his embarrassed accounts of his early courtships and some fluent but unremarkable passages of sermonising, have been left out; omissions are marked with a simple ellipsis, thus '...' There are a few places where we have been unable to decipher a word, which we have marked with '[?]'. To structure the narrative, and to carry the reader through omitted sections of any length, we have used summarising paragraphs differentiated by typeface; but we are conscious that an ideal procedure for this kind of transcription is elusive. We apologise in advance for any irritation our intrusions may cause, and, conversely, for any points where we do not seem to have offered enough explication.

Frowde's scribble was, presumably, intended for later transcription, hence his hurried and complicated procedure, with many corrections and additions. Thomas Lawrence, on the other hand, wrote carefully, fluently and in a clear hand, in a rational and deliberate order; he was making a tool intended for rapid use in dim light before he returned to the ring. The first gagbook, not transcribed here, is full to bursting and has lost its cover; when he began on the second, he copied out materials he was still using, apparently updating them in the process, and crossing them through methodically as he rearranged them in the new book. This later book, which we have transcribed in its entirety, is 8 × 6½ inches, contains 68 leaves, and is not full. He titles and numbers his 'wheezes', starting each on a new page, and he groups short fragments together under headings. Therefore his work presents very little difficulty on the page – except for the enormous effort of translating the bald script into a performance. Lawrence was less formally literate than Frowde, so his spelling is practical rather than orthodox; we have updated it for ease of reading and to avoid a factitiously quaint effect. Where it seems to us that the way he writes makes a point about pronunciation, or suggests how he thought about a word, we have added a note of the original spelling.

❖

Part I

❖

The Victorian circus

❖

Figure 1. James Frowde (1850s?).

1

❖

The Victorian clown

The professional comic exists in a semi-independent relationship to the Western institutions of entertainment. Comics may work with other performers, with writers and with technicians – but they do not need to; all they actually need, to make a living from laughter, is their own materials and skills, and access to audiences. A funny man[1] is not necessarily a team player. His particular ability, and his personal relationship with the audience, make him at best an auxiliary, at worst a loose cannon, in the dramatic theatre. The rewarding and institutionalisation of laughter-making has taken various forms over the centuries in Britain, and the comic performer has been dubbed accordingly – fool, jester, clown, droll, comique, stand-up. The role is not the same as that of actor, which breaks down into tragedian and comedian and perhaps farceur, but is confined within relatively stable, predictable relationships with the audience and the dramatist. The list of the names of the funny man has been constituted as a succession or tradition to be traced, a taxonomy to be established, both outside the theatrical space and as appropriated or recruited into

---

1. The masculine used throughout this introduction is not intended to subsume the feminine, and we are mindful of the heavily gendered nature of the images and concepts under discussion. There were some women playing the clown in the Victorian circus; their work needs examination, but it cannot be approached through the documents we have in hand in this book. Frowde and Lawrence, like the large majority of clowns at the time, were male; we intend therefore to work with the assumption that they are the norm under discussion, without forgetting that such an assumption is ideologically charged and significant. We are discussing funny men.

drama from Shakespeare to Beckett; and the institutional relationships in which it is framed also evolve.

To begin with the relevant item in a taxonomy of comic performance: 'Clown' initially signifies 'rustic booby', a simple man, the reverse of the savvy townsman who is the 'wit', or of the gentleman with cultivated manners and an education. 'The term', as David Wiles has shown, 'does not appear before the Elizabethan period. The word entered the language because it expressed a new concept: the rustic who by virtue of his rusticity is necessarily inferior and ridiculous.' Within the institutional frame, this figure is impersonated by the professional funny man who presents himself as the rude male creature who is the obverse, the underside, of civilisation and beauty, gentility, femininity. Idealisation of the beauty of the human spirit in the drama is overturned in the clown performance, which is associated with the grotesque, with the bodily functions (especially greed), with ugliness and stupidity; he is the butt and also the satire or parody of politeness.

Wiles notes that 'the clown' as a technical playhouse term dates from just after its first introduction in the general sense, and applied to a particular member of the professional acting company for whose individual act spaces were made within the work of the company and of the dramatists writing for the stage. Significantly, 'clown' roles did not occur in the boy players' companies, nor in the plays written for amateurs and university students. 'The clown' was a particular professional, and audiences might well choose which theatre to attend on the strength of their preference for one clown or another, rather than by the play on offer.[2] Wiles goes on to trace the interplay between 'the clown' and the older manifestation of the comic man as 'the fool' in the work of the comic men Tarleton and Kempe and of Shakespeare the dramatist, showing a developing interplay between writer and performers; but 'the clown' was not thereby subsumed into the drama permanently, and at later points – when, for example, a neoclassical aesthetic dominated dramatic theory – he was

2. David Wiles, *Shakespeare's Clown* (Cambridge University Press, 1987), pp. 61, 66, 67.

excluded and excised from Shakespeare's texts and institutionally othered.

But the comic man was still professionally at work, and the clown persona transformed to suit the demands of the time. In the fairground and the strolling or portable booth (arguably more important settings for entertainment than the permanent theatre from the seventeenth century to the nineteenth), he conventionally presented himself as Merry Andrew or Jack Pudding or some other variation on the greedy, amoral, irreverent simpleton. Despite perpetual complaints from critical advocates of artistic purity, the major London stages also always offered physical feats, singing and dancing as well as the drama, and comic men were part of that mix. The importation of *commedia dell'arte* into Britain during the eighteenth century made a further range of comic types available, and the clown began a second dramatic evolution within the institutional setting of the conflict between legitimate and illegitimate drama.[3] Richard Findlater attributes the creative move by which Clown came to be singled out from the other comic servants associated with the harlequinade/*commedia* characters to the personal genius and inspiration of one practitioner, Joseph Grimaldi. He argues that it was Grimaldi who invented the red-on-white makeup and the patchwork of grotesque clothes, as a kind of surreal version of the country servant brought to town and put into an elaborate livery.[4] The clown figure was thus used in the leading theatres (Grimaldi starred both at Sadler's Wells, the ancient popular venue, and the patent houses, especially Drury Lane) to parody the absurdities of Regency/Romantic high fashion and pretension.

Inheriting from Grimaldi (according to conventional teleology), clowns became central to the nineteenth-century development of pantomime. Whether or not the instantly mythologised Grimaldi was the reason, a skilled comic man was often the creative lynchpin of that genre. By now his irreverence, impatience with or refusal to understand romance, and his emphasis upon the grotesquely physical – his persistent tendency to bathos and deflation – no longer necessarily

3. See Maurice Willson Disher, *Clowns and Pantomimes* (London: Constable, 1925), pp. 232–74.

4. See Charles Dickens, *Memoirs of Joseph Grimaldi*, ed. Richard Findlater (London: Macgibbon and Kee, 1968), p. 21.

included a rustic simplicity. The early Victorian clown was often knowing and self-assertive, an ambiguously contained figure who invited audience identification, stepping out of the pretty fiction to refer to real life and to encourage scepticism and rudeness. Throughout the nineteenth century, London theatres might employ a manager/writer, such as Charles Dibdin Jnr, Planche, A'Beckett or Blanchard, to blueprint these major theatrical events, but frequently it was a clown performer – Tom Matthews, Frederick Hartland, Robert Bradbury, Richard Flexmore, or, later, Dan Leno – who invented jokes, organised the comic through-line in his own work and arranged all the trickwork, dancing and slapstick in collaboration with others.

The clown, deriving both from the fairground and the pantomime stage, from Jack Pudding and Joe Grimaldi, was also an important participant in the new nineteenth-century institution of the circus. Circus has recently become the focus of much interest to performance historians, partly because it is not a space of fiction, like the drama, but is about the admiration of bodily skills and extreme physical feats.[5] Developing from the riding school and displays of trick-riding, Victorian circus rapidly added acrobatics and other skills, but its mainstay was equestrianism. Horses were, of course, an important part of everyday culture, and the circus relied upon the audiences' personal interest in horse-flesh, horse management and skills in riding and driving. Much as the petrol engine defines the twentieth century, so the Victorian period was a horse-dominated culture. The circus was built upon admiration of the skill and the muscle of both horses and humans. As the institution developed its formal paradigms in the early nineteenth century, it was the clown's task both to assist and to problematise that admiration. His quite different skills and exaggeratedly unglamorous body and dress acted as distraction from the acrobat and the equestrian, masking illusions and shortcomings, and so challenging but also enabling their pretensions to physical transcendence.

5. See, for example, Yoram S. Carmeli, 'Performing the "Real" and the "Impossible" in the British Traveling Circus', *Semiotica* 80–3/4 (1990), pp. 193–220. Anthony Hippisley-Coxe posits this distinction in 'Equestrian Drama and the Circus' in D. Bradby et al., *Performance and Politics in Popular Drama* (Cambridge University Press, 1980), pp. 109–18.

In the ring as on the stage, the nineteenth-century clown was arranger of tricks and manager of audience attention; a tongue-in-cheek admirer, or an outright parodist, of dangerous and skilful spectacles, who worked from his personal relationship with the audience and their expectations, using not only slapstick, but backchat, elaborate monologues, inventive costumes, new and traditional songs and many kinds of reference to the real world beyond. He worked with the other performers, and mediated their feats fluently, and also safely, to the audience sitting close around.[6] Later circus practice made the 'clown entrée' – a group of men rushing into the ring for a slapstick routine with zany costumes and giant props – the main clown performance, but this was not the case in the early and mid-nineteenth century.

Our microhistory of the Victorian clown is built on two examples. Thomas Lawrence and James Frowde worked as circus clowns in the middle decades of the century, between 1845 and 1875, performing alone or interacting with the physical performers or the ringmaster. Both were descended from performing families. Lawrence worked as a clown in many circuses but came from, and returned to, the portable theatre. Frowde took comic roles in the dramas that were a regular part of the Hengler's Circus entertainments, working as an actor, though he notes, significantly, that he

---

6. Professor David Mayer, a senior theatre historian, reminds us of the analogy with the modern American rodeo, where the clown's task first task is to ensure safety. The Victorian clown, too, had to know about the possibilities of riding accidents, 'how to prevent them, what jokes to make if the rider mis-times a trick but isn't hurt, what to do to distract the crowd when a rider comes off and may be injured, what to do if a horse is frightened and/or has a hump in its back and may bolt into the audience. Yes, the clown is in the ring to be funny, but the clown is also there to read a horse's eyes and ears and head position, to make certain that a horse continues to canter and doesn't slow down to the point where the rider loses the benefit of the centrifugal force which is helping her/him to remain on the horse's back. The clown knows when to grab a horse's head or tail and slow it (exaggeratingly dragging his feet or bumping along on his bottom at the horse's heels) or to lead it into the centre of the ring. There will be imbecile/drunk/adolescent/stupid spectators who think it a jape to spook a horse. The clown doesn't have to be a horseman himself, but he has to know what can go wrong and to anticipate trouble before it happens and gets out of hand ... the rodeo clown always has his eye on the animals and, knowing the dangers the performers/riders/ropers/doggers face, is present and alert to the dangers.' Private communication, February 2005.

hated to learn his lines, and often suffered excruciating stage fright in these performances. He was happiest working his own material. He began as clown to Jim Ryan Jnr, who was a juggler; his function was to 'do some tricks' to give his principal rests and breaks, taking the focus from him when necessary, and ensuring that the performance was continuous, without breaks or silences in which audience attention might stray. On Hengler's bills the listing of turns often names the act and then below, in smaller print, adds 'clown: …' and names the assistant who is 'clown to the rope' or 'clown to the horse'. Lawrence's extraordinarily surviving ring material includes many snippets which could be used in this way, and also longer set pieces, called 'wheezes', which he records with linking material – a comment on the departing performer, an aside to the ringmaster – which make clear that he then had a slot of his own and could work through a longer routine or sing a song.

In his memoir Frowde stresses the physical grace of his Hengler relations, who ride, dance on ropes and even play Romeo or Hamlet, while he himself is lanky, pop-eyed and unkempt: intelligently, he chose to make his unpromising body a parody of their perfections. His act soon grew to include grotesque characters – the Red Man of the Ajax Mountains, for example – and work as a contortionist and comic equilibrist. Eventually he found his route to stardom via his physical oddity, and also by exploiting his voice and his wits, singing comic songs in character, including the improvisation of topical additional verses night by night. The songs that both men record are drawn from the newly expanding genre of the comic song which was, at the time they were performing, becoming the foundation of another new entertainment institution, the music hall.

In attempting to consider all this clowning, it is vital to see the setting, as well as the performances, as a continuum. Both these comics acted in plays. Frowde's account of his singing, and Lawrence's repertoire of songs, add significantly to our understanding of the roots of popular music and music hall song. Clowning itself was multilayered: there came to be a recognised distinction, which emerges in mid-nineteenth-century circus reviews, between grotesque or tumbling clowns and talking clowns, sometimes called 'Shakespearean', who were expected to say clever things and dressed in pseudo-archaic liveries suggestive of cap and bells. On the dramatic

Figure 2. James Frowde in costume for a character song, not mentioned in the memoirs. The poster attached to the railings reads 'W. Button, Tailor'.

stage the Romantic pantomime evolved rapidly, and by the 1850s the harlequinade, in which Grimaldi had made Clown the leading participant, was marginalised in favour of large-scale spectacle and an increasing inclination to tailor the show for children at Christmas by basing it on nursery and moral fables. But the comic man was never excluded, and the music hall comedians and circus trick-acrobats brought their clowning into these extravaganzas – accompanied by the everlasting complaints about innovation and debasement which can be regarded as the authenticating critical response to popular entertainment.

The institutional frame had, of course, a significant hierarchy of pay and esteem. Most performers insist upon the respectability and superiority of their particular rung of the ladder. When Henry Mayhew interviewed entertainers for his survey of the London poor, he spoke to a 'penny-gaff clown', who 'appeared not a little anxious to uphold the dignity of the penny theatre' for which he had written ballets and pantomimes, and who wished to make clear the superiority of playing to a seated audience of a thousand at the unlicensed Rotunda in the Blackfriars Road to the 'canvas clown's' act delivered from the parade outside the booth in a fairground. Mayhew's humblest informant was a 'street' clown, who hated his own work, but even he had the pride of the professional, having started as a supernumerary at Astley's. He knew enough old jokes to 'fill a volume' and felt that his profession was ruined by 'the stragglers or outsiders' who clown only at holiday times and 'are not pantomimists by profession'.[7] At the other end of the hierarchy were such men as Tom Matthews in the pantomime theatre of the 1840s, Tom Barry Snr in the circus in the 1850s, Dan Leno in the 1890s music halls; but it was still all one scale. The successful comic man could work in the ring, the halls, the pantomime; he went wherever space and pay was best. One of the most important understandings we glean from attending to the particularity of these two clown histories, located in a particular institutional moment, is that in a dynamic performance world our attempts to compartmentalise and hierarchise performance

7. Peter Quennell (ed.), *Mayhew's London* (London: Spring Books, 1969), pp. 497–8.

are confused and unhelpful. The contextual information that follows here, therefore, offers a description intended to break through received boundaries in our historiography, without ignoring the delicate web that put every element of Victorian entertainment in its place.

2

✣

Victorian travelling shows

Circus, as a formal institution, was created by Philip Astley around the turn of the nineteenth century, and by the middle of the century more than twenty circus companies were performing across England each summer season. Its architectural structure was based upon the 42 foot (13 metre) circle, within which a core of equestrian acts appeared in turn, supported by other physical skills (especially acrobatics), animal trainers and the ubiquitous clowns. The larger circus proprietors, like Frowde's relations the Henglers, regarded themselves as distinct from the mass of vulgar entertainers, and unimpeachably respectable;[8] but the circus was part of a much larger travelling body of shows, and could not really escape that rich and diverse kinship. From earliest times the exhibitors of monstrosities, quack doctors, peepshow men, mummers, acrobats and animal trainers displayed their entertainments around the country; but it was during the nineteenth century that the shows which temporarily occupied a field or a corner of the market square in villages, towns and cities became significant as institutions of popular entertainment. Although their documentary invisibility has tended to render them at best marginal in recent accounts of performance history, the evidence of their sheer numbers and the regularity with which towns and villages, both urban and rural, were visited during the nineteenth century suggests that here was popular entertainment at its most prolific and accessible.

8. See Brenda Assael, 'The Circus and Respectable Society in Victorian Britain', (PhD thesis, University of Toronto, 1998).

Animals

The nearest rival of the circus, both in size and respectability, was the menagerie. From the start, circus itself included trained animals in its programme. Dogs and donkeys (which were easily trained) and cats (which were not), accompanied the clowns in the ring, and lions, bears and elephants provided more exotic and dangerous entertainment. But outside the circus, mobile zoos[9] were the largest of the travelling shows, transporting their collections of animals in cages drawn by horses, and accompanied, as in the circus, by brass and woodwind bands, who travelled in purpose-built ornate band carriages. When they came to rest, the cage-wagons, containing exotic animals from lions and wolves to porcupines and parrots, formed a square or semicircle, around which the spectators would move, visiting each cage in turn. In the menageries animal taming took place within the cages of lions or tigers,[10] and tamers such as Maccomo, 'the African Lion King' and the elegant 'Delmonico' were hugely popular (and frequently injured) in their extremely dangerous acts. Their careers often encompassed both menageries and circuses.

In fact, the crossover between circus performance and menagerie exhibition is blurred, as is clear from the sensational court appearance by a four-year-old boy ('a little sprightly fellow, and dressed in Highland fashion') from Day's Menagerie whose performance (objected to by a group of reverend gentlemen) involved being shut with the lions in their cage and 'included . . . riding on the lions' backs and finished by his allowing the beasts to lick or kiss his face'.[11] The sensational nature of the show, the boy's costume (which suggests vulnerability and even a Celtic 'otherness', with overtones of Barnum's General Tom Thumb, who also wore Highland dress), the

9. Bostock and Wombwell's, Day's Crystal Palace Menagerie, Edmonds's (late Wombwell's) Royal Windsor Castle and Crystal Palace Menagerie, Manders' Grand National Star Menagerie, Stevens's Balmoral Castle Menagerie, Whittington's National Star Menagerie and, Wombwell's No. 1 Menagerie were all operational during the mid-century. John Sanger's Circus and Hippodrome also included a Menagerie.

10. The ring cage was not in use in the travelling circus until the 1890s. As in the menageries, a transportable cage-wagon was drawn into the ring and the animal trainer worked with his beasts in quite close confinement.

11. *Era*, 21 October 1866.

implicit danger, the attractive and vulnerable protagonist, the narrative, however flimsy: all these were circus elements replicated in this (and other) acts of animal training in menageries. In theory, however, menageries promoted an essentially rational and scientific exhibition, while circuses were all skill and amusement. Menageries were in lieu of zoological gardens, as the Provincial Correspondent for the trade newspaper the *Era* noted of Wombwell's Royal Menagerie visiting West Hartlepool: 'The number of rare animals it includes is surprising in a travelling collection, and it is an important advantage to those whose means or occupations render a visit to London almost impossible.'[12]

Smaller tent shows such as Mullett's, Tanner's or John Chittock's Dog and Monkey Circus featured another hybrid of performance and exhibition: monkeys which rode on the backs of the dogs in a parodic horserace. They were also to be found as acts within larger circus programmes, but as single-handed shows they offered the smaller proprietor a living, though they were frequently attached to menageries, such as Blight's Dogs and Monkeys Show which travelled with Wombwell's Royal Menagerie. Less flamboyant were the animal shows in which caged domestic animals were exhibited or displayed – dogs and goats, badgers and so-called 'happy families' of cats and birds.

Like the circuses, travelling animal shows were not confined to the round of fairs and feasts, though the great agglomerations of fairs around the country often gave a focus to showmen's itineraries. For example, in 1871 Day's Crystal Palace Menagerie was heading towards Manchester and its Easter Knott Mill Fair (commencing Monday, April 10th) from the beginning of March. Its steady progress from Blackdimond in North Wales, took in Chester, Frodsham, Warrington and Earlestown over three weeks. Clearly the enormous size of establishments such as Day's and Mander's made visiting small villages uneconomic, and even towns such as Frodsham risky:[13]

12. *Era*, 1 December 1867.

13. This particular stopover may have been purely expedient – a suitable point between Chester and Warrington, offering accommodation and a sympathetic local audience. Nevertheless, menageries such as Edmonds's could occupy an entire market place with its huge caravans and portable 'dens', and if a big enough site could not be secured, the advance agent was forced to look elsewhere.

though they might be *portable*, they were not necessarily easily *trans-portable*. Menagerie wagons were heavy and cumbersome; horses became tired. Poor roads or weather caused delays. However, the menagerie's itinerary differed from that of the circus not entirely for reasons of portability, but also owing to the audiences. Day's three-week itinerary seems modest in comparison with a week in the life of Powell, Foottit and Clarke's Great Allied Circus (the tenting circus to which Lawrence belonged), in March 1868: Monday 23rd, Ilkeston; Tuesday 24th, Belper; Wednesday 25th, Worksop; Thursday 26th, Ashbourne; Friday 27th, Uttoxeter; Saturday 28th, Rugby. They travelled around 155 miles over six days, the greatest distance being the 55 miles between Uttoxeter and Rugby.[14] Circuses were impelled to move to a new town on a daily basis, appealing for a new audience each day, an indication that audiences read menageries and circuses in quite different ways.

One might argue that circus and menagerie offered audiences quite different entertainments. The circus programme of equestrian acts, acrobatics and clowning had limited variations over the course of a season. The core programme remained the same, with changes in the personnel as speciality acts came and went. This is clear from a range of advertisements placed in the trade paper the *Era*: the following is typical:

> Wanted, at Pinders' Circus, Nottingham, for present and future dates, first-class talent in all branches of the equestrian and gymnastic profession, including sensation novelties.
> A good knock-about clown can have a constant situation.
> One preferred that don't expectorate every five minutes on the Ring Carpet.[15]

If the same (or similar) programme was presented at every performance, the entertainment encouraged only a single visit.[16] Where

14. *Era*, 22 March 1868.

15. *Era*, 15 January 1871.

16. This would also account for the strenuous efforts made by the clowns – Frowde and Lawrence – to be topical and novel. The grumble that the clowns' material was old generated the clown Charles Keith's riposte that 'if a few impromptu jests are indulged in, they are not always believed in to be such, consequently many stick to the old

circuses stayed on permanent sites they made efforts to vary their programmes, presumably because they had the leisure to practise and rehearse, with the possibility of engaging a changing selection of novelty acts.

The menagerie, on the other hand, whether fixed or on the road, was an attraction at a much slower pace. Visitors might make multiple visits on the understanding that they would, if they were fortunate, see something different: the creatures might be feeding, nursing their young, fighting. Wombwell's No 1. Menagerie, at Barnard Castle, had a wide variety of lions, leopards, bears and panthers plus a tiger, plus 'monkeys and exotic birds [which] drew the customary attention of the ladies and the juveniles'.[17] There was, in effect, something for everyone to look at and in which they might take an ongoing, even an intellectual, interest. But, as its programme and its many descriptions suggest, the circus appealed to the senses: the music of the band, the scent of the sawdust and the horses, the glow of the paraffin lights and the brilliance of the spangled costumes. It was the domain of the extraordinary – feats of strength and skill, wild animals tamed, ordinary human beings transformed into sublime sylphs on horseback or ridiculous painted fools in the sawdust. The circus was a feast of spectacle and skill; but its otherness, its magic, did not necessarily survive frequent repetition. It was better to remember the special moment, and perhaps seek to reinvoke the spell next year.

The fairs

Itinerant shows, arriving at random moments, taking possession of the market place, waste ground or farmer's field, presented an opportunity for the population to indulge in the essentially urban exotic and carnivalesque. The shows which travelled with their own portable premises transformed the landscape of a small Welsh or Yorkshire mining village. Their flamboyant presence – colourful booth

material, which they find pleases best'. See Charles Keith, *Circus Life and Amusements* (Derby: Bewley & Roe, 1879), p. 136.

17. *Era*, 2 September 1866.

canvases, highly decorated showfronts, paintings which advertised the exhibits within – and, particularly for the larger shows, their dramatic entrance into a town, challenged the cultural as well as the geographical landscape: as a Derbyshire journalist had it in 1905, 'The Market place, so staid and respectable in ordinary times, is now invaded by showmen. Here like a mushroom, there springs up in a single night a miniature city of side shows, wooden shacks, round-abouts and dirty canvas.'[18] He was describing not a single show, but the recurrence of one of the local fairs which, despite many repressive new regulations, persisted across Victorian England. The fair offered the chance for the annual transformation of the ordinary, and it was at the great fairs – Barnet Fair, Birmingham Onion Fair, Manchester's Knott Mill Fair – that the individual components of the travelling exhibition culture could be experienced *en masse*. Travelling shows of all kinds stood shoulder to shoulder in market places and on feast grounds. The more refined visitors to Hengler's or Cooke's circuses might regard fairs as abominations, making a distinction (often unspoken) between what was regarded as the legitimate demonstra-tion of skill in the circus and the perceived trickery of fairground exhibitions.[19] For them, the circus was, despite its superficial simila-rities, an altogether more respectable entertainment. Nevertheless, a large proportion of the population looked forward to the annual feast, the season of carnival excess. By the mid-nineteenth century, the industry of travelling entertainment was well established in both town and country, despite the efforts of 'rational recreationalists' to prohibit fairs and feasts.

For a limited time towns and cities like Lichfield and Nottingham were transformed, not just by the arrival of the showmen and their caravans, but by a great influx of the population of neigh-bouring towns and cities. Railway links made day excursions feasible

18. *High Peak News*, 8 July 1905, p. 8, quoted in Vanessa Toulmin, *Pleasurelands: All the Fun of the Fair* (Sheffield: National Fairground Archive, University of Sheffield, 2003), p. 13.

19. The eighteen-year-old Sydney Race, a respectable clerk visiting Croueste's Circus with his pal Will, found it 'crowded in every part & an admirable and dashing performance' (Sydney Race Diaries, Nottinghamshire Archives M24, 480/A/2).

to Hull or Nottingham specifically to enjoy the annual October fairs.[20] And Victorian fairs were neither the old annual markets nor the predominantly interactive experiences of rides and games that they have become. Shows of all kinds dominated: exhibitions of skill and strength vied with human monstrosities and out-and-out illusion. As the great showman Tom Norman wrote, 'You could indeed exhibit anything in those days. Yes, anything from a needle to an anchor, a flea to an elephant, a bloater you could exhibit as a whale. It was not the show it was the tale you told.'[21]

The culture of spectacle and exhibition, to which the circus undoubtedly belonged, was a powerful one. An inventory of shows at the late nineteenth-century Goose Fair in Nottingham made by Sydney Race, a local man, illustrates the variety of travelling amusements gathered in the Great Market Square for the three-day festivities in early October 1895:

1. Wombwell's (in its old place) [menagerie]
2. Burnett's (opposite St James' Street) [military display]
3. The Mystic Swing
4. Kemps Midgets
5. Buckleys performing birds etc
6. Radford & Chappell's Ghost
7. Amyes Mechanical Exhibition
8. Second Sight Show
9. Coxwain Terry's Crocodile
10. Ball's Midgets
11. Diver's and Naval Exhibition
12. Williams' Fine Art Exhibition (joining up the Avenue)
13. Johnsons Circus
14. Wadbrooks Ghost
15. Sedgewicks Menagerie
16. Norman's Varieties (top of avenue)

---

20. The great fair at Hull was held in the week preceding Nottingham's Goose Fair.

21. Tom Norman, *The Penny Showman: Memoirs of Tom Norman 'Silver King'*. Full unedited manuscript in the Norman Family Collection in the National Fairground Archive, University of Sheffield. Quoted in Toulmin, *Pleasurelands*, p. 46.

17. Marionette Exhibition (facing Long Row)
18. Walls Ghost[22]

Victorian shops, shows, fit-ups and voyeurism

The listing above of the Goose Fair shows offers a perspective on the nineteenth-century taste for the visual which privileges the enjoyment taken in the activity of 'looking'; Race demonstrates the diversity of shows which required nothing more of a visitor than that he or she should *look*: at original copies of 'old masters', at models or mechanical exhibitions, at ghosts created with mirrors or waxwork shows where contemporary celebrities stood cheek-by-waxen-jowl with historical figures: Napoleon, Dan O'Connell, John Bright, the late Prince Consort, the Prince and Princess of Wales, Oliver Cromwell and General Tom Thumb.[23] Like the circus, these inanimate shows, operating within precarious economic parameters, needed to attract as many spectators as possible, since most visitors would pay only a single visit. The difficulty was inducing spectators to pay their penny. The circus relied on a spectacular entrance into a town; 'all the auxiliaries that can be pressed into service, in their gayest character-dresses, preceded by the band, and accompanied by the den of lions', often attracting and bringing with them an audience for the afternoon performance.[24] Bands on the outside 'parade' of travelling shows on the fairground worked hard to compete with other shows and bands to entice spectators, and showmen often went to great lengths to find novelty attractions: 'Wanted, to travel with Purchase's North British Waxwork, four respectable men to play the scotch bagpipes. Must dress in Kilts when the Collection is open.'[25]

22. Nottinghamshire Archives reference M24, 480/A/10, text reproduced in Ann Featherstone, ' "Goose Fair is with us once more T/J" – The Journals of Sydney Race, a Nottingham Lad,' *Nineteenth Century Theatre* 28 (Winter 2000), pp. 161–95.

23. *Era*, 28 May 1887. For extensive discussion of Victorian scopophilia, see Martin Meizel, *Realizations* (Princeton, NJ: Princeton University Press, 1983).

24. Peter Paterson, *Glimpses of Real Life as seen in the Theatrical World and in Bohemia: Being the Confessions of Peter Paterson, a Strolling Comedian.* (Edinburgh: William P. Nimmo, 1864), p. 143. The memoirs of 'Peter Paterson' are an entertaining peregrination through the worlds of the stroller, booth player and circus performer of the first half of the nineteenth century.

25. *Era*, 8 March 1874.

Circus operated in this cultural mix of fairground and theatre. 'Peter Paterson' observed that circus 'worked entirely on the sensation plan';[26] 'sensationalism' permeated the show culture. Living and inanimate exhibits often shared the same exhibition space, moving between fairground booth and a room in a public house or an empty shop. Public houses kept their own museums, the landlord's personal 'cabinet of curiosities', to amuse and attract the local clientele. Added revenue might be gained from renting out a room to the proprietor of a freak exhibition, such as Madame Hartley, the Armless Lady exhibited in the front room of a public house on the corner of Queen Street, Nottingham, the Scottish Giantess who could be seen at the Howard Arms in Glossop, or the English Giant Youth, who stood 'in the bar' of the White Swan in London's Mile End Road.[27]

But mere monstrosity was not enough. Exhibits, whether animal or human, live or dead, were advertised by extraordinary 'puffery': 'the Ugliest Woman in the World', 'the Smallest Horse' and 'the Missing Link', in the same way that some circus performers were now 'startling novelties'. Paterson notes the pressure within the circus to be 'the modern Hercules', 'the wonder of creation', and within this sensational trap (to attract and retain audiences), to perform increasingly dangerous tricks. He cites the equestrian who, in order to draw a large audience for his benefit, announced that he would turn three somersaults in the air. On the night, having turned only two and a half somersaults and landed on his head, he died.[28]

The portable theatres

If the circus and the menagerie strove for a rational superiority over the lesser exhibitions on the road, they were kept in their place by the superior artistic claims of the portable and, especially, the fit-up theatres. The 'fit-ups', developing from the eighteenth-century strolling players, were theatrical companies who carried with them a portable proscenium and costumes, and who took a hall (in previous

26. Paterson, *Glimpses of Real Life*, p. 136.

27. Nottinghamshire Archives reference M24, 480/A/13 in Featherstone, 'Goose Fair'; *Era*, 24 September 1865; *Era*, 24 December 1865.

28. Paterson, *Glimpses of Real Life*, p. 140.

times a barn might have served) for a few nights and performed standard dramas until their repertoire was exhausted and 'the houses dwindle away'.[29] Portable theatres were distinctive in that the theatre itself was carried from town to town, upon wagons. Often a much larger enterprise, the portable theatres came into existence in the 1830s and finally disappeared only after the First World War. Their residence in fields and pub yards was frequently much longer than that of the fit-up companies: licences could be had for up to three months, and their semipermanency often rendered them part of the local community. The exoticism of the theatrical might be tempered by seeing the leading man buying fish or ordering a glass of beer, or by the involvement of locals in the performance, as a writer from Yorkshire remembered:

> I think one of the reasons why they [the portable theatre
> company] were so popular was that one of the actors was a
> local lad, and he used to get some of the other locals, men and
> women, sometimes children as well, to act as members of a
> crowd (supers) in some of the plays. I was a member of the
> choir at All Souls Church at the time, and one of the actors
> recruited about a dozen of us boys to appear on the stage
> and sing, but directly my mother heard about this she put
> paid to any public appearance on my part, as she was rather
> strait-laced. But I did envy those other boys, especially when
> the proprietor gave them 3d each and a free pass for the
> Saturday matinee.[30]

Frowde's account of his clowning life makes clear the rival claims of the sawdust-men and the mummers to artistic superiority; and he too found ways of partially integrating himself – as a small celebrity – into communities where the circus stayed long enough.

29. Paterson, *Glimpses of Real Life*, p. 7.   30. *World's Fair*, 7 September 1957.

3

✣

Circus buildings

Established circus companies, while they maintained their glamorous otherness within the communities they visited, were also vitally embedded in them, not least because they had the chance of long stays over winter, when they occupied purpose-built wooden or even brick premises. Frowde's account makes clear the structure of feeling within which each circus related to its two communities; that is, to the nationwide network of performers, and to the places where it put up. His narrative returns to these two focal points: his people and his places. People are vital to his security and feeling of belonging, on the one hand reminding him of the wider family of entertainers to which he belongs – the actors, music hall entertainers, managers and direc-tors, as well as circus performers – and on the other, the 'jossers'[31] who punctuate his life with incidents of relative normality – getting drunk with the naval officers in Portsmouth, first-footing in Bradford, attending church in Derby. The litany of town and village, of theatre and circus building, is also vitally important in his memories; he writes not about the performance (except to extol the excellence of others)

31. 'Josser': 'A circus word for outsider', according to Nell Stroud in *Josser: The Secret Life of a Circus Girl* (London: Virago, 2000), p. 10. She makes the important point that 'the boundary between the josser and the legitimate – that is, born and bred – circus person, is permanent. You can't step over that divide and claim the place that blood ties would have granted.' Frowde struggles with this 'divide' constantly, and the maternal Hengler bloodties are not enough to give him absolute legitimacy in his uncles' business. Hence, perhaps, the cruel and bullying treatment he constantly receives. On the other hand, he associates with jossers readily, which suggests that there was something in his bearing or speech which bridged the otherness of the circus performer, and rendered him sociable and popular.

but about the towns visited – 'Business was very bad. Always is in Leicester' – and the spaces in which they performed – 'At night we arrived at Leicester Amphitheatre.'[32] He offers a sometimes detailed insight into the travail of reaching the destination, the rigours, the miles covered, the hardship endured, the sense of ownership of this wandering life.

This preoccupation with the detail of routes and locations is more than a collection of topographical points in a picaresque memoir. Lawrence scrupulously annotates his notebook entries with people and places: 'Given to me by Mr Coleman, equestrian, Footit's Circus Liverpool, November 21/71.' Frowde's attention to precise location, even to the field or building, is essential to his recall: it is the permanent marker in any itinerant life: 'Newcastle was our next town. *We stood by the railway station and market*' (our italics).[33] Further, Frowde often recalls the actual building in which the circus performed: 'Our next winter town was Plymouth, at the Theatre Royal. I always enjoyed playing from the stage' (1854) or 'We arrived at Cheltenham and occupied a cirque built by a Mr Blizard' (1855).[34]

The importance of the performance space for travelling shows is often underestimated. In economic terms, the site or pitch of a booth or show at a fair or feast might be crucial to the showman's livelihood; 'Lord' George Sanger's account of the (literal) race for the best pitches at Henley Fair, and the battle which ensued on the Oxford Road between rival shows, illustrates the intense rivalry this aroused.[35] Frowde records the difficulty of following another show into a town: 'West Bromwich was not a fortune. We were opposed by one of Batty's companies [a rival circus] under the management of a

32. See pp. 54, 53. Of course, Frowde is by no means alone in this; very many of the autobiographies of travelling performers record in detail the itinerary of places visited. See, for example, Samuel Wild, *The Original, Complete and Only Authentic Story of Old Wild's*, ed. 'Trim' (1888; reprinted London: Society for Theatre Research, 1989); Jack Le White and Peter Ford, *Rings and Curtains: Family and Personal Memoirs* (London: Quartet Books, 1992); Walter Haggar, 'Recollections', in *Dock Leaves* (1953), pp. 8–22.

33. See p. 86. Compare, for example, Sam Wild's recollection of a portable theatre in 1841: 'I think it was during our first season at Bradford that Parrish came to the town, and erected his establishment in the Hall Ings, and facing to Leeds Road', (*Old Wild's*), p. 56.

34. See pp. 119, 127.

35. See 'Lord' George Sanger, *Seventy Years a Showman* (London: J. M. Dent, 1926), pp. 44–7.

Mr Thomson and we gave them best. We had a better run after the tents had gone.'[36]

Currently, showmen are allocated positions or hold a right to a particular site, all in advance. Showman Roger Tuby explains:

> We have a plan of where everything is going, we mark it out the day before. Each ride will have a mark where the centre of the ride will go, and we'll just say 'that's your centre' and then it's over to him and he puts his ride on his centre and just starts to erect it . . . There are certain rides that don't go together, one will take a lot of money and the other one will take nothing because that ride is too similar to that one or it's a bit better than that one. So you have to get the rides that suit each other at the side of each other.[37]

This modern perception of site and location reflects in many ways Frowde's recollections 160 years previously. For Roger Tuby, the siting of a ride is more than mere organisation; it is not, as he tellingly notes elsewhere, 'chaos', but a process requiring definition and exactness: he details the 'centring' of a ride – the point of control, as it were. In an itinerant life the certainty of place and site, the familiarity of the destination, have enormous importance. To the adolescent Frowde, the circus was his home and his family, and he is understandably (and literally) possessive in writing about it: '*Our* circus was built on King Charles Croft' and '*Our* circus was built in the market, near to [the] lane at the bottom of which was the Theatre' (our italics).[38] He is not alone here: one of Lawrence's pieces begins, 'Don't you think *our* circus has a very strange appearance this evening?'[39] Emotional energy is invested in the tent or the temporary wooden circus building.

Circuses today are associated with the canvas 'Big Top' tent, only a very limited number of shows locating in permanent buildings, such as the Tower Circus at Blackpool. During the nineteenth century, there was a shifting division between tenting circuses, those which predominantly moved between permanent or semipermanent

36. See p. 63.

37. Quoted in Toulmin, *Pleasurelands*, p. 64.

38. See pp. 58, 99.

39. See p. 172.

buildings, and those which utilised both. During the tenting season, which ran from 1 May[40] until the onset of autumn and wet weather, circus companies transported their circular canvas tent or pavilion, the entire company and animals to prearranged sites around the country. The tent was generally about 120 feet in diameter, supported by ropes, stakes and poles, and capable of holding anything from one thousand to seven thousand people. Advances in tent technology were few,[41] and the daily work of putting up and pulling down the tent in order to move on to the next town was a significant task. The *Era* carried regular advertisements for tentmasters,[42] the coordinating and supervisory element in the process. Tent men might also be recruited in this way,[43] but cheaper, if inexperienced, local labour might be used. The wear and tear on the tent canvas, supports and seating involved ongoing expenses. Poor weather might affect not only the movement of the wagons and coaches which transported the circus, but the actual performance itself. Charles Keith recalled the misery of performing in a wet tent:

> The ring ankle-deep in water; the riders, instead of gaily tripping in on foot, carried in on the backs of the horses or grooms; the clowns throwing flip-flaps in top boots, and splashing the people; being forced to dress under this soaking wet tent, with the canvas flapping against your skin before you have half got your tights on.[44]

40. Other sources claim April until October; see Paterson, *Glimpses of Real Life*, p. 141.

41. Frowde's reference to Jno. Hengler's tent innovation is tantalising, and never fully explained: 'The Govr. was experimenting in the making of a tent. He and O'Hara had their hands full. We used to go from Lewes to a small place 3 days a week and perform under canvas. It was very cold and evil and the new tent was soon deserted' (p. 74).

42. 'Wanted, tentmaster. Must be a sober man; no wife with him. A character required. Apply John Swallow, Chorley, Lancashire, Monday Tuesday and Wednesday, next' (*Era*, 21 April 1867).

43. 'Mons Maus' Circus, Dudley, Worcestershire. Wanted, immediately, four tent men. None need apply only those used to the business, strictly sober, and peaceable for the company. Never remove only once a week. Address the Proprietor' (*Era*, 7 May 1865).

44. David Fitzroy, *Charles Keith: The Roving English Clown* (Privately printed, 1998), p. 18.

There is some evidence that the tent – economically risky (unpredictable variations in ground rents, and the tent itself requiring constant, often expensive, upkeep) and logistically trying (single-day visits to individual towns, the unreliability of tenting personnel) – was becoming less popular as the century progressed. More circus companies performed instead in permanent or semi-permanent buildings.[45] Frowde's narrative locates Hengler's Circus in various such buildings around the country. Ordinary theatres, such as the Theatre Royal in Birmingham or Plymouth, seem to have given them no great difficulty, though an equestrian director might be engaged to deal with exigencies of dramatic staging. Frowde himself appears to have relished playing from a stage; at Plymouth he says that he enjoys having an audience 'before instead of surrounding you'.[46]

There were also many purpose-built circuses, though: from the 1850s temporary circus buildings, as opposed to tents, were a common feature on unoccupied ground in industrial towns and cities, proprietors taking advantage of a town-centre site and audience. They were built of wood, often with a corrugated-iron roof, and erected, occupied and then sublet by circus proprietors, or by enterprising local builders. Hengler's took, for instance, Cooke's Circus in Plymouth, and Pablo Fanque's Circus in Leeds in 1848 was originally built by the Henglers the year before, and sold on or sublet. The extant plans and descriptions for wooden circuses suggest that the Henglers adhered to a design which replicated their circular tent[47] – a circular building, with a gallery over the orchestra and stables, and tiered seating elsewhere, with the classes clearly kept apart. There were separate entrances for gallery, boxes and pit, and a smoking promenade was advertised as a feature of the building, a male habitat like the promenades in theatres and later music halls. Big cities were provided with relatively grand, brick-built edifices as the century progressed: even allowing for puffery, the 1855 Cheltenham circus, for example, was probably a substantial building:

45. See Assael, 'The Circus and Respectable Society', Appendix, for numbers of circuses on the road.

46. See p. 119.

47. George Speaight, *A History of the Circus* (London: Tantivy Press, 1980), p. 43, noting the lack of evidence for the widespread use of tents, suggests that it is more accurate to say that circus buildings imitated the circular shape of a pavilion.

The magnificent Edifice, erected by Mr Blizard for the reception of this celebrated Company, will be found a most unique Structure, capable of seating 1,500 Persons, and fitted up in a costly style, with every attention for the comfort of Visitors. The Building, being circular, affords an uninterrupted view from every part in the vast space. The First Class Compartment will be carpetted [sic] throughout, and cushioned chairs, of unique design, with ample room allotted for each. The Second Class and Gallery are set apart with commodious seating, and general view of the whole Building. A spacious PROMENADE, 200 feet in length, will be found a delightful Lounge.[48]

Despite this final claim for the promenade as 'Lounge', neither tenting nor permanent circus premises emphasised provision for entertainment *away from* spectatorship of the show. Circulation spaces on the plans are minimal and utilitarian, without saloons or bars (see Figure 3). As a lad, Frowde sold pies from a basket to the audience, and no doubt some brought in their own drinks; but the circuses cultivated a reputation for respectability, and did not cater for either drinking or the sex trade, avoiding grounds on which theatres and music halls were still attacked. Thus their spectatorial entertainments were offered as superior not only to the fairground on which they sometimes stood, but even to the theatres with which they vied.

It was partly the threat that theatre managements perceived in this upstart contender for respectable audiences that fuelled attempts to prevent the circus from offering dramas. Hengler's did not include a stage in their design, though they consistently offered dramatic pieces as part – often the climax – of their show. A hybrid theatre-circus building style, the amphitheatre, had existed since the early years of the century (and probably, at that stage, had a more theatre-like provision of circulation spaces). Astley's Halfpenny Hatch amphitheatre made permanent a site which had at first a movable stage on trestles in the ring. Then a permanent stage end-on to the ring, complete with scenery and lighting, was set up, rebuilt in grander style, and eventually joined to the sawdust by ramps to enable a free

48. *The Cheltenham Looker-On*, 27 October 1855.

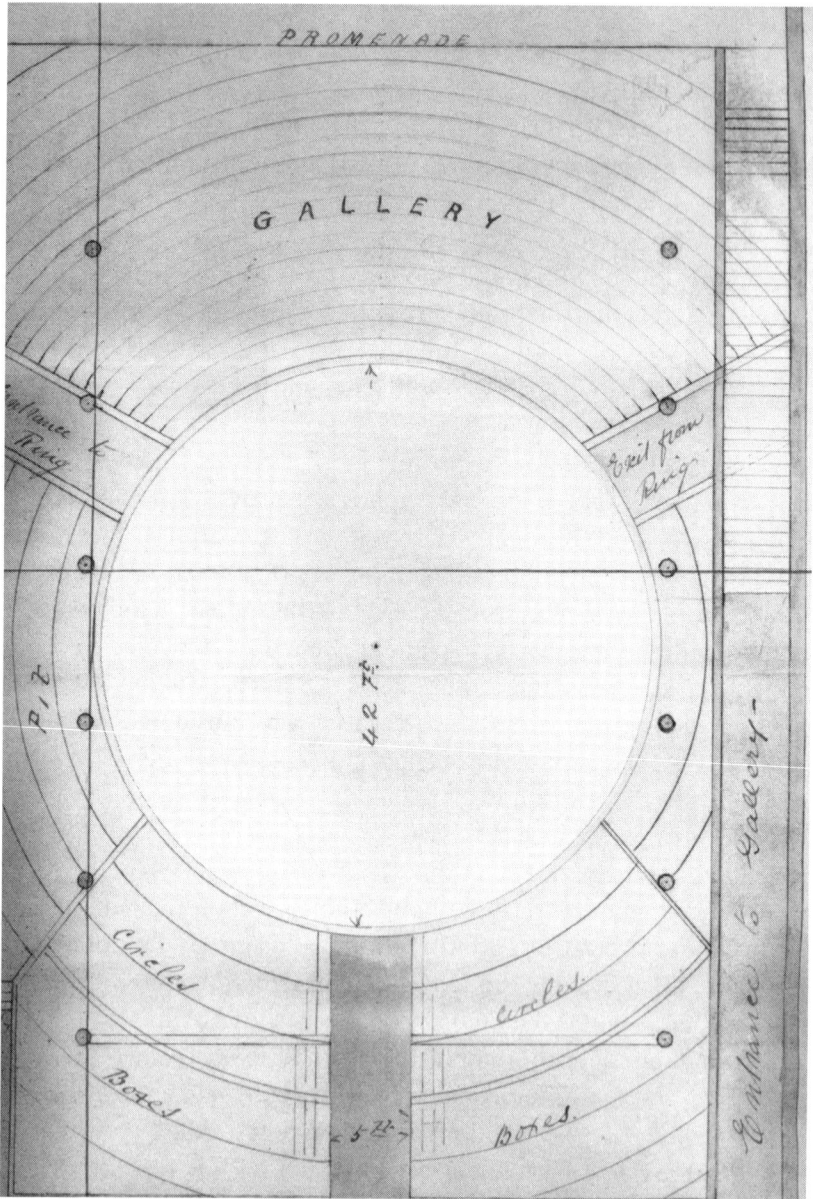

Figure 3. Plan of circus for Henry Swann, Fulford Road, York, 1883. This plan
is a typical design for wooden circus buildings for the mid-century, showing
the 42-foot ring and audience areas – pit, boxes, gallery, 'circles' and a
promenade. An entrance and an exit connect the ring to the
stabling behind, and under the gallery.

flow of action.[49] Modern theorists tend to regard the amphitheatre as essentially impure, an aberration; but they were widespread, and still being built sixty years on by hard-headed circus men such James Ryan in Birmingham (1847) and the Messrs Sanger in Dundee (1865). The *Era* offers a very full description of the Dundee amphitheatre. With an overall length of 175 feet, and a 70-foot stage, it was a sizable brick-built structure seating more than 2,500 people in pit, gallery and boxes. Moreover, it had the physical link between circle and stage that Astley's had invented to merge the horse and the drama. 'At each side of the stage', the *Era* reports, 'are moveable gangways, which can be lowered when the "spectacle" on the stage requires the presence of horses. One side will be used for the ascent and the other for the descent of the animals and their riders.'[50]

The binary that modern circus and performance-space theorisations pursue – the opposition of the performance of body (the physical feats of the circus) and spirit (the drama) – was clearly not built in by nineteenth-century practitioners nor recognised by audiences other than the dramatic critics.[51] The first-hand evidence of Frowde and Lawrence offers us a different approach to these theatres with singers, comics, horses and acrobats.

49. See J. S. Bratton and Jane Traies, *Astley's Amphitheatre* (Cambridge: Chadwyck-Healey, 1980).

50. *Era*, 3 December 1865.

51. For this theoretical argument, see note 5. A more sophisticated discussion is found in David Wiles, *A Short History of Western Performance Space* (Cambridge University Press, 2003), pp. 199–206.

4

❖

A microhistory from two manuscripts

The manuscripts

On 21 June 1894 James Henry Frowde (1831–99), a Gloucestershire gentleman aged 63, sat down rather self-consciously to write his autobiography, at the behest, he said, of his children, who wanted to keep him occupied. He worked quickly, covering the years from his first memories of the early 1830s to 1857 in, apparently, a few weeks' disorderly but extremely productive scribbling that filled five notebooks in faint blue pencil, which is written over, doubled-back, and sometimes corrected in ink; and then he stopped. Frowde was the son of a Portsmouth tradesman, also called James, and Georgiana Henrietta (née Hengler), a member of a family of entertainers springing from an eighteenth-century immigrant into Britain. By the time Georgiana married out, the Henglers had established themselves as noted physical performers, and had begun to intermarry with the leading equestrian families of Cooke and Powell.[52] They were on their way to the eminence which they enjoyed in the middle years of the nineteenth century. When young James ran away in 1847 at the age of sixteen, effectively to join his maternal family, he arrived just as his uncle Charles Hengler was about to regroup a business which would then take off, becoming a leading British circus of the day. After some difficulty in being accepted, and training himself secretly as a contortionist and novelty act, the boy became a professional

---

52. For a comprehensive history of the Hengler family, see John M. Turner, *Historical Hengler's Circus*, 5 vols. (Liverpool: Lingdales Press, 1989).

clown and took, eventually, a fairly prominent place in the family business before he married (in succession) two clergymen's daughters and left the ring once more. Frowde's early autobiography is therefore a detailed, if retrospective, account of growing up, working and touring with a large and successful entertainment enterprise during the mid-Victorian decades when the British circus was at its height.[53]

In February 1873, twenty-one years before Frowde wrote his account of his younger self, Thomas Lawrence (c.1820–?) finished the pantomime season in Nottingham with Foottit's Allied Circus, and decided to go into management himself. He advertised in the *Era* for 'an entire Theatrical Company' and 'a string band of Four or Five'[54] for a new portable theatre. In his current gagbook that Christmas, between the reference copies of his current wheezes and the songs and materials from other people that he had jotted down in the back, he wrote out a shopping list for the timber to build a portable. The new venture succeeded, though his finances almost collapsed under the strain, if we are to judge by the begging letter he drafted on the endpaper of his book. Lawrence's Great Allied Theatre (the name was doubtless derived from, and perhaps in homage to, his last employer's) was operational for the next twenty years. Lawrence was born around 1820, like Frowde into a family of entertainers. His father, also named Thomas, was in the business as a portable theatre proprietor, and, unlike Frowde, the son was never away from it. Tom Lawrence Jnr is just visible on the lowest rungs of the entertainment ladder: he first surfaces as an actor in both Douglass's and Latimer's portable theatre companies in the 1850s, and joined Maus's Circus early in the 1860s as a clown-comedian, performing dramatic 'business' in the ring as well as more traditional clown work. He appears to have moved between circuses – Maus's, Quaglieni's Italian and Manley's Chinese – before spending three years (somewhat discontinuously) with Powell, Foottit and Clarke's Great Allied Circus, which he joined in its Ipswich winter quarters in October 1869. It is

---

53. The great days of Hengler's were sharpened by competition from the American version of circus, whose arrival in Britain overlapped with the period of Frowde's membership: the first complete American circus toured England in 1842, and by the time Frowde's account ends, in 1857, competition with the incomers had become intense. See Speaight, *A History of the Circus*, pp. 104–8.

54. *Era*, 9 February 1873.

likely that he occasionally returned to work in portable theatres such as Carl Manges's Royal Pavilion, which travelled Wales, before he took the momentous decision to build a portable theatre himself. He never returned to circus clowning, but by amazing chance, both his last gagbook and its battered, coverless predecessor, from which he had revised and recopied material he carried over, survived. Both these rare manuscripts, Frowde's autobiography and Lawrence's gagbook, have been preserved by the descendants of the clown who wrote them.[55]

The microhistory

Here, then, are two manuscripts which together offer an unusually direct path into the culture of the mid-nineteenth century, via its underexplored comic dimension. We have in hand primary material, manuscript remains not written for publication, from which to extrapolate a history of one phase of comic performance and its wider context. The two manuscripts offer a new focus, one which gives us an opportunity to scrutinise and to generalise about particular entertainment acts and the institutions through which they operated. Our endeavour is to present the writings, and through them the performing lives and acts, of James Frowde and Thomas Lawrence, in order to construct a microhistory of mid-Victorian demotic entertainment in the circus and the nascent music hall.[56]

The issue of mediation of evidence – the problem of who is reporting any performance, and for what purpose – is always significant in performance history, and never more so than in the area

55. The gagbook transcribed here, containing 68 leaves, has an unused section in the middle (see p. 239).

56. Thomas Postlewait, 'Micro-history and the Writing of Theatre History Today' (unpublished paper for the Historiography Working Group: IFTR/FIRT: Worcester, England, June 2003), explains that 'the aim in microhistory is not simply to offer a biographical investigation of a particular person, but to probe the definitive features of the life in order to see what the case study reveals about the time and place. Even when the microhistorian focuses on a specific individual, there is no imperative that the life needs to be covered chronologically, birth to death. Instead, the aim is to discover the special aspects of the individual, whose situation, actions, and beliefs provide the telling traces of cultural, social, moral, and political conditions.'

of nineteenth-century popular shows. The critics, whether social commentators or press reporters, have always a purpose in recording the amusements of their social inferiors that imposes an obvious and often disguising bias upon what they say; and the published words of the leaders in the entertainment profession are always complicated, at this period, not simply by their various motives for self-representation but very often also by their defensiveness against the disapproval or at least belittlement of their profession by their social peers. To demystify the idea of clowning and achieve a material understanding of it through these two ordinary examples, who happened to work and to write about their work at an important moment in the development of the circus as it evolved within the entertainment culture of the West, will help to move discussion from cliché to history.

First-person accounts of the life and work of nineteenth-century comic men are not frequently found. Men of any calling who write autobiography most often wish to make a public statement laying out the contribution they feel they have made to their times. The undertaking is an assertion of success, of a sense of their own worth and importance. Whether they feel themselves to have been central to world events or acting radically on the margins, they are asserting themselves: the act of writing says 'I did it my way.' In the entertainment world as elsewhere, autobiography tends to be written by the most prominent men – indeed, such publications contribute to our sense that these are or were the leaders they claim to be. Theatrical proprietors, leading performers and/or managers are those who have the self-confidence and the leisure to write their own histories and so set out their claims, their stories of success; the obvious circus example is 'Lord' George Sanger's *Seventy Years a Showman*.

The nonmanagerial role of clown, on the other hand, while being much-mythologised and overdetermined by many layers of sentiment, has essentially inspired others to write, rather than being written about by the men who undertook it. The most distinguished nineteenth-century clowns passed into myth partly via published quasi-autobiographies, but these are heavily mediated: Charles Dickens, who professed 'a strong veneration for Clowns', was 'in a perfect fever' when he discovered that Joseph Grimaldi had spent the year before his death producing an 'exceedingly voluminous' account of himself. Thomas Wilks had already begun to edit and condense this manuscript when Grimaldi died. He sold it to the publisher Richard Bentley, who then passed it on to the novelist, who 'altered its form throughout' from first-person to third-person narrative, and admits that it no longer had 'any original manner' peculiar to its subject.[57] Charles Whitehead edited it once more in 1846, with voluminous notes which Richard Findlater discarded when he cut the text yet again for twentieth-century readers. Thus the account of himself given by the archetype of the pantomime clown reaches us through many filters and deflections. The writings of Dan Leno, the equivalent doyen of late Victorian comedy, are even less promising, '*Hys Booke*' turning out to be written by someone else entirely – it is a book of jokes incorporating shaggy-dog stories about his life which the great music hall comedian may have told.[58] Where a clown or comic actually published an account of himself during the ninetieth century, his declared motive tends to some sort of self-justification. Harvey Teasdale[59] aligned his text with the confessional subgenre of evangelical literature, in which the tale of a misspent youth is painted in lurid colours in order to set up Christian conversion as its triumphant denouement. Frowde's account tells several stories that stress his churchgoing and detail occasions during his performing career when his Christianity and respectability were recognised by the more liberal congregations among whom he appeared. After he retired into private life, he became a lay preacher and built a mission room in his Gloucestershire parish. But the MS is by no means equatable with the standard convert's narrative; it asserts that his circus days were hardworking and his calling harmless.

Other published examples of clown autobiography are Charles Keith's *Circus Life and Amusements*, which was serialised in *The Magnet* before publication at Derby in 1879, and *The Public Life of W. F. Wallett, the Queen's Jester*, edited by John Luntley and published by the same provincial press in 1870. Wallett's motive is

57. See Richard Findlater, *Joe Grimaldi, His Life and Theatre*, 2nd ed. (Cambridge University Press, 1978), pp. 11–12.

58. T. C. Elder, *Dan Leno Hys Booke, written by himself: a volume of frivolities*. (London: Greening, 1899). See Caroline Kershaw, 'Dan Leno: New Evidence on Early Performances and Style, *Nineteenth Century Theatre* 22 (1994), p. 31.

59. *The Life and Adventures of Harvey Teasdale the Converted Clown and Man Monkey, Written by himself* (Sheffield, [1870]).

transparently self-justification and, indeed, self-glorification, while Keith seems inspired by the wish to set the entertainment record straight, and to repudiate the romanticisation of his calling: as a theatre historian, he is an example of the tribal scribe. Keith, in particular, is a useful comparison with Frowde, and we have made much use of his writings in what follows; but there is a significant difference between his account, intentionally addressed to the public and making explicit claims for the realism and veracity of its account of his profession, and Frowde's rapidly written self-portrait. The fact that when extracts from Frowde's story began to appear in the *Gloucestershire Journal* after his death the Hengler family stepped in and forbade further publication shows how much less mediated this material might be.[60]

If unmediated autobiography is rare, records of the individual clown's professional material are like hen's teeth. Joke books are a distinct genre, put together for profit and not necessarily representing anything actually used by professional entertainers even where they are named after a famous jester in order to secure sales.[61] Occasional asides in professional reminiscences mention that circus clowns sometimes possessed – indeed, normally wrote out for themselves – a 'gagbook' to which they could refer in intervals during the show for inspiration,[62] but we know of no surviving example from the nineteenth century besides Lawrence's two volumes. The later book, which we offer here, is neatly written up, developing pieces from his earlier volume and adding more material, and it is not filled; it was apparently a working tool laid aside when he embarked on the next

---

60. See *The Gloucestershire Chronicle*, 2, 9 and 16 September 1899, and the discussion in John M. Turner, 'Frowde the Proud – the clown evangelist' *Gloucestershire History* (1994), pp. 9–14.

61. The 'Joe Miller' jest books, for example, are reprinted many times from 1830; in 1866 Herman Osterley published an edition of *Shakespeare's Jest Book* (London: John Russell Smith, 1866). Among materials from the Hodson portable theatre company, loaned to us by Sue Graves of Sheffield,

there is a very carefully written-out song book of materials used by the comic Jim de Marr who worked in the portables and in music hall; this will figure in our further work on the period.

62. See Frank Foster in collaboration with Willan G. Bosworth, *Clowning Through* (London: Heath Cranton, 1937), p. 64; and cf. the celebrated twentieth-century case of comedian Bob Monkhouse's gagbooks, which he left at a venue where he had been working, and moved heaven and earth to retrieve.

stage of his career. Moreover, the inclusion of versions of some of the wheezes from his earlier book suggests to us how he had developed and changed his material in use. Its value to us is inestimable, because publication was certainly not in his mind in compiling it, and no editor, journalist or anyone else before us has prepared it for a reading audience. It is by and for the performer himself and must therefore represent, as closely as the written word can, the actual material of the transactions in the ring between the humble comic man in a second-rate circus, and his lower-class audience.

The transcription that follows presents all that is relevant to his circus career from Frowde's manuscript. We have framed and annotated the extracts with some structuring and elucidation, but hope that others will make much further use of the story as a resource for understanding the culture it exemplifies. This is followed by an introduction to Lawrence's book, attempting some analysis of the material, before the transcription of his gags; and in this case, too, we have been restrained in our reading of the materials by a sense that much more work can and should be done to coax the Victorian clown into the twenty-first century – in this case, we hope, by practical exploration of the wheezes he has so miraculously left for our contemplation.

✤

Part II

✤

The circus memoirs of James Frowde, a Victorian clown

✤

Figure 4. Ink-and-wash portrait of James Frowde. Date and artist unknown.

1

❖

One: Childhood and youth, 1831–1846

To judge from his sound spelling and his attempt at an orthodox construction of his own story, Frowde was a reading man: he knew what was expected in an autobiography. He begins with a little self-consciousness and the facetious excuse that he is writing at the behest of his children. He does not wish to give the impression that he thinks his life important enough for a public record; but neither does the jocular manner with touches of self-deprecation that he initially adopts suggest he has in mind the serious evangelical conversion model of narrative. Even though at this point he describes his childish enchantment at his first theatrical show with (ironic) reference to its supposed sinfulness, he certainly does not go on to construct his life as an entertainer as having been the work of the devil. Later (pp. 117, 137–8), he is robust in self-justification and often speaks of the healthiness of the circus life and his own unimpeachable propriety, painting antitheatrical sermonising as rank prejudice.

My children, in order I suppose to keep me out of mischief, or possibly thinking there may be acts that I have committed which they would

---

The following abbreviations are used throughout these notes: *JT VA1*: John Turner, *Victorian Arena: The Performers. A Dictionary of British Circus Biography*, 2 vols. (Formby, England: Lingdales Press, 1995), I. *JT VA2*: John Turner, *Victorian Arena: The Performers. A Dictionary of British Circus Biography*, 2 vols. (Formby, England: Lingdales Press, 2000), II. *JT HH*: John Turner, *Historical Hengler's Circus*, 5 vols. (Liverpool: Lingdales Press, 1989).

avoid, and thus modify or improve upon a sanguineous inheritance, have expressed a wish that I should write my life, and in order to please my offspring, I, this lovely June afternoon, now 21 days of age, of this year '94, decide to obey them. Not that I suppose what I write will be read by them. I can hardly desire this, because my wish is, they may [not] have time to read of a misspent life, they using the time God may grant them for amusement or recreation, their thought may be engaged by study of nobler deeds, adventures and themes than my 63 years of experience can offer.

After this brief introduction he launches into his story, at first in chronological order. He was born on 17 April 1831 in Portsea, near Portsmouth, to Georgiana Henrietta Frowde,[1] into the famous circus family of Hengler: she was the eldest daughter of Henry Michael Hengler, and an equestrienne. His father James Frowde was a shop manager. He is aware of his paternal lineage, and sets it out in some detail, tracing it back to 1698.

Frowde's early life was a difficult one. His mother died when he was six. His father remarried, to a stern and unforgiving woman who seems to have treated the Frowde boys unsympathetically. James and his younger brother George ran wild, and came up against authority frequently. His father was hardworking, but unapproachable. Frowde writes of him spending long hours in his study, during which time they were forbidden to interrupt him – 'How I used to long for a time to speak or touch him.'

Contact with his maternal family in his early childhood is suggested in a vivid passage of infant memory, in which he is taken by coach to London, or some other city, sees an Italian organ-grinder, mistaking his monkey for a man, and later goes to a theatrical performance.

I remember a journey, some straw, a great jolting, finding myself in a strange house and people and a formidable looking gentleman with shock of curly black hair and a mouth covered with hair and he

---

1. Exact date of birth unknown, but she was baptised on 27 November 1808 in Lambeth. She married James Frowde on 10 April 1830, and died on 10 September 1837, aged twenty-nine.

opened the windows and talked to 2 men with an organ, he spoke a queer language, but the organ man understood him and one, the little one, on the organ took off his cap, there seemed to be much laughing and I fancy I was angered. I remember being taken somewhere and there was a large rock with a door in it and a handsome lady was outside fastened with a chain to a stake, by the door or entrance to the cave. Her long black hair, refined and yet withal a pronounced Semitic face, showed to me Aunt Eliza,[2] while spell-bound to see her under such extraordinary circumstances, a huge reptile, hideous in green scales and large fiery eyes made its appearance over the brow of the rock, flapped its wings and swung its tail, my scream of terror, my shout for Aunt Eliza's assistance, my puny efforts to go to her assistance made, it seems, quite a sensation, and the hero spoiled tragic effect, and caused much laughter. Thus early I made a melodramatic comedian's success.

He gives a detailed account of his early attempts to find employment – in shops and as a whitesmith – in Portsmouth, and includes an excited description (in which he characteristically slides into the historic present tense) of early theatrical enthusiasm provoked by visiting Richardson's booth theatre at the annual Portsmouth Charter Fair.

Emmanuel, the great silversmith of the Borough,[3] did away (amid strong opposition to it) with King Charles' Charter Portsmouth Fair. Oh King Chs.! In gilt enshrined in the walls of the semaphore,[4] looking down the High Street, no more will your glove be placed on view, a license for a fortnight's Saturnalia. They took down the grand

2. Eliza Ann Hengler, daughter of Henry Michael Hengler and wife of William Powell, equestrian and circus proprietor. She was primarily a rope-dancer; this instance suggests, however, a play (probably *George and the Dragon*, a favourite circus piece). Aunt Eliza is clearly cast in the role of the intended victim of the Dragon; whether this was part of a circus perfomance or not is unclear.

3. Emanuel Emanuel, silversmith and jeweller, who became Portsmouth's first Jewish Mayor, was responsible for having the Fair discontinued.

4. A bust of King Charles I was set into the wall of the Square Tower or semaphore, facing up the High Street. It can still be seen. The roof of the Tower was used as a signalling (or semaphore) station, linked by a chain of such signals to the Admiralty in London.

old building that stood in High St.,[5] and round which the market was held, where early culled flowers with the dew yet sparkling upon them were exposed to the gaze of semi-civilian sergeants, the staff, sleek and tight in undress uniform, the delight of the market women and hero of the dress-makers. It was the first fall … When the old Market was pulled down, the Glove (a large gilt wooden one)[6] was displayed at the window of the Council Chamber, over the New Market. Until then the fair could not begin. When it was taken in after a fortnight, [the] fair was over.

Soon as the Mayor and attendant hung out the glove at 12, then simultaneously there was such an unpacking of poles and canvas, such a row of sledge-hammers driving stakes into the ground and tapping of smaller hammers, fixing drapery, etc., '*all new*' for Portsmouth Fair … Yesterday the broad, quiet dreamy old street … was serenely quiet. The old fashioned bow windows with small panes looked deadly respectable. Today all one side of the street is alive with gaudy tents, the gutter was boarded over, the gilt gingerbread, gay silks and goodness knows what besides put the frowsy old shops in the background. At the back of the stalls are living carriages and canvas wall, hiding the cottages &c from passers by. Then the Parade:[7] Richardson's smaller mumming booth, fat women, giants, Fair Circassians, a Circus, Wombwells, and sometimes another, wild beast shows.[8] Perry St.[9] has its cheapjacks,[10] roundabouts, swings, and small gambling arrangements, too, there for 14 days.

I remember going into the shop, this was Fisk's or Clark's but Dad was manager. He was engaged [with] some fellow and they were

5. Probably the old Town Hall and Market House that stood in the middle of the High Street until 1837.

6. The carved open hand, or glove, signifying that the Fair was open.

7. The Parade, now Grand Parade: a square off the southern side of the High Street leading to the Garrison Church.

8. Frowde lists a variety of travelling shows found in nineteenth-century travelling fairs. Richardson's 'mumming booth': as well as theatrical performances, 'Muster' Richardson frequently showed freak exhibits. See Sybil Rosenfeld, 'Muster Richardson – "The Great Showman"' in David Mayer and Kenneth Richards *Western Popular Theatre* (London: Methuen, 1977), pp. 110–21). 'Fair Circassians': a popular freak exhibit, these were bushy-haired women, the epitome of slave or exotic beauty. Wombwells: a famous menagerie.

9. Perry Street ran off Grand Parade, parallel with High Street.

10. Cheapjack: travelling hawker.

laughing and yarning. I wished him further hanging over a brass gun.[11] I thought I should never get a chance of a fairing.[12] Presently the Gov. saw me and threw me a sixpence. Off I was going, when the commercial called me and gave me 2/6, a real half-crown. How I felt the burden of wealth – then I could understand the warning of 'beware pickpockets!'

Just another look at the show – how grand the Dukes and Queens, the Lords and Ladies, how majestically grand they move – how pretty the ladies. Oh how I would like to be rich and marry that lady in white. Oh to touch her hand. *'All in to begin!'* and the lovely one touches the arm of a grandee – Oh how I should like to go in – would it be very wicked? What a row in my breasts, what arguments for and against – but I wanted to go – and go won! How often it is we smother good resolutions because our desire drowns our reason and better nature. How many have made their lives miserable and their existence a sorrow, by yielding to the lust of a momentary pleasure – but the play – in the virtuous lady that now tempted me, I beheld in the mirror held up to nature a persecuted child whose passionate entreaty to a brutal man with long hair, black scowling brow was met by a yell as with half-drawn sword he called his minions to drag the victim to the darkest dungeon. They appeared more demoniac-looking than the Baron. The chains rattled, they approached, when as she gave an ear-piercing scream and heart searching pang, lightning filled the booth and thunder cracked as though it would shake the world off its balance and the rain came down in a deluge penetrating the canvas roof and flooding the concentration of sin! … Oh what a guilty wretch I felt, as though all that fearful storm was a judgement on my disobedience – poor boy – I felt I had sinned and grieved – no more thoughts of the beautiful actress.

He continues with random recollections of his childhood and teenage years, including the firework celebrations of Queen Victoria's coronation (1837) which were augmented for James and George by some amateur efforts of their father. This reminds him of the professional work of the first Henglers to come to Britain.

11. Sailors were tied face down over the breech of a cannon to be flogged (naval slang).

12. Fairing: money given to children to spend at a fair.

I also have some recollection of my g-grandmother Henglers death. She had an European fame as a pyrotechnic, and was in great request at Vauxhall. Here, I have heard, King George has fired some of her designs. In one of Tom Hood's volumes, which you may find among my books, there is an ode to Madame Hengler. It is headed by one of the comic wood cuts that illustrate some of his poems. She is depicted in sections each representing fireworks. It was prophetic – she was blown to pieces – went up with fireworks of many designs.[13]

This took place in 1845; a chain of free association takes him to 1846, when his brother George has already run away from home and joined his maternal relations.

1846

Now comes an incident that seems to have influenced my after life. In Waterworks Lane[14] the builders are putting up a large wooden structure, I hear of it, 'tis to be a circus. Presently in large raised letters of gold on a blue ground appeared the name of Hengler. These letters are now common, I believe were the invention of a Mr Rourke of Lambeth, who lived not far from the Church in which my parents in the early Easter of 1830 were, by the Rev. Lane, married. Mr Rourke, I believe, was a relation of Mr Hengler, and the father of the present celebrated actress Miss Rourke.[15] By and bye the Circus arrived and I was, by George[16] who came with the Company, presented to my grandparents.[17] I was much struck with my g-father's appearance and remember well the meerschaum protruding from his braided frock coat. There were Uncles Charles and Jno., Powell and Beacham, and 3 of the prettiest aunts a fellow need

13. Madame Sarah Hengler, equestrienne and pyrotechnist, who died in a fire at her firework factory and home in 1845.

14. Waterworks Lane, Portsmouth, derived its name from the waterworks begun there in 1811. It was later renamed Hyde Park Road, a remnant of which still exists.

15. Perhaps Kate Rorke (1866–1945).

16. George Frowde, born 1832 and James's younger brother. Already working in the circus at this young age (fourteen), he became a strongman athlete. He was working in Hengler's Circus, Edinburgh, in 1863 as 'The Modern Hercules.'

17. Grandfather: Henry Michael ('Mons.') Hengler (1784–1861). His fame as a rope-dancer was legendary.

wish for.[18] This was in July 1846. I spent a good bit of my time with my new-found relations at Aunt Beacham's. Henderson,[19] husband of Aunt Agnes, came for a day. He was travelling with Lord Jem Lee,[20] an extraordinary man, one of Batty's education was his companion. I can remember how he made them all laugh as he told of Jem's exploits. I met Lee in after life. I was at the circus one eve and saw Dad, listening and watching Billy Taylor,[21] the clown, a funny but very coarse clown, I met him after in Plymouth, landlord of a pub. I saw my father laugh and thought how I should like to be a clown. Jem Franks[22] was playing 2nd clown and working with a school of acrobats. I can remember g-father coming before the audience to work a trick horse, Prince. I never have seen a man make his obeisance to an audience with the grace and command that he did, save perhaps his son Edward,[23] who was not then with the concern. ... The circus, through some difficulty of Powell's, was sold and Geo. came home.

18. Uncles (Frederick) Charles Hengler (1821–87) and John Hengler (1831–1919), and William Powell (1816–1900) and Richard Beacham (dates not known), the latter two being uncles by marriage, marrying Eliza Ann and Henrietta Frances Hengler (both daughters of Henry Michael Hengler) respectively.

19. John Henderson (1822–67), equestrian, married to Agnes Selima Hengler. He was to become a friend to Frowde.

20. Possibly Tom Lee, an equestrian with Batty's Circus. Wallett, the Queen's

Jester set his dislocated shoulder after he had fallen from his horse.

21. 'Comic Sayings and Doings by the Funny Clown Mr TAYLOR' appears on Hengler's Circus Royal, Union Road, Plymouth, playbill dated 31 December 1846 (University of Bristol Theatre Collection, TCPB/000456).

22. James W. Franks, clown, born 1818. With Hengler's from c.1846 (JT VA2).

23. Edward Hengler (1819–65).

2

✣

Two: Running away to join the circus, 1847–1849

Having met the Henglers, James was drawn into the circus world, leaving behind the cold neglect of his stepmother and his unbending father for a more physically direct but also a harder life on the road, starting, aged sixteen, at the very bottom. Before long he was effectively confined to his new place in life by the failure of his father's business. But the circus world was unremittingly harsh, and it took years to prove himself there. As an untried boy he was given odd jobs, including menial grooming and cleaning, and also money-taking at the door, an important function in which his quickness and intelligence proved indispensable, though he always resented being confined to something he regarded as no task for a man.[24] In this masculine and competitive milieu, enforcement of authority by violence seems to have been entirely accepted, and Frowde records its application to others besides himself, but he is still concerned to point out that he did not always deserve the treatment he received. He was bullied by his cousins and frequently beaten by his 'Govr.' Uncle Charles Hengler, who was, it seems, a quick-tempered man with a strong sense of the standards of obedience, smartness, behaviour and 'respectability' that his new enterprise needed in order to present itself successfully to the public.

24. Women usually managed the pay-box. Mrs Pablo, for example, was holding the pay-box containing the night's takings, when the circus collapsed in Halifax. See *The Public Life of W. F. Wallett, the Queen's Jester: An Autobiography Of Forty Years' Professional Experience & Travels in the United Kingdom, the United States of America (inc. California), Canada, South America, Mexico, the West Indies, etc.,* ed. John Luntley (London and Derby: Bemrose & Sons, 1884), p. 76.

Frowde records here not only his own early years in the family business, but also the emergence of the Henglers' important circus and its place in the nexus of mid-Victorian entertainment. Charles Hengler's company was starting small when the boy joined at Stamford in Lincolnshire, with a multiskilled company largely made up of family: six performing or working horses, three riders, a clown, a strong man. Their father, Henry Michael Hengler, in his mid-sixties, was still travelling with them, and one day, upon provocation by a complaining rope-dancer, frightened his sons by leaping up on the tightrope and showing how it should be done. Uncle John was the star rider, and performed and postured on horseback in the same style as Andrew Ducrow the famous equestrian and manager of Astley's. Gradually more performers were recruited, either as visiting stars – Frowde admires the famous clown Wallett whom they engaged in 1848 – or more permanently, like the apprentice equestrienne Miss Chart who arrived in 1849.

They were travelling extensively, sometimes setting up at fairs: at Newark Fair in 1847 they bought an extra horse; Frowde records an adventure at Coventry Fair in 1849 with a son of Batty's Menagerie who tried to impress him by getting into a lion's cage. But they also set up independently, designing and erecting wooden circus buildings and, importantly, they worked in theatres, and even in collaboration with theatrical companies. In 1847 Charles began to mount 'pieces' – that is, plays; it was for the first of these, about Dick Turpin, that the new black horse was bought. The young Frowde had a small speaking role. He looks back with amusement upon the uneasy alliance/rivalry set up at the Theatre Royal, Birmingham, where they mounted the play in collaboration with the acting company there, under the direction of William Broadfoot, who played Turpin for his own benefit but could not manage the Henglers' frisky colt.

At Brighton in 1849 they fell out completely with Maynard's company, who, according to Frowde, were jealous because none of the actors could work a horse and thus could not star in George and the Dragon. *The result of the dispute was that the actor cast as Timour the Tartar absented himself after the last rehearsal. Uncle John Henderson, rider and acrobat, had to learn the role in half an hour and perform in the play after he had done his own vaulting act in the first half of the programme. Frowde also mentions that they played*

47

Cinderella and The Battle of Waterloo. *At Portsmouth in 1848 the manager of the theatre attempted to put an end to competition by prosecuting them for playing drama without a theatre licence, but they got away with their dramatic presentation.*

You will see why Geo. was home and that the circus was dismembered. Uncle Charles had joined Mr W Cooke, Uncle to Aunt Charles. Charles, in his old mumming booth days besides being a musician got a knowledge of scene painting, and was a fair property maker – consequently of great use to a concern of Mr Cooke's magnitude. A circus was being sold up and Edward bought the nucleus that forms Hengler's, now of world renown repute. Aunt by this time, 26 July 1847, had given birth and I think in September Uncle Charles' show was started.[25] In October of that month, I found myself with him in his first town of Stamford.[26]

October 1847

I am to make myself useful – what was the stud? <u>Judy</u>, the Dun mare I called <u>Mrs Hall</u> because she had a wart on her nose, and bore the same kind of expression,[27] <u>Spot</u> mare, the ring horse <u>Wellington</u>, a cream, named <u>Stargazer</u>, <u>Dolphin</u>, a flop ear'd skewbald, and <u>Spot</u> the trick pony – carriage none – but a very pretty gig. Here I took cheques, counted tickets, various jobs and amused myself with the baby. We became great chums. We had a small but good company, Palmer, Charley Adams and Jno. were the riders. Swan I think was the

25. Charles Hengler married Mary Ann Frances Sprake, a member of the Cooke circus family, in 1846, so the daughter was probably Susannah Jane, whose birth was registered in Coventry in 1847. She married W. Henry Powell, her father's general manager, in 1867. When Powell died, she married David Abbey Seal, clown. See p. 83, where she is 'Susie', and 'much grown'.

26. Charles's circus (Hengler's Circus) was formed in 1847, from the original Hengler's Circus formed by his older brother Edward, in 1844. The link

between 'Uncle Charles' and William Cooke, circus proprietor, was familial – William Cooke was the uncle of Mary Ann Frances Sprake, Uncle Charles's wife. The passage shows how multiskilled were the personnel in travelling shows, as Uncle Charles was musician, scene painter and property master, as well as an equestrian.

27. See p. 53. Mrs Hall was the wardrobe keeper. Frowde frequently makes comparisons between humans and animals (see Ryan and the monkey, page 95).

principal clown.[28] The Gov. was very particular, at this early stage everything said or done before the public has to be decent and good order. So with the dress and behaviour in private life. He was always particular to get the most decent people he could.[29] Certainly our ring was not that of after days, neither baize nor velvet covered the padded top of the ring fence, in fact it was not added and often nothing but the edge of the board and stakes formed the ring's promenade.[30]

Frowde continues to be mischievous; in this company he is 'whacked' for his impudence, and his suffering causes 'many a grin'.

Our season was over and the tilt[31] removed from the cirque, things were packed, Aunt, Uncle, G-mother and Baby had started, [all] save g-father and C. Adams, a musician who could [not] ride. For as far as I know the first time in my life I was on horse-back,[32] following, with others, g-father and Adams in the gig. I found a great difficulty in keeping my feet in the stirrups. I felt sure the whole system was a mistake and invented in my mind many improvements in stirrups. Presently my trousers, which would persist in assuming corkscrew shape, distressed me. A portion, and a long portion, of what should

28. See p. 55. Swan was probably Tom Swann, equestrian, grotesque and talking clown. Palmer: Adams, born Alfred Palmer, equestrian whose speciality was a sailor's hornpipe on a bare-backed horse (*JT, VA2*). Charles Adams, born 1828, equestrian clown. He was with Ryan's, Batty's, Ducrow's, Powell's, Hengler's and Cooke's circuses in the 1840s and 1850s, and married Mary E. Cooke, daughter of circus proprietor Thomas E. Cooke (*JT VA1*).

29. Compare with p. 126: the 'Govr.' was very particular about how the company presented themselves to the outside world, respectability being the key.

30. The ring fence (about 3 feet in height) literally divided the ring space from the auditorium. In some establishments it was a substantial structure, sturdy enough to allow the clown to leap on and run around it.

31. Tilt: the roof, often canvas, sometimes wood, of the circus, booth or travelling show.

32. This incident clearly shows the difference between the Henglers, born to the circus, and outsiders such as Frowde, and is one of the roots of his future troubles. Many accounts of nineteenth-century circus life point to the importance of early training for equestrians and acrobats, though clowns, according to Charles Keith, are a different matter: 'Some people have an idea that all clowns are bred clowns – that is to say, that clowns and circus artistes must be taught when young. It is completely wrong. I own equestrians must be taught when young, and require a deal of practise … [But] not one clown in fifty was, perhaps, ever brought up to be a clown' (Keith, *Circus Life*, p. 8).

have been calves were exposed to view. As I was too chafed one of the grooms commiserated me and several times dismounted to rearrange my trousers and alter my stirrup straps. For the horse's sake we went at a slow pace: Uncle Jno.'s mare must not suffer, [f]or how could he in safety ride and impersonate sailor, soldier, highlander, upon a tired horse or with a strained sinew?[33] After about 3 hours walking, jogging, we halted. How stiff and sore I felt! I went into a stable to see what ailed my knees, calves and thighs. Good gracious, they were raw ... I had 3d given me to get some food, and for a penny I had a bowl of milk sufficient to last a family with the strongest lacteal sentiments for a day, the good woman cruelly but with kindest intent gave me more. And now came the time to mount and start. Ben was at my side altering my stirrups. The grand-dad looked behind, and impatient of the delay, wanted to know the reason and I was called to the gig. 'What is the matter with you sir?' I explained the stirrups were wrong. 'Vell the D – you ride without.' Out came my feet and out went my toes. 'You tailor, turn in your toes'[34] was the injunction, crack went the whip and off jogged the horse. I seemed to want another pair of hands, one to hold the reins, the other to hold on to the saddle. Why on earth, thought I, could they not have a rail from the saddle to hold on by. The horse I was riding was a pad horse[35] and like most of that profession the animal had a hard mouth. Whilst riding in the rear a rein in each hand I was enabled to hold on but now under the eye of g-father and worse under the lash of his whip – I was told to let the horse have its head. One would have thought, being an uninitiate, that I had its head in my pocket. After much jeering and [being] called a tailor, I was allowed to fall in the rear, wondering whether all tailors off the board and from behind the counter were on the saddle and outside the horse[36] as

33. John Hengler's 'hippodramatic sketches' in which he represented characters while on horseback, in the manner of Andrew Ducrow, the manager of Astley's 1824–42.

34. If 'tailor' was a circus term for a nonrider, that perhaps explains why the incompetent horseman in the comic riding act 'The Taylor Riding to Brentford' is of that occupation; or of course the explanation could be that the

famous sketch gave rise to the use of the expression more generally. See Speaight, *History of the Circus*, p. 24, and George Speaight, 'Some Comic Circus Entrees', *Theatre Notebook* 32 (1978), pp. 24–5.

35. Pad horse: mount used in an acrobatic or balancing act executed from a padded platform on the horse's back.

36. Outside the horse: on horseback.

miserable as I was ... Some may think my first riding lesson a severe one – but I think it was a good one. I taught my boys on something like it, it gave me a balance and a grip which in time gave me as secure a seat as though I had been brought up in the saddle.[37]

The 1847 summer tour continues round the Midland towns. Frowde recalls his boyish interest in food – 'We halted at Melton Mowbray and I had for the first time a real Melton pie' – and in fair play, with a story about getting even with a servant girl who blamed him for raids on the jam pot (he treated it with a laxative, and she was sent home to her mother to recuperate). He records his increasing acceptance in his new family, albeit on their terms,.as boy and often scapegoat; and his sorrow at his unbending father's continued harshness towards him.

Newark

I have no notes and have to trust my memory and hints from Aunt Charles ... Aunt was very kind to us and saved us from many a row with the Govr. I have been busy writing to my father, of course, letting him know what a 'John' he had in his son,[38] and other details of my prowess. I waited patiently as I could for a reward. It came. But Oh such an indignant epistle with a strong ultimatum not to write to him again, till my syntax and orthography was improved, spoke of what my schooling had been and intimations that there was a grammar by Cobbett, to be had for 2/6.[39] I purchased one and ever since have kept a copy or edition ...

Uncle was anxious to bring out pieces, in particular 'Dick Turpin' who was and doubtless is a hero of the town here. There was in my days an old public house called the 'King's Head', at the back a small window from which Turpin emerged, when his pursuers had entered the front of the house, the ostler in league had Bess at hand.[40] Turpin from the window could reach with his feet his horse and sliding into his seat, pistol in hand, was off:

37. Frowde's clowning career does not extend to being a ring rider, of course. As Wallett says, 'As a rule clowns, acrobats and gymnasts and the like are bad riders' (Wallett, *Public Life*, p. 29).

38. John: a man.

39. William Cobbett, *A Grammar of the English Language* (1818).

40. *Dick Turpin or the Death of Black Bess* (Milner, 1836), from Ainsworth's novel *Rookwood*, was a favourite circus play, for obvious reasons. Turpin supposedly stayed in Newark for three

Pursue me you blood hounds, in rear and in van,
My foot's in the stirrup now catch me who can.

There was a horse fair during our stay and Uncle and g-father purchased an Irish black colt, about 16 hands, a fine specimen, of course too frisky to do much with, and yet Turpin must be played and a trained horse was wanted, one to feign lameness and death,[41] we had no black horse to do this, those that could were a cream, and others were spotted. It was suggested we should black the cream but there were difficulties and so instead an apology was offered to the public, that on account of an accident, Black Bess would not be able to play, but the part would be sustained by the highly trained horse 'Wellington'.[42]

So finished a bad season. In pulling off the tilt, after the night's performance, Charley Adams from the ridge dropt his hammer used for drawing the batten nails, that held the tilt, so near the head of M. Rivers,[43] the strongman, as to occasion a scene, no blood was shed, no blow received.[44] . . . Uncle Jno., Tom Swan and a spot pony were the favourites.[45]

years, and a number of escape routes, all from public houses in the village, were mythologised. The King's Head was on Chain Lane. Dating from 1735, it was demolished in 1967.

41. The dramatic crux of the piece – the horse had to feign death and, frequently, submit to being stretchered out of the ring.

42. Wellington was the ring horse, a work-a-day animal (see p. 48). A ring horse, according to Speaight, 'is a plebeian broad-backed animal, a Percheron or Belgian, similar to the cart horse, and often piebald in colouring' (Speaight, *History of the Circus*, p. 62).

43. Mr (or M[ons].) R. L. Rivers: equilibrist and strongman, and billed as the 'Herculean Wonder' and the 'Great Bottle Equilibrist'. In the Theatre Royal, Birmingham, season of 1848 a playbill describes 'his Extraordinary Performances forming graceful positions on real Glass Bottles, Tumblers, Basins, Plates & Feats of Balancing Unequalled in Gymnasia' (30 March 1848, Theatre Royal Playbill Collection, Local Studies Library, Birmingham). He was still with Hengler's in 1849, when he was ringmaster (*JT VA*2).

44. The tent was taken down after the evening performance in readiness for moving on. All the male personnel were involved in this, as indicated by Charles Adams, who was an equestrian. Charles Keith recalled 'Many times have I been last in the ring, and on coming out have found the dressing tent half pulled down by the tent men, who were eager to get their work done' (Keith, *Circus Life*, p. 45).

45. Uncle Jno. – Jonathan, i.e. John Michael Hengler, tightrope artiste. Tom Swann, the equestrian clown, was with Charles Hengler's re-formed circus in 1847.

Now for another long ride but with a lighter heart, but still a heavy hand. I was riding the Dun mare, over 16 hands, a well-bred creature, who chaffed at having her mouth so roughly handled. I tried to dismount and change horses with one of the performers and a good job I did, for before we had gone far, down she went, but no harm done, yet I felt thankful 'twas a more proficient hand that did the forespring. At night we arrived at Leicester Amphitheatre;[46] here I made my first appearance on a stage. I was called front, the front of the house, put on a Chinese dress and was a super in the Chinese fair.[47] Nothing to do but form in a group, a spectator in a theatrical crowd, witness Chinese representation of a fete. I never suffered more from stage fright than I did on that eve, and yet but a unit of a lump. Uncle was much engaged in breaking Black Bess (Johnny); rehearsals were many and everything done to command success but at the last rehearsal Bess would not die – jump the turnpike gate as often as you liked, go lame as long as it had the cue, but neither carrots or morris stick would make it die. I told you uncle could paint and make properties.[48] He was also cast for Turpin. Suddenly, as though by inspiration, off I was sent to a draper for unbleached calico. Mrs Hall, wardrobe keeper received orders to arm herself and sweepers with thread and needles. Hall to make unlimited lamp black paint, strongly sized. I am back with a roll of calico – the height, length, girths, etc., had been measured. The calico was unrolled. The Govr. had sketched out the profile of the horse, life size, on double cloth. The women stitched up the sides, the property man had stuffed it with straw, sewn in it. A tail, the only thing left of a Black Bess of past days, was sewn on, and there was a dead horse! A rehearsal for position was called – home – tea – theatre – a good house – ring performance over – the curtain up and all done to perfection – the young horse leaped the gate – Dick had led him on to the stage – made his speech of love, begged of her to cheer up – 'Look Bess, yonder is York Minster – one

---

46. This may be the 'Splendid new Amphitheatre' erected in 1839 in Humberstone Gate. See Helen and Richard Leacroft, *The Theatre in Leicestershire* (Leicester: Leicestershire Libraries and Information Service, 1986), p. 101.

47. This is odd but not impossible. It would seem to mean that he stood in the ring and performed the role of picturesque audience – in front of the real audience, in the boxes – while the fete was presented on the amphitheatre's stage.

48. Uncle Charles Hengler.

short mile dear Bess, then all thy troubles are over.' He has passed to the wings – tears were being wiped from the eyes of the more emotional, and rounds of loud applause, and calls for the actors, had subsided – another scene – night – woods – Luke Rookwood and gypsies – another – Turpin in an agony of grief, was apostrophising his dying mare – he raises her head – kisses her lips – but alas no response – she has breathed her last, and with a heart bursting with grief, the highwayman exclaims 'Best mare that man ever owned is dead – I have killed her!' In his grief and remorse he falls upon her corpse – down comes the curtain and cheer upon cheer. And so Black Bess for a short time was a success. Bess, however, was used for another purpose. We had with us a lad called Polaski, nephew of William Powell.[49] Dan was a clever lad as a trick act rider. We utilised the dummy horse for another purpose – of an afternoon when all had gone to tea, we used to practise from the springboard using the mare as a bed to alight upon. Unfortunately by some means we tore the canvas and before we had time to repair the damage we were disturbed, so we dragged the dummy to the property room and made good our escape. Night came. As each act passed my qualms grew greater. Presently came the last scene. Judge my horror and fear when I beheld straw protruding from the horse's stomach, none however noticed it and the curtain fell with the usual plaudits. It was the last night of 'Turpin' and the dummy was no longer needed for the public. Dan and I had a good laugh over it.

Business was very bad. Always is in Leicester. Wallett[50] in his autobiography gives his opinion of the town and concludes it by saying 'In due time I bade adieu to my Leicester friends, assuring them that I would never again erect a circus within sound of a stocking frame.' Wallett was very honest with an audience. As great a failure as a manager as he was successful as a jester or actor.[51] He had come to

49. Polaski: possibly the equestrian Jean Polaski, who was with Batty's, Tournaire's and Hughes's circuses and at Astley's, as well as Hengler's.

50. William Frederick Wallett, born 1807. Originally an actor in portable theatres (see Wallett, *Public Life*, Chapter 3, and Wild, *Old Wild's*, pp. 24–9), he joined Samwell's Royal Circus as a clown. He was the 'original' Shakespearean clown, famous for his intelligent monologues and biting wit and sarcasm.

51. 'Every theatrical season in this town terminates in bankruptcy, and music halls have like success. A dirty penny show may exist in it, but no circus with a horse and a half' (Wallett, *Public Life*, p. 89).

the end of a wretched season in Yarmouth and told, in his farewell speech for which the audience called, the audience of their short-comings. Someone in the boxes answered and the gallery cheered the speaker and told Wallett he had not done as he ought. Wallett pulled himself together and with a scorn and voice peculiar to him, turned to his assailants calling them a set of herring-catching beggars, made his defence, finishing by saying . . . he was glad to escape from the meshes of the ill-flavoured smokers of bloaters.[52]

Well, business was bad with us. Tom Swan's benefit was announced and as a gag he was advertised to drive a team of cats. Uncle painted a large billboard for outside the theatre. I assisted by holding pots, brushes, &c. He did not work in the scene room but on the stage and I was much interested in the work of art and thought I would like to have a daub at it. Fate favoured my desire – he was called away and left me in charge of pot and brush. I made a few strokes where they would not be observed and imitating him walked back to see the effect – but unfortunately stepped a little too much to the left. He reappeared, saw Mr Clever, he shouted 'another step to the rear', and head over heels I fell into the orchestra. No harm was done, not a scratch – but the drum! from the contents of the pot was another colour. He, Chas., was too much amused to be angry. I neither got kicked, hit or bullied.

If Leicester was a bad spec. to the Govr., it was absolute ruin to my refreshment venture.[53] I had work to do in front. Cheques to take at boxes, boxes to attend to and other duties that prevented me looking after my refectory arrangement. So I arranged with a boy to carry round my refreshment basket, giving him a 1d in a shilling. That worked well for him and kept me from insolvency, but on the very night of our departure my agent not only eloped with the night's takings but took off my stock and trade.

52. Wallett's 'honesty' was an uncompromising bluntness. In his autobiography he records beginning his managerial career in Yarmouth, where he erected a circus building. Little support was forthcoming, and even the Mayor was miserly in his patronage. Wallett records that he 'bade adieu to the intellectual herring-catchers, with an earnest prayer that I might never again fall into their meshes' (*ibid.*, p. 87.)

53. Of which this is the first we hear. Circus establishments did not include refreshment rooms or bars (see p. 27) but the antique theatrical practice of selling food from a basket in the auditorium enabled the boy to augment his income.

Leeds [1848]

Another ride, a cold journey. I cannot remember any incident on the road, more than we stopped all night at Sheffield. Pablo was there at the Amphitheatre.[54] Circus people when they get a chance always prefer a circus to any other performance. I suppose they know the difficulties of the performances and so they better appreciate them. We went and for the first time [I] saw and heard Wallett. To say I was delighted is but a weak phrase whereby to express my admiration. I remember one of, and give one of his impersonations.

Young Pablo was riding a trick act. His Uncle was ringmaster. Both were of the Negro type.[55] The younger had missed several times a trick and getting into his fork[56] pulled up his horse, looking defiantly and angrily at his uncle, who also was looking desperately angry at his nephew. Wallett got between them and asked the Master 'Are you looking black at him, Sir, or is he looking black at you?' Both performers grinned, the house was convulsed. It was not always the words of Wallett that touched the audience to scream, laugh or cheer, but his inimitable acting.[57] I have seen lots of men emulate him by dress, words and position but they were but dull sticks.

When I got to Leeds I was questioned as to last night's performance. Wallett was my theme. I little thought that I ever should have

54. Pablo Fanque, born William Darby in February 1786. See John Turner, 'Pablo Fanque, Black Circus Proprietor' in Gretchen Holbrook Gerzina (ed.), *Black Victorians, Black Victoriana* (New Brunswick: Rutgers University Press, 2003), pp. 20–38.

55. Probably William Banham, aka Billy Pablo, Fanque's sister's son. A tightrope dancer, vaulter and bareback rider.

56. Getting into his fork: coming down astride the horse. See Antony Hippisley-Coxe, *A Seat at the Circus* (Connecticut: Archon Books, 1980), p. 53, for this usage. It was not unusual at this time in British circus practice for a difficult trick to be tried repeatedly, during the performance, until it came off: the always-perfect acrobatic and equestrian display was an American import. See Speaight, *History of the Circus*, p. 104.

57. There are many anecdotes about Wallett's performances. A correspondent to the *Manchester Evening News* recalled: 'He would declaim witty selections from the poets, quote Shakespeare with telling effect, a favourite feature being his praise of women in the home and in social life, and the influence she could exercise. After an impassioned outburst on the influence of the wife and mother in the home he would suddenly relax his posture, and slouch round the ring with shoulders raised and arms hanging loosely by his side, and exclaim, "'Owt u'll do for a feyther."' Newspaper article dated 23 February [1930] in a scrapbook in Manchester Central Library; with thanks to John Turner.

Figure 5. Bill for Hengler's Circus, Leeds, December 1847, soon after James Frowde joined. Many of the artistes are mentioned in the memoirs.

fought with him for public favours – and obtain a respectable defeat. Our circus was built on King Charles Croft, on different lines to the last. The audience were at one end. Under the best seats were the money-takers and lobbies. Pablo had the circus after we left. Wallett was a great draw and things were prosperous. I think it was on his benefit night befell a dreadful accident. The gallery fell in and a falling timber crushed the life out of Mrs Pablo who, with Mrs Wallett, had been taking money. This was on 18th March 1848. No other person was seriously injured. Some wretch robbed the dead of her watch and the money box.[58]

About this time Mr Ryan had come very low, was at Nottingham, salaries were unpaid or only as far as the takings would share. Of course the musicians struck, they are the first, music may soothe the savage breast, it does not wake up in the breast of its mechanics' charity ...[59]

I took the gallery money in a wooden box outside the circus. The weather was very cold and I suffered very much in that draughty box. Uncle happily came one eve for money, my fingers were frozen. I was out in a jiffy, something warm administered, but better next day, the box was made weatherproof and lined with baize. I got another kind of warming. Jno. was poorly and I had to sleep at one of the performers. A lie was told of me. One morning after I had counted the checks, &c., the Govr., with whip in hand asked me a question. I would not answer. In the presence of Aunt I might have done. He swore, I should. No dog ever got a worse whipping. The door was locked, no one could come in, but the landlady kicked up a row, my

58. The wooden circus on King Charles Croft had been built and used by Charles Hengler the year before. At the inquest it was revealed that, though the building appeared sturdy enough, it was the builder's original intention to dismantle it after Hengler's Circus left. The collapse of the gallery, holding six hundred people, was attributed (by the builder) to 'Hengler's men removing props under the beams supporting the gallery when they went to get their things out' (Turner, 'Pablo Fanque', p. 25). Pablo Fanque had taken the circus 'as it stood' (*ibid.*, pp. 25–6).

59. Wallett confirms this: 'I next joined Mr Ryan, at Nottingham. His establishment appeared then on its last legs, for the bailiffs took possession that very day; and, to mend the matter, the bandsmen struck because their salaries were not paid. So I had to play clown and music too' (Wallett, *Public Life*, p. 77). See also note 115.

skin and bones were in a miserable condition, as was my shirt. Powell, who had been hors de combat, guardian of Dan Polaski dined with us. We lodged at a confectioner's and lived sumptuously. On this occasion calves head was the principal dish but aching bones and wounded spirit revolted against food, and the whip already frayed was threatened, but a word of pity and supplication from the liquid eyes of Aunt prevailed and after mercy, some choking, I took my miserable body to solitude.

After this slightly mysterious instance of his pride and ill-treatment, Frowde relates a jolly incident about a Christmas meal, and recollections of his dead mother. There is also a tale of how they saved the life of the daughter of their lodging house, who had taken poison, and who in later life became 'an actress of some position'. He met her again when she was playing the theatre at Scarborough. Then he returns to the narrative of the tour.

Soon as things were ready for starting, after my professional work, I had to visit the stables, tired and longing for an hour's sleep.

The other side of the ring was a stage, on either side of the ring was a passage to stables, &c., boarded to shut out the audience. We brought out 'Cinderella', often the juveniles sitting 'in state' were observed to scratch and rub their aristocratic carcasses while from the throne royalties gave spasmodic starts and ejaculated 'oh'. Accident solved the mystery. Chas. hurrying from the ring doors to the dressing room caught [?] pea-shooting the poor little beggars, he was fond of jokes.[60]

To raise our funds, Wallett was engaged. He came to tea. I can remember his coming into the room and my veneration and admiration. Aunt had Susie in her arms after the introductions, to her he most kindly enquired after her farm and then to the babe. Said Uncle, 'That's no. 1' 'To be renewed annually,' said Wallett. It did make Aunt blush and smile.

60. Tantalisingly, the name of the pea-shooting marksman is illegible.

February 1848

Derby does not present, at present, anything striking. Only a cuff on the ear from g-mother that knocked me off the corner of a box simply because I stared at Uncle who had come to see her, instead of answering a question.

'Twas here I heard of my Father's failure. Near all was sold and all were paid . . .

Wallett was our star. He gave a mock lecture on mesmerism – calling from the audience for help. A cocky sort of fellow came in a Dr. and sitting took off his gloves, gave Wallett a look that meant mischief. Then taking off his hat placed it on the phrenological chart, or head. Wallett removed the hat, looked at it, at its owner, then replaced on the model says 'Tis not the first block it has fitted,' his bye play &c. got a great laugh, as did the rejoinders. There would be a consequence, frequently got, till he sunk in silence and with a more modest demeanour left the ring for a back seat.

We had a good-natured old fellow for a landlord and a dear old woman who smoked a short pipe in the kitchen after each meal. Both were very good to me. Mr Etches and Madame were our patrons and took some interest. With them we left our performing spot pony [when] we went.

October 1847[61]

Coventry fair
Miss Chart[62] was apprenticed and rode a grey mare Uncle Edward had brought from Scot. I was off to the fairground. Susie was lying on the sofa tucked up; I kissed the babe. Miss Chart only was present and larkingly said 'You don't kiss me', a neglect I hastened to rectify. Oh fireworks! I can just remember some long legs, finding myself bundling down the stairs and then busy painting or rather

61. Frowde's dating is not very clear – here he appears to take a step back, having arrived, above, at February 1848.

62. A Miss Chartre is with Hengler's in Brighton in March 1849, dancing the

Highland Fling and 'Pas de Jenny Lind', presumably on horseback. See *Brighton Herald*, 3 March and 10 March 1849.

whitewashing the pony pedestal. But [in] favour to the City I was sketching its [coat of] arms, an elephant, and was wholly absorbed in my artistic pursuits, when I was called back from a brutal idea to a brutal fact. Uncle Edward, thinking I was larking came behind and gave me across the ribs such a whack with a stick as left me writhing on the tan.[63] Charles came in just as this affectionate attention had commenced and stopped further display by an explanation I think might have put his brother to shame.[64] Whatever lickings I got from Charles was as his idea all right, but I don't think he would allow others to bully me and Aunt, gentle and beautiful as she was then, was always my champion and often shielded my faults. I was not the only victim to relatives' rough rations. Next to our show was J. Batty's[65] (brother to the celebrated W. Batty) Wild Beast Show. Before the show commenced I went in with young Batty, who to show his pluck, or a desire to interest me, went into a den of an untutored lion. Ere the first growl was over in came the proprietor. Down he went to the den, 'come out' he hissed, in his fear, and out he came and whilst the old man was fastening the door off he was, well for him. But he got the whip after and well deserved it. Next time I saw [him] he was a big fellow and had a circus in Gloster, on a piece of land called Wildman's Ground. Wildman's father had a mumming booth,[66] in fact there were other mummers, circus and all kind of shows. The Coventry Fair was the greatest remembered. It was, I think, a revival. Anyhow,

63. Tan: oak bark used to bed the circus ring.

64. This tale seems to be confused, possibly by his embarrassment, either at the time or in telling it to his children, about kissing a girl; what emerges clearly is the Hengler impulse to knock the boy about on general principles, rather than wait for him to commit any specific crime.

65. Perhaps George Batty Snr, proprietor of Batty's Menagerie.

66. Frowde is evidently writing about seeing Batty nearly forty years later, since Wildman's Ground did not come into use until around 1885. It was a plot of land 40 yards by 40 yards on the corner of Barton Street and Park Road, and opposite the Bell Inn, where Mr Fred. William Wildman was the publican from 1885. According to Miss G. M. Davies of Gloucester, 'As no-one owned the piece of land travelling players would ask at the Bell Inn to pitch their tents. Mr. Wildman gave permission and the players were not charged any rent. [It] was used until about 1930 by small fairs, vendors of patent medicines, fortune tellers etc' (Gloucester Local Studies Library). Although Edward and Frederick Wildman owned portable theatres in the mid-century, there is no evidence that the Gloucester Wildmans are from the same family.

the celebrated Madame Wharton[67] was engaged to personify the historic Lady Godiva. She was a magnificent woman clothed by her luxuriant hair and silk tights.

[March/April 1848]

Birmingham found us a nice little circus. Here Uncle engaged a man called O'Hara as architect.[68] A man to go ahead, arrange with timber merchants and erect the buildings. Here stands the building that was erected by Mr Jas. Ryan of here perhaps. By and bye he married a lady of Cheltenham by the name of Dangerfield. Her people had, I think, something to do with coaches and some position in that town. Another of his Circuses, still at Shrewsbury, after was, and I suppose is still, used as a market place.[69]

Here we had our first small pony, a black one, 'Tommy'. We went to West Bromwich. I remember in the vaulting O'Hara made his appearance with a square face, flat head and a great rotundity. To my surprise he did a somersault and I found out that once he had been a rider of some ability. His figure prevented him being fit for any decent Co.; too proud for 1 penny shows or mountebanks,[70] he had retired to

67. In answer to an enquirer regarding Madame Wharton or Warton, the *Era* offered the following: 'Madame Warton, who appeared in the *Poses Plastiques* long ago and exhibited in Leicester-square, was on one occasion the representative of Lady Godiva in the Coventry procession. The names of recent representatives were not made public, but it may be here recorded they were not known on the London stage' (*Era*, 11 April 1875).

68. Probably the Mr O'Hara who was still with Charles Hengler when he opened his circus in Dale Street, Liverpool in 1857. The architect, as Frowde indicates, was more than a draughtsman, but travelled with the circus, and supervised the erection of these temporary wooden buildings.

69. Ryan's Circus at Shrewsbury may have been the building by the Welsh Bridge. It was a large brick building used for equestrian performances, etc. and for the sale of butter and cheese on fair days. It was later used as a brewery – named the Circus Brewery – and survived until after the Second World War as a warehouse. See note 115.

70. A mountebank show is a display, often in the street or market place, by a few acrobats and other acts who do not charge for the exhibition, but sell things to the crowd that assembles – either goods that they try to pass off at an inflated price, or raffle tickets to be drawn for miscellaneous prizes.

private life and had by his honesty and shrewdness obtained a responsible position in a builder's yard.

West Bromwich was not a fortune. We were opposed by one of Batty's[71] companies under the management of a Mr Thomson and we gave them best. We had a better run after the tents had gone. We were joined by Jim Wild[72] and a return of C. Adams who brought 2 beautiful spot horses.

1848

Now we are [at the] Theatre Royal Birmingham. Mr W Broadfoot[73] was engaged by the Manager Mr Simson, to bring out equestrian pieces. He was a dreadful man to have to do with, most exacting and excited. Would, if things went wrong, ... stamp and actually foam with rage, and would keep actors and actresses hours after the performance to re-rehearse something that had gone wrong. As stage manager he was more autocratic than the general run of such big pots. I have seen him after a storm rush to the prompter's box and the boy rush to him with a foaming pot, till the 2 foamers settled down. I think our fellows had the best of it by one dismounting, taking him by the collar and taking him to orchestra, saying 'My wife is among the ladies you have addressed, and for 2 pins I would pitch you head first into that drum!' So said he, 'Jno. and Mr Hengler's horses all may go.' 'Yes' said Mr Hengler 'it's now nearly 12. I never work, nor my

71. William Batty himself was manager of Astley's in London at this time.

72. James Wild, equestrian clown. His brother Sam Wild, owner of Wild's portable theatre, wrote: 'Our brother James ... had visited Adams's Circus while we were at Huddersfield, and fascinated by the cream-coloured horses, the elegant dresses of the performers, et cetera, went and joined himself as a clown and vaulter to that establishment ... He achieved considerable popularity in his time as a clown. He travelled with Batty, Cooke and Pablo Fanque. His last engagement was with Hengler, with whom he remained until his death' (Old Wild's, pp. 14–15).

73. William D. Broadfoot, equestrian actor and manager. Wallett recalls him at Astley's: 'He was the best stage manager for spectacles that ever lived in our time – except his great original master Ducrow – but a man of irritable temper, and a great tyrant ... During the second week of his management he compelled us to rehearse a piece over and over again till it became unendurable: when a stuffed Astleyan cannon-ball came into violent contact with his head, and prostrated him on the floor. He stamped, he raved, and offered a reward of two pounds to any one who would betray the projector' (Wallett, Public Life, p. 81).

people, or horses, if avoidable, on Sunday. Grooms take your horses home. Good night,' and good luck thought the people.

Mummers and showmen fraternised. Atkins was the favourite comedian, and properly so. There was a real old mummer there named Barlow,[74] of whom many anecdotes are told. He was spinning a yarn of his early days, evidently the scene was a mumming booth which he described as a kind of 'Wooden Town Hall'. That wooden town hall was a standing joke against him for years. The horses were at a public house stables in the Bull Ring. (Geo. and I were on board wages with the paid grooms.) Horses did not leave the stage till the audience were dispersed and then a trap was opened and they descended by an inclining platform. 'Lincoln', a spot, objected to this delay and having perceived his biped professional brethren descending to the street below by a staircase running parallel by their mode of egress determined to reconnoitre. Accordingly down the rickety stairs he went, pushed the hall door open with his head and appeared unabashed before the horrified stage door-keeper, with as much confidence as a *lion comique*[75] of the present day. The door-keeper knew not what to do. Presently some ladies opened the door and gave vent to screams and other ways of expressing their terror. Then it was that Lincoln was missed. There was no getting by him. There he stood boldly at the letter rack and notice board, till a groom opened the street door and led him out.

One funny episode which I must miserably fail in describing – Broadfoot chose 'Turpin' as the play for his benefit, he to play the hero. Rehearsal was called and Broadfoot, with a courage worthier of a nobler field, booted and spurred somehow got on the saddle of Black Bess (Jack). I cannot say he got in the saddle, he was anywhere but there before his leg was well over. [Uncle] John had a taste of the brums[76] and [Black Bess] Johnny had not taste for the titillation they produced and showed a frantic desire to tear himself from the groom. At last the word was given, let go! Oh, what a sight! Oh how the victims of Mr Stage Manager, jeers and insults presented – there was

---

74. Joseph Holloway's Theatre of 1849 has Barlow in the company.

75. *Lion comique*: music hall performers like Alfred Vance and George Leybourne with a brash, swaggering man-about-town persona, were a byword for self-assurance.

76. Brums: spurs (slang).

Figure 6. Woodcut from a playbill showing Dick Turpin and Black Bess leaping the turnpike gate. The bill is dated February 1852.

the tyrant jostled about – now being turned round – now backing into the scene and now nearly into the orchestra from which the musicians, to the danger of their instruments, were scrambling into the pit (there were no stalls then). Presently the Govr. got the horse by the bridle, 'Get off' said he to Broadfoot 'or take off your spurs.' 'What! I,' shouted Broadfoot, 'take off my spurs' – this was answered by a voice from the boxes, 'You had better be advised by Mr Hengler, Broadfoot.' The voice was the voice of Mr Simson, Lessee. Horrified, Broadfoot slid from the horse and with a stride that the great Irving (had he then been on board) might have envied, struck an attitude and addressed the Chief – 'What! 'Turpin' without spurs!!! Whoever saw a highwayman without spurs, such a [spectacle][77] would draw down upon my head the disgust of the audience, my reputation would be destroyed.' The intensity of this tragic [sic] was just hovering between the sublime and the ridiculous. All were in smiles, even the discomfited musicians, save the owner of the bass viol that in the stampede had to leave his portly instrument to its fate: the eccentricities of Broadfoot or maddened instincts of the big black horse.

77. Frowde leaves a gap in the original, presumably at a loss for the word to make his story tell.

Broadfoot subsides, he became, after blowing the head off a foaming tankard, for him he became mildly satirical. He resigned his spurs, curbed his pride and with a slack rein went on to rehearse. All was peace, though every detail was duly enacted till the gate scene. Gate and toll house were erected, the cue was given and up should have come Turpin, full gallop, but no, Johnny came on, head like lead, and action tame as a cow's.[78] Then was Broadfoot triumphant, 'Now Sir, are spurs required?' Then came the argument – spur or failure. Then did the faces of the musicians elongate and then came a happy thought [perhaps of Uncle John, deleted] – 'have a double' was suggested. One of ours most like Broadfoot in figure was selected, the costumer was summoned, coat &c. to match Turpin's was demanded; in a wardrobe of the T[heatre] R[oyal] of Brummagem this was not difficult. Comfort was resumed, but there was a glare lurking around the eyes of the night's hero, the set and scene went well. Turpin, among Ainsworth's heroes, was fairly acted. Broadfoot felt the joy that warms the heart and thrills the veins of a successful actor. Oh that such moments of triumph could be established; but alas, the spirit that fires the imagination to place expression in every feature, the soul that gives unction to [expression, deleted] sentence, labour but for a moment. The eye of the spectator sees a picture, hears the sound, the imagination is excited and admiration of the pleasure given is genuine – but oh for how briefly! A beefsteak, a bad oyster, a blue pill and black draught – the actor is a thing of the past. The actor has fretted his hour soon soon to be forgotten; how much better the fate of the sculptor, the painter and the engraver.

All went well the dummy, or rather Broadfoot's second, with face averted from the audience, did the racing and Broadfoot mounting at the wings, made his appeal to the gate keeper – back to the wings to dismount – hurry scurry the second mounts – a high and a long leap excited the sporting instincts of the Gods. Loud was the call for Broadfoot, hearty the cheer he got for another's skill. This wounded

78. Leaping the toll gate was an important and dramatic scene in the production. Playbills frequently illustrate it. See Derek Forbes, *Illustrated Playbills: A Study with a Reprint of* A Descriptive Catalogue of Theatrical Wood Engravings (1865), (London: The Society for Theatre Research, 2002), which has two illustrations of the episode (pp. 52, 53) and an entry in the 'Descriptive Catalogue', no. 463.

his susceptibilities: now was he more certain than ever that Hengler had in jealousy robbed him of glory – from the 1st objection to the spurs evidently Broadfoot attributed his spurless position to jealousy. Now came the scene where Bess' strength has failed her. The virtue derived from the steak Turpin at the King's Head Newark had put round her bit was gone and pulling the mare (Johnnie) on the neck, Broadfoot made public his wrongs and improvised as thus, 'Come on Bess, only 1 short mile and glory waits us – 'tis a struggle I know, my dearest, nature has been outraged, we have done more than horse and man has done before. We would still do more Bess, but Mr Hengler has taken away my spurs, he won't let me have a whip and ...' but here all acting and oration was drowned by the perfect thundering of laughter from house, actors, musicians and people.

Now drop the scene at Brum, only I would observe, I had a very idle time of it and resolved to learn tricks of posturing – but how to begin? I enquired and for reply was told to practise. I commenced with the splits – at all times, in all places, Church, home or abroad, from the time I awoke till I went to bed was I training my muscles. I tried a very drastic method to bend my back. I put the backs of 2 chairs together, then standing on my head on the seat of one, back of my head to the back of the chair, I threw my body over the back. Rolling over in the most positive agony from the chair I writhed in pain and was sure that I had broken my back. I dared not speak of it. My Leeds experience was a lesson so I suffered in secret.

Oxford

Here I slept at a pub by the circus, which stood in a field by Giles' church.[79] Uncle Edward slept in the same room, we had food at Charles'. It was a busy house and for a young wife[80] a great trial, for she was busy enlarging the wardrobe, quite sufficient without catering for so many of us. Aunt Kelly, grandmother's sister, was busy assisting. We did fairly. 'Turpin' and 'Cinderella' were the strongest draw, as pieces, but Uncle Edward and Selim Bridges were

79. The pub was probably the Horse and Jockey on Woodstock Road. St Giles's Field refers to the whole area of open land north of St Giles's Church, between the Woodstock and Banbury Roads.

80. Young wife: Charles's wife, Mary Ann Frances (née Sprake), daughter of a bandmaster and an aerialist (JT VA1).

favourites.[81] G-father's advance to an audience was good school, Edward's another.[82] A handsome head well set on his shoulders, a fine face and good figure every movement was a study. He could not make an ungraceful motion, on rope he was clever, but his style alone would evoke admiration when clever feats by the less artistic dancer would be met with silence. His muscles were beautifully laid on; his arched instep aided the beauty of a pointed foot, his pantomime was excellent, but he was a bad mummer. John was the superior in this.[83]

It was at Oxford and in Turpin I first spoke a part – that of a tinker trying to evade a toll – if I had stuck to the text all might have been well, but I did a mild gag and told the gate keeper he ought to let me go through without toll, out of respect to my cap and gown. I thought I had done something wonderful. I had got a gag (viz. a laugh). I got something else, soon as I got out of the audience's sight. Turpin and Tom King gave me a taste of their whips, both thinking I had committed a species of sacrilege, and insulted the University. At Oxford, some philanthropist took an interest in me and would have put me to some business, and in order to find out what I was best adapted for he took me to a phrenologist to have my head charted. I expect the professor found more bumps than were described on his chart. His ultimatum was that I might do in a bank as far as honesty went, but neither behind the counter or at the books would I be of good. In a shop I would disturb other workers. I had no application, no veneration, would make a good friend but for a time a dangerous enemy. The stage would be the only fit place for me. I never saw my would be friend after.

My little cousin Sue had been badly treated by the nurse and I resented cruelty. I had counted the cheques and arranged the boxes for night, I was writing out orders for bill board displayers, when I recd. a command to go to the circus. There was Uncle Edward with his fiddle and some performers sitting round the ring fence. As soon as I appeared he called me into the ring. In the centre was a rough.

<hr>

81. Selim Bridges, equestrian, who played the character of 'Mercury'.

82. Both Henry Michael and Edward Hengler (grandfather and uncle respectively) were rope-dancers. Frowde seems to mean here that their deportment set him a good example.

83. John Michael Hengler, Jno., Henry Michael's son.

As I came into the ring Ed. played a chord of introduction, and then described me as 'the boy that pushed the nurse, over head and heels into the cradle' and 'now' said he 'let us see how he can push the Oxford chicken'. I had to take off my coat and vest, tuck up my sleeves from my skinny arms. I don't think over all my body was sufficient fat to grease Edward's hair. (He used a lot, he was proud of his close curly hair. In Church, waiting to be shown a pew was he and Jno. 'Jno.', said he, as though he was the Saint of the Church, 'Jno., is my head tidy?' 'Yes,' said Jno., 'a tidy size.') But we were not in Church, but in a ring and my opponent grinned, as he took stock of me and contemplated which part of my physiognomy he would first attack. He soon made up his mind and I found myself on my back, again and again I received his gracious attention. At last I resolved not to spar but receive and give. This tactic was right but my opponent wrong, and I gave him one on the nose, that made him smile with tears in his eyes. I got in another and then I became dazed. Uncle Chas. coming, the fight was over, but he did let Ed. and others have the length of his tongue for many days. I was quite ill and very sore, unable to practise. G-mother heard of it and she was angry. That fight had this effect; one of my tormentors, on the last night, we were pulling down decorations and he shoved me, we were both in the ring, the performers and musicians were in various parts of the building, and in their presence I gave Bridges as big a hiding as probably he ever had, evidently to the secret pleasure of Uncle Charles and the dismay of Edward and others. Never from that time anyhow, no one cuffed or bullied me.

Next morn we started for Portsmouth and [I] got a good share of chaff for my riding and fighting – neither of them very brilliant. We halted at Petersfield; I was Charley Adams' guest. Portsmouth: I cannot remember anything of importance. I had a great deal of walking to do, seeing bills delivered at Shelford, etc., etc. Hogg, the Manager of the Landport Theatre which was then situated in a narrow street at the back of Russell Terrace, summoned us for playing pieces without a Theatrical Licence, but Mr Lord, our lawyer by his logic got the Magistrates to entertain his expressed views. He showed it would be impossible for Mr Hogg to produce the plays we did, and argued the dialogue was only to show the training of the horse, and produce spectacular effect. I think it ended in their giving us a licence. The opposition did us a great deal of good and Hogg much harm.

Bill Shalders[84] was here, at the height of popularity. He was a good all-round comedian ... At Portsmouth I received a salary and lived in my own lodgings, 12/-.

Guildford

[I] had a comfortable lodgings. Here I gave my first dinner party. A rider called Macket[85] was my first guest and boiled rabbit was the piece de resistance. I think it was to him I confided about practising posturing. He told me I was much too old for it, that my bones were set. I don't think bones have much to do with it, yet sometimes my ribs will crack like a piece of artillery and often in Church or when I have been sitting still.

1849

Our next town was Windsor.[86] Our stud was increased by 'Battleaxe' and 'Alfred', a pony from the Castle, and 2 of the prettiest ponies, Sir Quattro a stallion and a mare. Alfred horse was a spot. Battleaxe was a large lean headed skewbald and was the cause of a most serious accident, a dreadful roadside scene, Hayden Bridge to Haltwhistle (see p. 87).

Parish, a slack rope vaulter, was of our company.[87] There was some dispute as to a trick that grandfather spoke of. It could not be done! 'What' cried he in his rage. He let down the rope and in less time than it takes to write he was on the rope and executed the trick. Uncle was in a rare way because of grandfather's age and health. We played Waterloo.[88] Some officers made themselves very objectionable in the Boxes. Henderson halted in one speech and asked for a little consideration. The audience backed him up and called that they should be turned out. Soon as the performance was over, the officers came round to kick up a row, but nothing serious occurred. The Eton boys took a

84. William Shalders, actor and scenic artist. He appeared with Robson at the Olympic theatre in 1853.

85. W. Mackett, equestrian (*JT VA2*).

86. In January–February 1849 (*JT HH*).

87. George Parish, born 1811, Rope-dancer (*JT VA1*).

88. Probably *The Battle of Waterloo* (J. H. Amherst, Astley's, 1824).

great dislike to Rivers,[89] used to mock applaud him and call him fatty. Henderson, among his many performances, used to throw a great number of somersaults in succession on the vaulting board. All the company used to compete in this. Rivers never could do more than 3 or 4 and they all over the board. The boys too assisted, one day brought pea-shooters and made some painfully good shots. He took it good-naturedly and the boys at last only in good temper chivvied him. I lodged by the Batchelors Acre, at the pub and most kind they, landlord and lady, were.

Brighton Theatre.[90] Here the actors were a little envious. We played 'St Geo. and the Dragon', and Henderson played St Geo., this the actors objected to and foolishly, for none of them could have sustained the part, which was done in pantomime, or work the horse. I forget the leading man's name, I think it was Maynard.[91] We had rehearsed the last rehearsal of 'Timour the Tartar'. Timour was anything but pleasant and of course was not happy. Night came, there was no Timour. The Manager came in a great fright to the Govr. Said he, 'Never mind, either I or Henderson can do it.' The costume was too short for the Govr. Henderson had to do it. 'Give me half an hour to read it up, and quiet,' said he. But before the piece, he was advertised for vaulting. This he did and was called to front. Some other act of gymnastics took place. This gave Henderson time to dress his part. The mummers in groups were grinning sarcastically, expecting to see the sawdust hero flounder and mull, but to their amazement he made a great hit . . .

89. R. L. Rivers the strong man. See note 43.

90. Late March 1849 (JT HH).

91. The Theatre Royal, Brighton, was opened in 1807. Advertisements from the *Brighton Herald* (3 March, 10 March and 17 March 1849) announce *Mazeppa, The Runaway Horse of Savoy, Timour the Tartar, Dick Turpin* and *The Battle of Waterloo*. Unfortunately the performances are not reported.

3

✣

Three: Out into the world to learn his trade, 1849

By the spring of 1849, the concern was thriving. Frowde was by now eighteen, and had begun working towards an act of his own. His lanky and unlovely appearance (he mentions his 'big eyes, red nose, lantern jaws') was well suited to 'posturing', that is, contortionism, parodying the cult of the beautiful and athletic body cultivated by his relations. The Henglers were unimpressed, and he had a row with the 'Govr.' and went off to his parental uncle's home in Portsmouth. But once there he soon took fright at the idea of being regularly apprenticed to an ordinary trade, and walked away to seek his fortune alone on the stage. He went to London and plunged into the cut-throat underworld of the entertainment boom in the capital.

The 1840s and 1850s were an interesting passage in the development of the entertainment industry. The previous generation of humble professionals were still more or less dependent upon the old strolling life described by Dickens in The Old Curiosity Shop, *where Little Nell and her grandfather, tramping the roads, fall in with performers whose ever-shifting pattern of self-employment cannot have varied greatly over many generations. They walked, alone or in their family or partnership groups, from town to town and fair to fair, gathering occasionally at friendly pubs on the way and setting up their shows – everything from puppets to ballad-singing to performing dogs – whenever and wherever they found a few people assembled and so might hope to earn a few pence by passing round the hat. This network was still to some extent in place when Frowde took to the road, but it had begun to grow, becoming involved with small capitalists who provided premises in which larger audiences might*

*gather in greater comfort, and where more profit could be made.
A growing concern like the Henglers' formed business links with
innkeepers all over the country who profited from their need for beds
and, especially, stabling. During his ramble Frowde was greatly
helped by these friendly publicans, the first of whom gave him a bed
and a lift onwards, and later welcomed him back and converted his
skittle alley so that Frowde could get up a 'free and easy' entertainment
there. Such enterprising conversions were the basis of what was about
to mushroom into the music hall boom.*

 *When he reached London – a grim metropolis in 1849,
overexpanded, overcrowded and in the grip of cholera – Frowde headed
for Astley's, the premier and original circus, that stood amid a muddle of
entertainment venues in the lower-class districts immediately south
of the Thames. This area had been a centre of metropolitan amusements
for centuries – the bear- and bull-baiting pits and the Globe theatre had
been located there, outside the City's jurisdiction. Now it was dominated
by Astley's Amphitheatre and the Surrey and Victoria theatres, but
offered many other venues as well, a mixture of purpose-built circuses
and theatres, and rooms or other temporarily empty spaces where a
concert could be got up – the semiprofessional 'Free and Easies' of
which Frowde speaks. Seven years later, Henry Mayhew collected
the observations of a 'penny-gaff clown' whose life was, Mayhew
discovered, 'wrapped up in these cheap dramatic saloons' including
'The Rotunda in the Blackfriars' Road ... the largest in London, that
holds one thousand comfortably seated ... at one penny ... a
first-class entertainment it is, consisting of a variety of singing and
dancing, and ballets, from one hour and a half to two hours' (Mayhew's
London, p. 499). Frowde got a job there, and records that he had a
working day of seven or eight hours. This was, in effect, where he
created his act and hardened himself to the life he had chosen. He also
recalls brutal conditions in the lodging-house he shared with other
performers, including a vicious exploiter of children. He made some
friends, including a clown, Stonette, whose round of work in
miscellaneous halls and suburban arenas struck Frowde as 'slavery'.*

 *He eventually tramped to join Henderson at a Hengler's
satellite in Rugby, but found he was still not ready to settle into his
subordinate role. Taking off again, and meeting acquaintances from
London, he began a round of the Midland proto-music halls, which*

*eventually reduced him to near-starvation in a Coventry winter –
again sheltering at a pub where the Henglers were valued customers. It
was there, while he was painting an announcement on cardboard for a
desperate venture he was about to make, that his Uncle Charles found
him and scooped him up. He submitted to a haircut and a new hat
before returning to the family fold at York.*

We left Brighton for Lewes. Here Jenny was born.[92] I lodged with
some of the performers. The Govr. caught me practising and gave me a
good slanging. By now I could do a few tricks in posturing. This
I could practise in my bedroom. But I wanted to do a forespring which
means throwing yourself on your hands and turning over on to your
feet, a kind of flip flap, but a forward instead of a backward action.
I made miserable attempts at this and deserved all the compliments the
Govr. gave me on my clumsiness. Lewes is a place to visit. A peculiar-
ity in diet was cheese at every meal. We did very bad business. The
Govr. was experimenting in the making of a tent. He and O'Hara had
their hands full. We used to go from Lewes to a small place 3 days a
week and perform under canvas. It was very cold and evil and the new
tent was soon deserted ...

I had to submit to much hardship and having a row with John,
I determined to see whether I could not get a living as 'posture master'.
Accordingly I started off, got to Portsmouth, went to my Uncle's for a
few days, heard him discussing as to putting me apprentice to a
draper, got alarmed and having a half-crown in my pocket determined
on starting for London ... I got a lift to Guildford. I went to the pub
our performers used to frequent. The landlord made a guest of me and
next morn, thanks to his good nature, or gratitude I was enabled to
ride to London. And now what to do, or where to go; I did not know
(certainly not to relations) till I could get a situation. I enquired for
Astley's, thinking I might hear of something. I met Dick Moffat,[93] he
has a penny cirque in a gaff in the New Cut,[94] lived in the square that

---

92. Jenny: the daughter of Charles
Hengler, born 1849 (*JT VA2*).

93. Richard Moffat, equestrian, with
Hengler's in the 1840s (*JT VA1*).

94. A gaff is one of the *bêtes noires* of the
Victorian social commentator, a cheap
unlicensed place of entertainment, often
in a disused building, attracting a young
and rowdy audience. It quickly came to
be used to signify the bottom of the scale,

was entered by the New Cut, houses of some pretension, I forget the name of the square, call it Lambeth. Then I went to see my Father, Mother, sister, brother and Harry. They have a gutta percha shop in Oakley Street . . .

Frowde's father was distressed that his son was working in a gaff, so he went to live and work with his aunt, who sold fruit and vegetables in a shop in the Westminster Road.

Mrs McCarthy, a star then at Astley's, with her maid, had rooms with us.[95] Soon as I let them in I used to retire to my bedroom. It was an improvised one, the room at the back of the shop from where, in the daytime, like spiders in their den, Aunt and I looked out for flies (customers). This room formerly had been a back yard, but was now enclosed by a roof, of glass. When the coast was clear, I used to undress and have a good practice at posturing. One night, after hopping the frog, I rested sitting down with my legs behind my back. By some means I fell over, on to the fender, which made a great clatter. I feared I had disturbed the house and in fear I listened, for I had the gas burning which ought to have been out an hour ago. All was silent, so at it I went again. I was sitting in the chair, preparatory to hopping to the ground on my hands, when I thought I heard a noise. I looked up through the skylight and through it I saw 3 ladies looking at me from the passage window! Down I came, out went the gas and they gave their smothered laugh which had disturbed me, full vent. In despair and shame I listened to their peals of laughter. Next morn I was off to Lambeth [crossed out] Church Square off the New Cut. At night [I] was performing at the gaff. My turn was come, but I wanted to be announced. 'Oh, I'll announce,' said Fuller the clown (one of the readiest I have met). And he did, saying 'Ladies and Gentlemen, I have the honour to introduce for your favours, His Grace the Duke of Limbs.'[96]

and has remained a term of abuse in subsequent histories: 'There was a penny gaff of a circus called the Olympic in Lower Marsh, Lambeth, which seated 1,000.' See Antony Hippisley-Coxe, 'The Lesser-Known Circuses of London,' *Theatre Notebook* 13 (3), (Spring 1959), p. 96.

95. Perhaps Mme Marie Macarte, equestrienne, who was with William Batty's company at Astley's in 1849 (*JT VA1*).

96. Duke of Limbs: a gawk, fool or awkward person. Frowde's lanky and unprepossessing appearance is turned to comic advantage.

Figure 7. James Frowde in his posturing routine.

When I appeared to the view of horrid crew and they saw my skeleton form, I was greeted with a roar of rough laughter and slang, but left the ring with éclat.

Frowde describes living in London in the grip of a cholera epidemic in the summer of 1849. In his own lodging house a Risley performer (a kind of acrobat) called Professor Hemmings dies, and a woman goes mad and tries to seduce Frowde, and then jumps from the window.

My next experience was at the Rotunda, by Blackfriar's bridge.[97] Stonette, who was clown with us, was out of a situation and to fill up time started a gaff.[98] He was very kind to me. There was a great powerful wretch, with miserable kids that he was torturing to do what he was never capable to do. In my indignation at his cruelty I expressed myself for which I received such a blow on the nose as stunned me. Years after this I read of his being committed to hard labour for cruelty to some other victims. Performing 6 or 7 hours a day was good practice though battering. Stonette got a situation and worked at fairs often a long journey of miles home after a day's slavery.

Then I thought I wanted to go into the country. My old landlord was glad to see me and helped me to rig up his skittle alley for a show, self &c., free and easy.

The theatre was opened. I went to the manager and was put on the staff to make myself useful. I went on the stage at the first rehearsal. A black man was lording it, sending actors about to this and other positions &, with much haute, directing them how to stand, look or gesture, to suit his reading and acting and personal success. 2 young men whispering excited his wrath because one was gently swinging a cane. His manner of addressing the gentlemen was so fearfully autocratic that in sheer disgust I walked off and this probably is the reason I am not a Compton or Buckstone.[99] That coloured individual was Aldridge, after Chevalier Aldridge, who years after told Wm. Cooke he had no right to keep me off the stage (of that in its place).[100]

I returned to London, all the better for rest and pure air, and did work at the Free and Easies ... Clarke had opened a Circus at the

97. See John Earl, 'The Rotunda: Variety Stage and Socialist Platform' *Theatre Notebook* 58 (2), (2004), pp. 71–90. In 1844 it had been refused a theatrical licence, and continued that decade as 'a variety house, with a magistrate's music and dancing licence' (p. 83).

98. Charles Stonette, Shakespearean clown (*JT VA2*).

99. Two popular and famous comic actors of their day. John Baldwin Buckstone (1802–79), dramatist, actor and manager, was a fine low comedian.

Henry Compton (1805–77) was best known for his Shakespearean clowns. Frowde, tongue in cheek, blames his failure to rank with the leading legitimate comic performers on this bruising encounter.

100. Ira Aldridge (1807–67), African-American actor. His reputation in Britain increased after he replaced the dying Edmund Kean as Othello at Covent Garden in 1833. Unfortunately, Frowde never returns to the subject he suggests here.

Lambeth Baths.[101] There I met Uncle Henderson, who told me he had, with Jno. Wells[102] and Dick Moffat, started a circus. If I liked he would give me something to do. Aunt Powell found me and I went to help her. Soon as I got a few shillings I resolved to walk to Rugby and join Henderson and Co.[103]

There follows an account of Frowde's farewell to his father, who desperately disapproved of his son's profession, and gave him nothing but his blessing. Frowde never saw him again, and only heard from him by a letter after his death (see p. 86).

I was quite willing to work as an apprentice would do, but saw no prospect of advancement. At Rugby I had the temerity to go to some swells in the boxes and tell them to behave and warn them. One of those fellows was Johnny Broome, the then celebrated who became after notorious in some law case of which Brighton was the scene[104] ... I saw no chance of getting on – one of the managers (Moffat) hated me. He left the ring for something. I was by, and he struck me. Aunt Henderson saw this, she being in the ring. When Moffat came out I was waiting for him and at once went at him. Mrs Henderson had left on the other side of the house, and in hot haste went to her husband and complained demanding satisfaction. He came round and found me helping myself – Moffat did not appear before the public that week. I got a tip from Uncle, but at Stourbridge I left them.

101. John Clarke, equestrian, clown and proprietor. He had a circus at Lambeth Baths in 1855 and had early associations with Astley and Ducrow. He was at Bartholomew Fair in 1825. Noted for his wheezy, gruff voice, he is said to have been the model for Mr Sleary in Dickens's *Hard Times*. See also Keith, *Circus Life*, where he is recalled as having 'procured an engagement at the Lambeth Baths, Westminster Road, which, in the winter months, was turned into a circus' (p. 20). Keith has great affection for John Clarke, and writes about him at length.

102. John Wells, equestrian and circus proprietor. He had early connections with Charles Hengler, and then with John Henderson (JT VA2).

103. It appears that John Henderson was heading a circus company in Rugby that was, perhaps, an offshoot of Charles Hengler's, as both he and Frowde were to do later. No other record of this venture has been found.

104. Broom was a prizefighter. In a celebrated bare-knuckle match which took place somewhere between Birmingham and London, Johnny Broom fought J. Hannon in January 1841 for the Lightweight Championship. The fight was over forty-seven rounds and took 1 hour 19 minutes, being stopped when Hannon was unable to continue. We have not been able to trace the incident in Brighton.

Here I was so hard up that I was hungry and without a place to sleep in. I slept in the stables, of course up before the grooms came, fearing Henderson might find out my destitute condition. Strolling along I met the clown Fuller. 'Well Cully,'[105] said he, 'what brings you up so early?' Question answered by a similar one. Fuller was the clown who introduced me to the audience of New Cut as the 'Duke of Limbs' and sometimes addressed me as 'Your Grace'.[106] I went home with him to b'fast. I told him I had no situation, no one knew me. So after b'fast he wrote for me. I stayed a day or two with him and went to Brum. At one of the best halls I got a turn on trial and got on well. But my dress was objected to.[107] I got a few shillings for my turn. Xmas Day my money was gone. I started for Coventry, it was a miserable day and awful travelling. Snow was thick upon the ground, it took me all day to get to Coventry and it was dark when I got in. I went direct to the Red Lion; I think our horses had stood there – the landlord was a friend of Uncle Edward's. I went direct to the tap room. The bright hot room made me feel faint. Some men were having some Xmas drink, hot and spiced. I enquired for the landlord, told him who I was, he remembered, said I could have a bed, went and had a wash and joy, sat down to good Xmas cheer. Next morn after b'fast I went to see Judd, a publican who had a concert room. As luck would have it they wanted someone that night, on account of a disappointment. So I was to go on trial. He eyed me very curiously. My hat was a Spanish one and my dark hair turned up in a lazy kind of manner, over my shoulder, which with my big eyes, red nose, lantern jaws and general make-up would be enough in these days to have got me locked up on suspicion of being an American Fenian.[108] I went to a little

105. Cully: mate.

106. See note 96.

107. His dress may have been too outré for the saloon theatre, either because he was in the full flood of adolescent rebellion against conventional clothes, or because he had acquired it with the circus in mind. More probably, however, his clothes were just too shabby to make a good impression.

108. American Fenian: a member of the Irish-American organisation dedicated to the overthrow of the English government of Ireland. The Irish were frequently depicted in Victorian cartoons with simian or brutish features, which included a pronounced jawline and long, unkempt hair. Sympathisers were, of course, regarded with enormous suspicion. See L. Perry Curtis Jnr, *Apes and Angels: The Irishman in Victorian Caricature* (Washington and London: Smithsonian Institution Press, 1997), especially Chapter 5, 'Irish-American Apes'. Additionally, there seems to have been a theatrical, if not othered, form of

shoe-maker and got him to make me a pair of pumps by night. He did, and the best fitting and comfortable I ever had. Night came. I stood trembling at the wings for my turn. The house was crowded. At last my time for bravery came. I got a cold reception, everyone frowned. My first tricks went without a hand. I used to be able to hop very high holding my left knee in front of my face. I used to hop over it, it invariably told. I would stand directly under an object inches above my head and with stiffened left leg and with my other kick the object. For fun, in a strange house or a public room, I would sit down, hands in pockets, raise my leg perpendicularly by my side, knock off my hat and pretend to scratch my head with my foot. But to the audience: I got a round – this cheered me, and perhaps my face warmed to a better expression – anyhow, I was engaged. Being over I started again for Brum. I had been able to give some information of importance to Uncle. Back to my lodgings. I had made arrangements with a mummer to go to West Bromwich. We were going to learn some dialogues, sing songs and conduct a Judge and Jury,[109] he to teach me. We had some cardboard, and I was engaged in painting a show card, when the maid came and said, 'There's a gentleman wants you.' I heard the voice I knew was Uncle Chas. 'Show him' said I aloud as though it was a common thing to be interviewed. 'No,' said the voice, 'come here,' and I went. You know how prim Uncle was, in dress and appearance, he was more so then. Just fancy his thoughts as he saw my ungainly self and sweeping hair. 'Well,' said he, 'have you had enough of vagabondising, Jim?' 'Well,' said he, 'meet at such a time and come and for [word omitted] sake get that hair cut. 'Here,' giving me half a sovereign, 'and get some grub into you.' I went and had some grub, then with pain to have my hair cut. The barber cut off enough to stuff a cushion and I stayed his relentless hand and murdering scissors.

dress that distinguished the circus performers. At a hotel in Alford, Lincolnshire, Wallett finds himself recognised as a circus performer even though he was not wearing 'those outward signs which distinguished performers of [the] circus', that is, 'a comforter round my neck, ... long hair ... jack boots ... Birmingham jewellery' (Wallett, *Public Life*, pp. 40–141).

109. Judge and Jury: an entertainment originated by Renton Nicholson at the Garrick's Head, Coal Hole and Cyder Cellars in London. It involved mock trials of cases of sexual misconduct, often performed by cross-dressed actors, with much licence and bawdy dialogue.

Then to meet Uncle. Franconi's Cirque[110] was in Brum, Stonette[111] was 2nd clown but I had not, for reasons, called him or made myself known at the cirque. 'Well,' said Stonette, 'why did you not look me up?' 'Because I was too down.' 'Well, Jim, be a good lad,' said Uncle, '& come with me.' He took me to a hatters. 'I thought I told you to get your hair cut.' 'So I did.' Says the presuming hatter, 'They must have cut it longer.' 'Well cut your interference,' said I, '& look for a hat, large enough.' He wanted to gammon[112] me to one too small. We got to York, I had a kind reception from Aunt, a good supper, see Susie tomorrow morn, it was Sunday.

110. Bastien Franconi, circus proprietor. He was in Birmingham for the 1849–50 winter season with Marie Macarte, Pablo Fanque and Jackson, a clown from Astley's (*JT* VA2).

111. See p. 77. Stonette was 'very kind' to him.

112. Gammon: to trick, talk into.

4

❖

Four: At last a clown with Hengler's, 1849–1851

Returning to his old inferior position as money-taker and dogsbody was not acceptable to the nineteen-year-old Frowde, and the old man's narrative now offers the conventional moment of the big break, when his youthful self came into its own. He does his act in the after-hours ring and impresses the 'Govr.', who gives him the much-longed-for chance to appear. One might surmise that this was in fact not the accidental audition it appeared to him to be when he seized his chance, since the family knew that the returned wanderer needed to be on a new footing. They were perhaps happy enough to have his new, original act as an addition to their repertoire, particularly as he had now come to understand how hard the world of a single and unsupported entertainer could be, and thus how lucky he was to be a Hengler.

His test was to perform as clown to the juggling act of young Jim Ryan. Jim was the sole support of the Ryan family, whose amphitheatre's failure in Birmingham had led to the Hengler's Theatre Royal engagement there the previous year. When Frowde succeeded in this, he was immediately given more status and a stage persona, in the form of a costume – he became a grotesque/comic clown, the Red Man. The ensuing account of his first working months, beginning with the comfortable winter berth in the city of York, records something of an emotional rollercoaster: he is trusted, and sent on vital errands – to sort out a problem arising from the advance man being robbed, and to fetch a horse that had been left to recover after a nasty accident on the road – but he also has not yet completely shaken off the hated chores like money-taking, and he still flares up when his creative work is criticised. He is also faced with the sobering experience of the death of his father and his stepmother's unrelenting rejection.

Nevertheless, performing gives him a different place in the Hengler community, and he records practical jokes he shares with Jim Ryan, with whom he works closely, and the beginnings of the knockabout rapport and mutual respect he was to establish with the musicians of the circus band. A new role, and one he seems to recall with some tenderness as well as amusement, was the custodianship of performing apes. He expanded his range, learning on the hoof about several kinds of clowning, including acting in farces like The Merry Millers. *Trying to learn tricks of horsemanship was not successful, however; perhaps he did at this point come up against the disadvantage of his late start. This section is interesting for his memories of other clowns and of his own developing range of skills, as well as for the sense it affords us of the close and sometimes painful physical interdependence between human and animal members of the circus community. At the end of the summer tour in 1851, Frowde was laid off, along with several other more established performers including, apparently, his uncle and aunt, William and Eliza Powell. Even for Henglers, it was an uncertain life.*

December 1849

[York]

Went to the Circus, saw the horses, saw Susie much grown and very pretty. Monday I got lodgings. The circus stood in a meadow, between the castle and river, not far from the mill and pub,[113] such a cosy pub, big fires, real old York miller with wife and daughter, a little further on remains of the city wall and there I got lodgings. My wages were 15/- a week, my duties to count the cheques and make up cheque boxes for night, to help the Gov., attend box office, take money in the eve, and see horses feet are cleaned out and comfortable for the

---

113. The circus was probably located in St George's Field, and the pub was the Windmill Inn. Newsome's Circus, while in York in the 1850s, used a circus 'on St George's Field, an open space between the castle and the Ouse' (*Era*, 11 November 1911).

night and to eat Sunday dinner with them. All very well but about perform[ing]. I had alluded to it in a most modest manner but got so chaffed that I had not the pluck to mention again. In course of a few weeks after box office was closed, I saw Uncle and Edward in the promenade, intense on some business of partnership. I slipped into the dressing room and finding a performer's dress, I doft my clothing, took 2 chairs into the ring and then went out to come in as a performer. I could hear Edward and Uncle. I made my bow, and did all my tricks as though I was before the public, finished, made a bow, heard a laugh and applause. Edward came down, patted on the back and otherwise praised me. Charles came after. 'So you think you would like to be a performer. I'll give you a chance. I have put James Ryan in for juggling, you can do some tricks between his and give him rest.' Jas. Ryan was a lad of my age and almost as thin, with a strong, sallow face, slack lips and a long nose. He was the only son of the once celebrated Ryan,[114] performer and proprietor, a worthy rival of Ducrow, but now past work ... His daughter,[115] quite a child, was not capable of carrying much and Jim I have just described.

Two pretty objects we were for public affection. However the many headed monster[116] gave me a good turn and the Govr. came round front and told me I should perform on his benefit night and he would make me a present of a dress. This was ordered and delivered, a red pair of tights with a head piece and horns, only eyes, nose, mouth and ears were at liberty. I was now duly advertised and known as the 'Red Man of the Ajax Mountains', and received 20/- per week. I was very happy in York, kind, generous people, the dear old walls, the grand Minster, the castle and river. What scenes, what tales they could tell. One seems although divided from the stirring scenes still to have

114. James Ryan (1799–1875), equestrian and circus proprietor. Charles Keith said of him, 'Old Mr Ryan was rather an eccentric character, and of a very excitable disposition' (*Magnet*, 7 August 1875). But he had been a successful performer and proprietor: 'In his time (and perhaps since) he never had an equal.' He was a prodigious builder of circuses in major towns and cities but, having built a brick circus in Birmingham, it failed, and he lost everything. He worked for Hengler in later years, and died impoverished in Paris. See note 69.

115. Susannah Ryan, equestrian. She worked in circuses on the Continent, marrying Alfred Moffat, the elephant trainer (*JT VA2*).

116. Many headed monster: the mob, hence audience – an actor's Shakespeareanism.

some connection with them, almost a desire to call upon the time worn stones to reveal things they have witnessed. Outside of York they show a thicket in which they say Bess died in.

North Shields

Here I lived close to the Cirque with a virago for a landlady. She objected to my opening the window because of her flower stand, pots and plants. Jim Ryan was in my room one day, the window was open, in came Mrs Bosam and opened a broadside on me and closed the window. Said Ryan, 'When I leave, shy the plants out of the window. I'll catch them.' Open went the window, up she came, boiling over with rage. 'If you say much,' said I, 'I'll chuck them.' 'Just do you dare!' screams she. With that out they went! I had to dodge her round the table or I believe she would have chucked me out. In came a neighbour who had been watching our larking. 'Why, what is the matter?' 'Oh,' said she, 'he has thrown all my flowers out of window and smashed all the pots, look out of window and see.' And there sure enough were the plants, nicely arranged by the wall in front. The amazement of the woman was pretty comic. How they fell in that order puzzled her, till she knew the secret, and then was there peace. I was struck with the beauty of the Easter eggs, they were to be had in all the little shops which were many. It is also common on a certain day to eat parched peas.[117] There is some kind of legend concerning this practice which 44 years of wear and tear has obliterated from my mind. It had something to do with a ship in distress, all hands for some time were fed upon hard peas. Hard lines and hard I should think are the digestive organs … At Shields I had a row with Govr. as to the manner in which I had painted the dragon, a basket-made monster worked by a man inside. Much and hard work it was, not only in carrying the machine, but working the wings, tail, head, mouth, eyes and ears. I had done my best and felt the injustice of his remarks and expressed myself. If I did [not] like, he said, I could leave. Down went the brush and off I went. Some of my young northern friends were getting up a benefit for me.

117. Carlin or Care Sunday, the fifth Sunday in Lent, when carlins or dried peas were eaten.

1850

When I received intelligence of my dear Father's death I must have been in his mind near the close of his time. In a letter dated 8 April 1850 to me he says, 'Dear James, 'tis but a few lines you desire of me and but a few I shall send and that you will find badly written. Your last was received just as I was recovered from what was mistaken for death by a <u>Person</u> who is always at <u>her</u> post, watching my looks and attending to my every word and every look, and by <u>her actions</u> showing her entire devotion and care for me. I have said this much about her that you may be induced to <u>speak</u> and <u>write</u> of <u>her</u> with something like <u>decency</u>. With respect to my goods, there will be nothing for any of you. The Likeness of your Mother, your uncle John will have to keep in his charge for <u>you</u>, which he will give you when he considers you old enough to take care of –' and here his [pen] stayed, he had written his last word to me . . .

He transcribes a second letter, from his stepmother, telling him that his father has died, just a few hours before reaching the age of fifty.

Whilst we were at Shields our star was Edmund Jackson, uncle by marriage to Mrs Cooke, and Aunt. He was a very neat clown, spoke well, danced well and played violin, but was not very original – do for a star or clown of the present day with no more than 2 or 3 turns a night . . . Seal,[118] a popular clown in the north, paid a visit to the circus and was recognized by some of the audience and got a good cheer. He played one night with us, but to appreciate him it was necessary to see him frequently. He was very original and sometimes intensely comic . . . .

Newcastle was our next town. We stood by the railway station and market. The station then was a wooden arrangement. Whilst there we were preparing for tenting. The 'Stag Hunt' was to be the gag, and vans from a railway carrier had been purchased. They were covered and well-built. We repainted them and had scenes of the chase painted on

118. William B. Seal, born in 1808, was with Cooke's throughout the 1850s (*JT VA1*). Frowde's 1894 comment on the inferiority of modern entertainers is old man's pessimism, but it appears to reflect a real codification and hence limitation of the clown's role towards the end of the century.

their sides and thus made them objects of admiration. We had also a model of the Prince's shooting brake. This was well-made and painted. On the parade it was used to drive a team of ponies. We had also a high stylish dog cart. The next thing required was a stag. We got permission to capture, I am not sure whether 2 or 3, but it was rare fun. I was one told off to drive the deer. We had some galloping that day and succeeded in netting some deer. Only one lived. For him a cage was made in which he rode his journeys and paraded with the rest of us.

Whilst at Newcastle, Mr James Cooke[119] with a tenting party visited the town. Of course there was after performing, the fraternisation. Jim Franks was with Cooke, had left us sometime. He wanted to be cheeky as Chas. gave him a hiding. When he was with us, in York, he was playing a part in 'George and the Dragon', I think it was the King, but he drawled out his words as some dissenters do their prayers. When he had finished his lines, Mr Hengler, in the same tone and style, said 'Amen', to the amusement of one and all, save Jim. We started, things were getting into working order. The 3rd day, on our journey to Haltwhistle from Haydon Bridge, an awful accident occurred. Charles was driving the Band carriage, Edward was on the box by his side. I was riding the spiteful mare and leading a pony, when all at once a succession of screams were heard, and from the rear of the cortege, coming at an awful speed was 'Battleaxe' with 6 of the ladies in the dog cart. Aunt Powell was on the driving box. She was not driving, for the horse, tormented by the flies, had shaken her bridle off &, uncontrolled by reins or bit, mad by fright, was coming towards us at racing speed. Aunt Chas. was on the rear seat, Mesdames Thatcher and Young were in the back seat from which they fell. As they passed me, Chas. turned round, saw what had occurred and in a moment as the runaway came along side leapt from the box seat and had the horse by the nose and held like grim death, stopping the horse but running the cart up the bank when over went the trap and Aunt was thrown out – this would not have mattered but, in the agony of the moment, the Govr. or Edward let the reins go, they fell on the wheeler's back – Edward was of course powerless in a much less time than it takes

119. James Cooke, equestrian and later circus proprietor, also with Hengler's during the 1850s (*JT VA2*).

to describe, he had descended, gathered the reins and regained his seat. The carriage came up as she fell, her head against the spokes of the wheel. To me they seem[ed] to have struck her head back 2 or 3 times. The next moment all hands were around, and her face but a few moments [before] a perfection of womanly beauty was bathed in blood. The skin of her forehead seemed to have fallen over her face. To describe the scene is I believe past description. Wm. Powell had replaced the bridle, jumped in the trap and was off hard as he could make the horse gallop for the doctor. Chas. was wringing his hands, women were weeping and horror stricken, men could not without emotion look upon her, and all, so much respected, with dry eyes. There were some gypsies there. Never would you scorn those mystic and much maligned wanderers if you had seen the Samaritan-like spirit they showed, rushing for water in their vessels and in awe and love doing their best. I was sent off at once for the hotel, to prepare a bed, and met Powell and the Dr. I don't think the Dr. looked as easy as he would in his study or surgery, for Powell was rushing the horse. The whole is to me like a hideous dream. Presently, as I sat in despair and fear, expecting to hear of her death, Uncle came to me but so broken . . .

Frowde was then sent on an errand to make good the failure of an advance agent ('he was a joss to the business') who had been robbed.

I got back to the concern and learnt Aunt's injuries had been sewn up and subject to Dr. and nurse, she was living at Haltwhistle. In a letter I received from her, yesterday, July 20th,[120] she reminded me she came to the concern at Aspatria [in Cumbria], saying, 'You will remember Jimmy the monkey running away before the parade and the joke you had with man in the field.' Just a word as to that creature. He was a large sized white-faced monkey, low forehead, small sunken restless eyes, flat nose, long upper-lip, strong jaws, and receding chin, he was a hideous likeness of these parodies some 'comic' papers love to make represent Connaught men – very strong, treacherous and spiteful.[121]

---

120. This date fix suggests that Frowde wrote up to this point in a month (see his opening, p. 40).

121. Again, the caricature equation of the Irishman with the ape (see note 108).

In my reference to North Shields, I should have told you during our sojourn, a fair was held there. At it was a conjuror's van, by the side of which was a penny circus. It was here I first made acquaintance with Geo. Sanger. He was dressed a la Hamlet and doing conjuring tricks in his living carriage, called for the time the 'Hall of Mystery'.[122] In the circus was Jimmy the monkey, star rider of the company. He did other tricks, such as catching candle sticks with lighted candles in them, etc. The Govr. bought the wretch and the blood thirsting diurnal vampire became one of our principal attractions and the promoter of more laughing than either clowns or comic acts. He used to ride on a pony in the parade. The pony, set at liberty, going in any part of the procession where we could tell at what part of the procession he was in by the noise of laughter. But we only did so for a time or two. He caught at people as the pony passed, pulled one or two children under the pony and severely bit another. This cost the Govr. a good sum of money[123] to square the parents. And yet I have known the creature, when he has got loose, to be as affable as possible. He has even, when led up, allowed performers to say a kind word, to pat him on the head or give him food. But if he heard me approaching, away went toleration and in monkey came. Well, to Mrs Hengler's reminder. We generally halted a mile from the town, if a pub was near so much the better, dress and wash, if not hedges were our protection. I have seen more gold and chains hanging on the hedge than would be found in the shops of some towns we visited. Mr Hengler was most particular as to how his performers appeared on parade. No low-crowned hat or coloured shirt collar would be tolerated. Stick and gloves were insisted upon. Nor dare a performer be seen smoking a clay pipe in the street. Any infringement was a sure fine on the next treasury.[124]

122. 'Lord' George Sanger of circus and menagerie fame. His adoption of the Hamlet costume arose when he set up a travelling show of his own: 'I had a fine black velvet tunic, trimmed with black bugles, which at that time were very scarce and expensive. My hat, also of black velvet, carried 3 nice ostrich feathers, and my Hessian boots had 4 inches of black velvet round the tops, trimmed with black beads, with bunches in front to form the tassels. In this garb, with a large turn-down collar and white linen cuffs, and my long hair manipulated with the curling tongs, I was indeed a showman dandy!' See 'Lord' George Sanger, *Seventy Years a Showman*, p. 137.

123. This is a correction – 'poney' in the original.

124. The Henglers, like many travelling showmen, insisted on propriety and

We were outside of Aspatria, about 12, preparing for parade, the ladies were in the vans dressing, the gentlemen behind hedges, or in friendly cottagers' residences, ditto the grooms were cleaning down and decorating horses. Those that had gone in first with luggage etc., were brought to meet us. The musicians were sucking their pipes, as we should have been had we not been engaged. I won't include myself in 'we', I was at that time a non-smoker. At Leeds I bought a cigar. I took it into a dark and secret place and smoked it. I was very ill and received some commiseration, till the remains of the cigar was found and then in spite of my misery I got something else. I was not at this time a smoker, nor for some time after. I had put myself tidy and now attending to Jimmy's dressing. Something was the matter with his breeks. I took them to the wardrobe van for repair, leaving Jimmy to the care of Adrian, the clown,[125] who volunteered to mind him. On my return, the monkey gave Adrian a grin and Adrian dropped the chain and the monkey was off, I after him, but he got into a coppice, on the right hand of the road going to Aspatria and was lost. There was an awful consternation, parade was delayed till the last moment. Then off they went, I left behind with injunction not to come without Jimmy. I was left alone in the misery of isolation. Walks about the wood and in most endearing words trying to square Jimmy. Presently a young farmer came, to know my business. I told him and said I dare not go to the Circus without the monkey and begged his assistance: to solicit interest I told him of the monkey's tricks, reason, etc., but he got tired and was giving up the search, when to my fevered great joy I found Simson's, a musician's, pipe. 'Oh,' said I, 'he can't be far off, here is the pipe he was smoking when he ran away.' 'What,' said he, 'do you mean to say he smokes?' 'Half oz. a day is his allowance.' 'Well Jim, I'd like to see him' and he renewed his assistance. Search was useless, we had to separate. Said he, 'Will he do any harm to the game?' 'No,' said I. I was afraid he would go for his gun and shoot Jimmy, 'he won't touch game unless it is well hung', and so interested

respectability. Charles Keith claimed that two sets of clothing – 'performing dresses and ordinary wearing apparel' – were a necessary minimum 'through having to attend at the circus and often practice [sic] in the latter, they get soiled by the dirt which comes through the seats into the dressing room and the dust and whiting that is ever to be found in a circus' (Keith, *Circus Life*, p. 43).

125. Le Petit Adrian, equestrian clown (*JT VA1*).

the farmer that he conducted me to the nearest road out of the wood to Aspatria. Here I went to Aunt Powell and told her I would leave at once. She advised me, all were going to search after the monkey, going to search the wood after performance. 'Your Aunt Chas. has come,' said she. I was anxious to see her and went to do so, but an immense load of faggots passed me and on the top was Jimmy, holding the end of his chain with as much grace as the girls now hold up the rears of their skirts. I think Jimmy was as pleased to see me as I was him. I carried him in triumph to the tent, performed my act of posturing and all was well. Then to the Hotel to see Aunt. She was very bad, but not so much disfigured as I feared, but yet marked for life and always, I think, different in temper. Of course her nerves were much shaken.

A few weeks after, we were at Kirby Stephen ... The morning's performance was over and I was having tea dinner when the pony groom came to say the monkey was loose and injured a boy. The village was in alarm and many ready to do fight, or had shut themselves in. You should bear in mind that monkeys or any other foreign animal was a much greater rarity than they are today. This monkey had been the talk of the village since parade and the report of the damage done to the boy was much exaggerated and soon spread. 'There he is,' said one, 'on that house.' I got to the roof and was after the demon, when down he scampered into the arms of the Govr. I returned to the ladder but had to get round a huge chimney, not a stack but one big open chimney down which I saw [a] cauldron on the ember and from which I could hear a woman holding forth, declaiming against circus people and all other vagabonds. Anyone in those days that had travelled 50 miles from the family porridge pot was a ne'er do well and any stranger subject to as much suspicion as they would have been in Lord Harry's time. I heard the uncomplimentary allusion and felt that one of the big stones on top of the chimney was loose. So loose that when I touched it, it lost its balance and down the chimney he went, smashing the pot upon the hearth fire and sending the inmates screaming out of the house, swearing the damn monkey was coming down the chimney.

After this lengthy aside about the monkey, Frowde returns to describing the aftermath of the accident – the fate of the horse that was drawing Aunt's trap.

Judy Mare was staying in the stable – she was much injured. Before having a foal she was a grand padhorse and could make a wonderful finish. In the earlier days, Alf Palmer[126] was riding and she fell – throwing him a regular purler. Horse remained motionless, and all hands flew to her rescue – they got her up, trembling – she all right? Yes, sneered Palmer, the poor horse is all right, but poor b – of a man is half killed! No one had gone to [his] assistance – he fortunately did not require any.

Of course the mare had to remain where she was. I wish I had the route we took, but goodness knows what has become of it. Some time after this, we were at Barnard Castle. The Govr. came to me and said, I have altered the plot for the day, put you in for an early turn. When you have done, come to the hotel to me. I went. He gave me some money and told me to go to the hotel at Kirby Stephen, and bring back Judy Mare, giving me money to pay for keep and veterinary. I was to be careful they did not nail me [charge too much]. I was to ride a bay thoroughbred, look sharp, and I should be back in time for the show.

Off I started – but I had not gone far before the threatening clouds legitimated their promise and it commenced to rain. I got on the mountain, and such a deluge of hail I never before or after can remember. The mastery of the mare frantic, always a nervous fidgety creature, she was now almost unmanageable. It was impossible to keep my cloak over my knees and, in a moment, my boots were filled. So, independent of the awfulness of the storm, the black barren hill, and feeling according to my frailty, I felt the awe. I had a scared horse to contend with and now, to make matters worse, I had lost the road, and no sensible creature or sign to direct me. This was a position to wake the memory of the past, and to recall holy instruction and to cry unto God – His voice and presence in the storm did away with desolation. The storm soon cleared and the sun smiled, and Nature seemed to laugh at her late experience. At last an aboriginal made his appearance and in course of time directed me to York. I had gone two or three miles out of my road . . .

Well, ultimately I got to Kirby Stephen, very tired and drenched. I went to the hotel, put the mare up and ordered Judy to be ready that I should be able to start as soon as the mare had fed and rested, and went into the hotel. Saw the landlady and request for the bill of expenses as

126. Alf Palmer: see note 28.

quick as possible, as I wanted to be back by seven. 'Lord!' said the barmaid, 'See the water is dripping from him.' 'Look here,' said the missus, 'look here my boy, we buried one of your mates, we won't have your death at our doors.' She rang the bell. 'Get such a bed warm and tell cook to make some gruel' – giving me from her table some tea. Presently bed was announced – it's ready – I went to the bedroom. By dint of perseverance and a boot-jack, got my boots off. Had a wash, a warmed nightshirt and the luxury of a good bed. Was asleep in a moment . . .

I was awakened from my sleep to eat gruel, and such as I never enjoyed before or after. And then off again, to be awakened by the landlady. 'You cannot have your bill as early as you request, nor shall you start till a reasonable time. Now have some supper and wait till you are called.' Supper in bed!!! Well!

I woke early in the morn, had porridge, ham and eggs and coffee, but no landlady down, no bill ready. I was getting into [a] funk – I ought to have returned last night, I must be in time for Parade – and how about my expensive living? Presently I was called to the bar – I wish it had been to the Bar – went over the bill for Judy's maintenance, etc. It was heavy – more than outsiders would perhaps have given for the mare. Bit two pounds off the bill, paid it, asked for my own, and got laughed at. Not a penny would she charge, gave me some rum and milk, saw me start and shouted me good luck.

I am not sure of the town, perhaps Darlington; it was across country. I got to it in time for parade. Had lunch with Uncle Charles and Edward, explained why I had not returned to Barnard Castle, gave an a/c of my stewardship, all to their satisfaction, and off to the Tent for the overture, for I was drummer as well as performer etc. We had a good band and as the parade broke off, they used to play some favourite piece. This would invariably be listened to by the musicians of the place and our leader and men made good sums in selling bandmaster's scores. I used to be pretty free with the drum-stick flourish imitating the drummers of the Regimental Bands I had seen, at Portsmouth, and used [to] create a great deal of attention, smiles, laughs, and admiration, but woe to me if my time was faulty, or piano parts[127] infringed upon. In Yorkshire nearly every village

127. Piano parts: sections played softly, quietly.

93

has its Band and every Band a good player of some instrument. I think the Ophicleide[128] was then the favourite. Our man was very clever, we got him from Hemmings,[129] his was a dirty copper instrument, his name was Bailey,[130] his nickname Dr.; a tall nice fellow, but short-sighted. He wore glasses. You may have noticed in all bands there is either a bald-headed man or a fellow wearing spectacles, most of ours had moustaches; every Sunday afternoon would find ours lying on their beds with their mouths covered with cabbage leaves. They had been anointing their hairy lips with lime and litharge.[131] No matter what the natural colour of the hair was, their moustaches would be either purple or a blue-black. Yorkshire was a great harvest for the musicians, for in that county nearly every village had a decent Band. I have been to Church where the brass and string band was the music, and a pretty nuisance they were. Lessons or prayers, psalms or hymns, was nothing in their modesty, compared to their tunes. Our villages may thank [the] High Church Party anyhow for the reformation and sanctity that assist our devotions. Of a Sunday it sometimes happened that the village Band would meet our(s) for practise, always I think sacred music. Of course neither [?] was wanted or the drum allowed. Old Ryan used to go to these gatherings, and once insisted upon what he called the 'Halleujah Polka'. He thought the drum the principal instrument in the Band. All showmen believe in the drum. It was he or [some other manager][132] or Ducrow who seeing one of his musicians quiet went and asked him what he meant by such laziness. I have got, said the wind jamber, so many bars rest. 'Rest be hanged,' said the

128. Ophicleide: powerful brass instrument developed from the old serpent, and similar to the euphonium, with a horn, doubled-over tube and eleven keys.

129. Perhaps one of the Hemming or Hemmings family who were clowns, jugglers and acrobats during the nineteenth century. Henry Hemmings, clown, worked at Hengler's Circus in Sheffield in 1859 and remained there with Frowde at his Cirque Modele when Hengler's closed (*JT VA2*).

130. Tom Bailey, circus bandsman. He worked for Hengler's, Transfield's and Sanger's circuses (*JT VA2*).

131. Patent hair dyes being unavailable, the only method of dyeing hair, facial or head, was with a mixture of powdered lime and litharge (lead monoxide) bound with water. The resulting paste was applied thickly to the hair, and had to remain in place (preferably overnight), and covered with brown paper and a handkerchief.

132. Deleted in the original.

irate rum cull,[133] 'I pay you to work, not rest!'[134] Another wished the band to cease as soon as he had concluded some piece of pantomime, they did not. This riled the performer. 'Twas at rehearsal. 'Why don't you stop when I give the cue?' 'Why,' replied the leader, 'we can't stop in the middle of a bar.' 'Can't stop?' was the passionate reply. 'Pull the d – things out of your mouths, and they will stop of their own accord!' This was said with so much action and vehemence that the band and all joined in a general roar. But of the Dr. He was very irate at my drumming. We had words. He showed fight – I got him down, and took off his spectacles, fearing to hurt him; amidst general merriment. He stood up, and denounced me as a coward, saying I took away his specs so that he should not be able to see where to hit me. Bailey could get a wonderful tone from his instrument, and had good education. I found a pair of his socks ready for his laundress, and put them in his ophicleide. 'Twas some days before he discovered them.

[During the summer in the Lake District] we were at Ulverston. Uncle John had been starring at the Theatre, as Hamlet, Romeo, and Rope dancer, and left a good name. We had a crowded house. Jno. was, when with us, our leading actor, but of course we never played Shakespeare, save some scenes in Richd. III. Edward was not long with us. He came for a few days, bringing a horse, [and] a monkey, female. She was one of the most old-fashioned looking women you ever saw, always smiles, chatter or scold, she bore, as animals of a lower order often do, a comic likeness of Jim Ryan, especially when she implored for a favour. She was very fond of Jimmy the other simian, who used to treat her in a most churlish manner. It was funny to watch them. She would, as far [as] her chain would allow her, get as near to him as possible and, in subdued manner, converse with him, showing by tender glances she bestowed on the brute, how loving her communication was. He used to get as far from her as his chain would permit, and in solid silence only broken by a sound like a Dutchman's 'yah' looking straight before him all the

133. Rum cull: a manager; low theatrical, from c. 1860. Especially the master of a travelling troupe.

134. The story is attributed to Astley and Ducrow. See A. H. Saxon, *The Life and* *Art of Andrew Ducrow and the Romantic Age of the English Circus* (Connecticut: Archon Books, 1978), p. 397.

time. Poor Mary got into a sad mess or two. We were leaving Durham, I went into one of the stables to look round, and there I found poor Mary, stiff and cold. The man whose duty it was to put her in the travelling cage mistook, and reported her as dead. I picked her up and as one might speak to a wooden doll, spoke to her, and I found her eye-lid quivered. In a moment I was in the Hotel kitchen and her before the fire, pouring rum and milk into her mouth. Then back to the stables, took one of the horse rugs first to hand, got it hot, folded Sally[135] in it, took her to the stables, pack her in a box, putting [it] inside of the pony break.

This resulted in a delay to the company's departure, an ostler asserting that a rug had been stolen, and the 'Govr.' eventually finding it and tipping the monkey out.

Chester le Street was our destination and our last tenting town for the season, which was late, and as the day was a very cold one we went straight into the town, to dress for the parade. The town only boasted of one broad street, and parade for that day only consisted of Band and their carriage, drawn by 8 horses.[136] Soon as the pony carriage got into the ample yard, I proceeded to look after Mary, got the box out of the boot, and there to my surprise found Mary tail uppermost. The Govr. in his rage and hurry had put her in upside down and in this undignified manner her ladyship had travelled from Durham, and to this I attribute her prolongation of life. I soon had her out and before a tap room fire, that did credit to a coal district, where coals in comparison to present prices were almost given away. Had her rolled in a rug and I dosed her with old beer made warm and gingered. I had no idea of chaining the poor thing, left her, and off to the Tent. Thank goodness no one came, or so few the Govr. would not let the horses work, so their money was returned and we returned to our lodgings. On my way I met the Govr. 'Here,' said he, 'is another row through you and that infernal monkey!' 'What's the matter?' 'Go and see.' I went to the hotel and found the landlady, her husband and others just getting over an excitement. It appears 2 men, after my departure, had gone into the tap room, in order to eat their mid-day meal, and not observing, or

---

135. Frowde here gets mixed up, calling the monkey Sally instead of Mary.

136. See pp. 89–90 for parades into town.

caring to examine the bundle before the fire, had sate down to the table, called for their beer, unpacked their Tommy and were recuperating their tissue,[137] when poor Mary (this was the name of my sick friend) had crawled to the table, stood and putting her hands on the hospitable board, gave the two boors a Jim Ryan look which instead of awakening hospitable sensations, or charity, so filled the men with alarm that they scuttled out of the room, locking the door, and calling for the landlord. When the Govr. arrived from the tent there were these men and some others outside the tap room window, waiting for the landlord with his gun. Govr. was just in time to prevent murder. It cost him a trifle to the men to get some food, and a little temper at the unreasonableness of the host and hostess. Mary had satisfied her beery inclination, raised the cup and mauled the food. Had we brought an epidemic in their village, we could not have committed a greater atrocity. He gave the usual benediction on Jossers, and went his way. I managed not only to appease our friends, but to gain their interest and favours for Mary. The Govr. had called a groom to take the monkey into the cold stables. I showed Mr and Mrs Boniface[138] how unjust and cruel this was, and they ordered a fire in the back kitchen and before the day was over, Mary not only became a pet, but a patron. She had become the talk of the place, and many visited her, and many extra quarts were drawn. I may as well finish with Mary. We got to Sunderland for our first winter town. Jim Cassidy and I for a time boarded with Mr and Mrs Adrian. I squared the old landlady, and kept the monkey in the kitchen, so that I could attend to her. All went well till Mrs Adrian offended Mary in this wise. Mrs A. was taking a dish out of the oven, when Mary rose and took hold of it. Mrs A. gave a scream. Whether Mary was angry with Mrs A. for screaming, or considered Mrs A. was the cause of her burnt fingers, I don't know, but she was very savage, and tried to throw a wooden coal box at her. She could not do this, so she shied lump[s] of coal at, and after, the retreating Mrs Vampo.[139] In came the landlady to know what was the matter, and seeing the coal over her nice clean kitchen, got waxy

137. Tommy: workmen's food. Recuperating their tissue: eating.

138. Boniface: landlord of an inn or a country tavern.

139. Vampo: clown. Le Petit Adrian was clown with Hengler's (see p. 90).

and notified me and Mary to leave. So I took Mary (she was standing tall as the table) to the circus and got a fresh lodgings. That monkey never forgave Mrs Adrian.

1851

(February) At Bradford she nearly got me into trouble. I fastened her to a rope that was used to facilitate the flights of the Dragon, and which the property men had neglected to put in its place. She ran up the rope and got on to the false ceiling made of variegated calico and as Jim and I had been larking with her, we thought in her skylarking she would bring down the ceiling onto the chandeliers, but she came down in time to save a row. A few mornings after this, the property man found her, near an expiring coal fire, having been confined during the night with a baby in her arms.[140] No one dared go near her, when I went to see her. I saw such a sight I did not forget, the young one was exactly like a small human baby, if it had been shown to anyone unacquainted with simians he or she would have taken it for a child. The poor mother kept it to her breast and moaned and caressed it, her appeal to me was most pitiful. I got it from her, but the poor mother did nothing but fret and moan for days. She died.

I began to feel that my posturing act was not sufficient. I got permission to practise the bar act. To explain: a horse bare of furniture save a surcingle[141] at full speed gallops round the ring, jumping bars and gate, the rider vaults from the horse with it, leaps the object and vaults on the horse again.[142] I could get the horse but only at an early hour. So soon as it was light I had the horse in the ring.

The weather was intensely cold and on this occasion horses that were used out of doors were roughed. The one I practised on had the day previously been so treated. I had no ring master, and could not

---

140. The infant monkey was still-born, as appears from the context.

141. Furniture: the trappings or decorations of a horse. Surcingle: the girth or strap for holding the saddle on a horse's back; in this case the strap is used on its own, so that the rider, who is supposedly helpless and prostrate upon an unsaddled horse, can control his mount.

142. This describes a form of voltige act: it requires 'a sound knowledge of both riding and acrobatics' (Hippisley-Coxe, Seat at the Circus, p. 48), and was very difficult, necessitating many hours of practice.

keep the horse at a regular pace and the consequence was a bungle over a leap and I down under his feet. The sharp calk of his shoe made a hole in my left leg and for a long time I had a most dangerous sore ... Well of course that accident did away with my running vaulting. We were very jolly in Sunderland, the people were very kind, Old Ryan thought them too attentive. He on more than one occasion received police attention and hospitality, for which he however had to pay. He told the magistrates, on being fined, that their apartments were most uncomfortable and their charges exorbitant.

Frowde himself got into trouble in Sunderland by drinking whisky (with the chief of police) and then following John Hengler to a ball, where they and Jim Cassidy (also from the circus) got into a fight with local men. A policeman was injured and Frowde was accused of killing him: 'I got off all right save a wigging from Henry of course I was to blame not John.'

I was daily becoming more disgusted with my work of the morn and had a detestation of counting checks and making up the house. In after years I did not even check against the money takers. Aunt Chas. used to do it for me, any one could trust her ... From Sunderland we went to Bradford. Our circus was built in the market, near to [the] lane at the bottom of which was the Theatre, a very primitive affair, mostly I think, of wood,[143] but then Bradford was very primitive, no St. Geo. Hall, no grand rail station or shops, offices or stately building of any kind ... At Bradford I resented counting checks and someone else took the money or relieved me. One night I found the Govr. in a regular state of worry and rage. A scene, or rather equestrian ballet of action and words. The principal characters are the Miller, his Wife and Son, Dickie. All of the mill are at holiday, for 'tis the anniversary of the Miller's wedding day. At last a prize shall be given to the man who can imitate what they saw the Mountebank do on the green. Accordingly old Dobbin is brought in all caparisoned as though he was going to take the Master and Dame to market, and sent cantering round the

---

143. The Theatre is probably the Old Theatre Royal, Duke Street, 1841–67. It was known as the Liver Theatre and operated by Sam Wild. See Wild, *Old Wild's*, p. 55, 60–9, and Geoff J. Mellor, *Bradford & District Theatres and Music Halls*, n.d. (located in Bradford Local Studies Library).

ring, all the Millers vaulting and doing different tricks. The fun of the farce depends upon Dickie, who is always in the way, and imitating in a comic manner the tricks of the performer. Well Dickie had been fined in the morning, for it was Tuesday, the day on which the ghost walks.[144] Dickie left the treasury all right, no threat, no complaint. He was justly fined and could not growl, but at night when all were assembled and ready to commence, there was no Dickie. The Govr. was at wits end. I went to him and said, 'I think I could play it, Uncle.' 'You!!!' and then such a tirade of abuse. I went away. He did not know that my Sunderland winter morns practice had born any result, but I knew, I could do sufficient as would be required from Dickie. Presently the wardrobe keeper came with a dress. 'Quickly,' said she, 'the ring waits.' I even had on the big cap and pinafore, and proved myself and did the part. One would have thought this would have pleased the Govr., but no, he was riled. Every time I made my appearance at the ring doors, it was 'Bravo Dickie.' Hurst was the name of the man that had been playing the part. He never came again and I know not what became of him. *The Merry Millers* had run its length and another piece announced. I had made another step to the front.

My cousin Alfred was christened in this town [Bradford]. I had woefully offended the Govr., by refusing to do the checks, and was not invited to the ceremony or party . . .

April 1851

Uncle took the riding school at Halifax. My memory bears recollection of the Linen Halls; our tame fox that would lark with all of us and the dogs, but kept clear of the monkey and out of doors; Jas. Bristow, Ryan, Rivers our strong man,[145] lodged next to the Theatre, the Shakespeare.

Frowde's co-performers play a trick, by hanging his stuffed Red Man suit out of the window and spreading a rumour that he had hanged himself.

144. The day on which the ghost walks: pay day.   145. R. L. Rivers (see note 43).

Whilst we were at Halifax we had Edwards,[146] who had made a name at the Olympic[147] as clown, he was clowning with us, he could [do] a number of acts, and had some very clever performing dogs.

The fair was on at Leeds,[148] and the Govr. reopened his place there for a short season, sending W. Powell to manage it. I went with him as did some of the others. The rest of the company was made up by fresh performers, duffers. I had to [do] the Red Man and I think for the 1st time an act on champagne bottles.[149] Said Powell to me, 'This clown must have help. Do you think you could take an act?' Old Ryan pantomimed to me, 'Say yes.' I did. 'Well your Aunt will see to a dress,' so I did my best, but not a success. Then he came, 'The man can't play Jerry,[150] you must do it.' Don't know the words, and only part of the business. 'Oh,' said Ryan, 'I'll put you right.' I did. My figure in black tights and make-up got shouts soon as I appeared. This gave me confidence and my nervous horror and pains left, though the nervousness made the character more real. In the character I redeemed myself for bad clowning, and was more than repaid by the encouragement of a generous audience. Next morn the Govr. came over to advise, with Aunt Powell. He had engaged Broadfoot[151] to produce a new piece, 'The Afghan War'. They had had a reading rehearsal and failure for want of an acting company seemed inevitable, then he had brought out Turpin and was amazed at the manner in which he crabbed the part of the Beadle – could not act. He asked her husband

146. Edward Edwards, clown and pantomime player, working in the circus with a troupe of dogs (*JT VA2*).

147. Astley's Olympic Pavilion off the Strand in London, opened in 1806, soon lost its ring and became a theatre, but continued in that guise to make much use of comedy and clowning.

148. The main fair at Leeds is 8–9 November, but there were others; the company is apparently spreading itself between Leeds and Halifax at this point in spring 1851.

149. A move from contortionism to a balancing act (see Figure 8).

150. This may mean simply that he was no good, but it might suggest that they were enacting a sketch based on characters from Pierce Egan's bestselling novel *Life in London* (1820). Clarke's Equestrian Circus, for example, offered *Tom, Jerry and Logic* at the end of its programme in 1823, with the ironic proviso, 'if the Riding Master, Clown and Tailor are sufficient for the Title' (Birmingham Playbills Collection). So Frowde may have played Jerry, the country cousin, kitted out as a comically exaggerated man-about-town.

151. For Broadfoot, see note 73. Uncle Edward Henry Hengler had been performing at Astley's in 1843 when Broadfoot produced 'The Afghan War', and so had some knowledge of it.

Figure 8. James Frowde in his bottle-balancing act.

[to] come over, in time to play the part. No, wasn't at home. Said she, 'Let Jim do.' 'Oh, he,' in contempt. Then she enlarged upon what was done last night. Well said [he] I met the printer as I was coming here. He said I had kept my best man to the last. (Billy Powell told me of this, so I was prepared.) Chas. came, and in an off-hand manner said 'So you clowned last night?' 'Yes.' 'And did?' 'Yes.' 'Well if you like to clown you may, and I will give you a dress. But go to your Aunt Powell.' She told me what I already knew, adding 'I have promised to coach you for the Beadle tonight.' This took the whole of the day, or near. Powell was in a wax, but they altered the programme and put the last first and putting on my clothes, went as quick as my legs would take me to the station and as swift to Halifax as the train would allow. I was bustled into the dressing room and dressed and painted and succeeded in playing the Beadle sufficiently well, and got a 10/- rise in my salary and within a few weeks of 20 years of age, so of course began to think I should be looking for a wife. But my time was occupied – how to lick the old ramps was my study. Beside which Broadfoot had cast [me] for Tandillo, the Afghan Chief, and I had to study, always a nuisance, but I gave a little thought to it and was rewarded on the first night of the piece by breaking down. Oh the agony and perspiration I was in during the first few seconds of silence; it seems ages. In desperation I said something and got out of the trouble with [the] audience, but not with Govr. Old Broadfoot however came up [and] thanked me. 'What' said the Govr., 'and break down.' 'That's nothing,' said Broadfoot, 'experienced actors do this. What he did was done well.'[152]

Summer 1851

The season at Halifax was concluded and we out a-tenting. This was good for me, grand practice. Of course if one liked to be lazy, he might as a talking clown just stick to his old wits.[153] But I wanted to get on. So I, without their permission, used to play to the Band, and coveted

152. Given his reputed irascibility, Broadfoot was here both professional and kind towards Frowde.

153. Or hits, maybe – the sense is clear enough. Interesting, coupled with the remark above about it being a nuisance to have to study a part.

having a smile from them, than a big laugh from the audience. Tenting, with all its drawbacks, is as a whole a most pleasant time, if you can shut your eyes to the contumely of the huxter shop keepers. Anyhow, it is a most healthy life – or I should have been eaten up with rheumatism. I wish that I could find my rough diaries – they would assist me … It seems a slur on a man's intelligence that so many glorious opportunities of seeing and learning should be lost – but there is this excuse – we had always to start very early at the time I have written. We travelled for the horses' sake very slowly, always as near as possible halting at 10 miles to give the horses oatmeal and water and look to their collars. When we had finished parade, we had to seek for lodgings – not always so easily obtained. Then a snack at some refreshment, then to the tent some[times] a mile and more from the town – then our dinner – then a rest till 7. Then performance to near ten, then tired and weary to bed. I had to be at the tent at times early to take money. Then after night's work to go round to the various stables to get in bills and see horses were fed – feet cleaned and bedded. Often in the morn to go round, see nothing was left behind and to pay bills. So save Sundays there was very little rest – and then in pursuant with my father's wish I went to church. I never neglected this so much as I have since I retired from the profession – and my absence from church, you know, was seldom, no matter what the weather was. I cannot recall any incidents of that tenting tour that [are] amusing. I only at present remember at Peterboro':[154] I was sent for to be dismissed. Powell and Aunt also left. I remember as I rec'd my salary Edward being in the room, but the sorrowful injured face of Aunt Charles was all that excited my thoughts.

154. October 1851 (*JT HH*).

5

❖

Five: A spell with Cooke's circus, 1851

Finding himself out of a shop through no choice of his own, Frowde took the professional course of action and answered 'wanted' advertisements in the trade newspaper, the Era. *He does not seem to have had any more success in the concert rooms than he did when he went a-rambling. Invited to join another large circus, Cooke's, then working in Plymouth, he accepted and immediately felt more at home. His lack of broad experience in this profession gave him a few awkward moments when he arrived there – he did not know how to take part in a simple acrobatic turn, the 'Egyptian pyramid', and was intensely nervous as he began to undertake the multiple duties of clown to the ring. But he recalls the growing popularity for his own act of chair balancing and contortionism, and the beginnings of audience recognition and a personal following.*

I went back to my Inn and wrote to advertisers for performers. We all had the *Era* of a Sunday morn, every line was read, every criticism was recriticised. Much devotion was paid to the *Era*, [the] only credited paper for the profession. Jno. used to call it the Showmans Bible. Whilst waiting for answers to my applications, I stayed in the good old cathedral town . . .

      The first reply to my *Era* advertisement I accepted and went at 40/- a week to a concert room in Rugby, sang and postured. I would draw a veil over Rugby. From there I went to a Concert Room in Sunderland, where I received an offer from Mr W. Cooke who had a large building in Plymouth. I went to the manager of the room who was very kind and cancelled the engagement. Henglers at

Cheltenham,[155] stayed the night or some time, got to Plymouth, got
lodgings and went to the Circus. Jackson[156] was the premier clown
who introduced [me] to Mr Cooke.[157] A rehearsal was on and the
company were practising. The performers there were Barnes the greatest Summerset thrower ever known, Connor the next best, Jameson,
Russell and P. Adams, Ted Hemmings and some of the Cooke
family.[158] I was called upon, being a slight figure, to be top mounter.
Never did such a thing in my life and had no idea of how to proceed.
I got to the top and, standing on the shoulder of the 2, came down with
a run and sent the whole lot on their backs. Some rubbing, some
swearing and some laughing and I was called to the promenade to
be questioned by Mr and Mrs Cooke. They were pleased at my willingness and altered their plans. I was free from checks etc., but had to
assist by box-keeping and assistance at opening of the doors. They had
announced [me] as a Dutchman, Mynheer Frowde.[159] I was to do the
best I could by my tricks and not to understand the language when
spoken to. This put me out. I was anxious to get ahead with jesting but
Jackson was a favourite brother-in-law, and Poney Adams was his
foil. When my act came, I was in an awful funk, wet through with
perspiration, in positive pain and all of a tremble. The circus was a
very large one and the house very crowded. Half acting and half dazy
I got into every one's way. I got confidence and from that time became
a favourite. Mr Cooke was a famous ringmaster and declared 'if he
could only speak Dutch, he would' and then I would catch the word
Dutch and Scaramouch. I used to keep my trick and posturings for
entrée and my chair trick, using my elastic powers for striking comic
attitudes. If I threw my hat in the ring they would applaud, sometimes

155. They were there from late
November 1851 to January 1852
(JT HH).

156. Perhaps Chatteris Jackson, musical
and talking clown, with Cooke's Circus.
He joined Hengler's in 1856. Extremely
successful, he was reported to 'surpass
Wallett as a comic orator, being at the
same time more refined in his diction'
(JT VA2).

157. Alfred Cooke (1821–54), a noted
equestrian. He performed at Astley's but
died of cholera in 1854. His brother
William was lessee of Astley's from 1855.

158. Arthur Barnes, vaulter and
somersault thrower. Harry Connor,
acrobatic clown. Thomas Jameson,
aka Mons. Zamezou. Henry Russell,
aka Henry, Russelli, equilibrist.
P. Adams, probably Charles Adams
(see note 28). For Ted Hemmings, see
note 129.

159. Three years later, Frowde is still
using the Dutch persona. See
footnote 189.

Figure 9. James Frowde using his 'elastic powers for striking comic attitudes'.

I would get some one to throw it in and appear almost at the same moment from the other side of the ring or pit. I was very happy, in favour with the public, and manager and family, living well on 40/-!! If I could do, now as then, well I draw my breath and say if! Alfred Cooke,[160] brother to William was an artiste. All that he did was done with intensity, and laboriously practised. One of his acts was 'Shaw the Life Guardsman', a character that riders often performed, after a style, long after the style of Alfred. Musicians, horse and grooms were drilled, for every look and movement was to time and music, his death scene was very pathetic, soldiers in uniform at his death used to come in and in due form carry him out, his horse following him at slow time, to music of 'Saul'. Audience used be awe bound, and then to applaud. In this act, Cooke would not allow a clown and quite right. I followed him and keeping well on one side, till he passed. With a face and actions to the time, I used to come in and affect an idea the applause was for my appearance and got shouts. I only enjoyed this for 3 nights I was going it. He stopped, and panting out 'Fair play, wait till the

160. Part of the great Cooke dynasty of circus proprietors and performers. See note 157.

applause has finished.' But now our regular patrons were expecting me, and there was none, at least not as there should have been. I looked him in the face as innocently as I could and asked 'When is it going to begin?' An expletive and his hands relaxed their hold.

I had a reverence for him that none in the place had … I saw the practice of his daughter, Emily,[161] a dear graceful child, she developed into one of the most ladylike equestriennes I have ever seen. Her trick act always won the people, not so much from the daring of her tricks, but for her grace, becoming dress and womanly bearing. She married John Henry Cooke,[162] a cousin, who was also learning his profession and now the proprietor of a first class establishment.

161. Emily Cooke, equestrienne, noted for her grace and elegance. She worked at Astley's in 1852 for her uncle, William, the proprietor (*JT VA2*).

162. John Henry Cooke, equestrian and circus proprietor. With Hengler's from 1860, he became equestrian director at Hengler's in Hull from 1885 (*JT VA1, VA2*).

6

❖

Six: The end of the story, 1851–1857

Having made his journeyman step with the Cookes, Frowde was able to rejoin the family concern at Exeter in the spring of 1852. Professionally, he advanced little there, finding the audience 'unsympathetic' to his jesting. Riding in an entrée, the horse slipped and fell, smashing his instep and knee. But he was still not allowed to 'spout', 'play the talking clown', as he wished.

The account now falls into a rhythm that is no longer driven by the Bildungsroman *model of autobiography. The narrative alternates several elements. He recounts a succession of seasons of tenting and, especially, winter quarters, marking his benefit nights and their triumphs. Woven into this is a pattern of memories of personal relationships, some of them within the profession, like that with his uncle John Henderson, or with other performers, such as the tale of accompanying the young dude Hernandez, a star trick-rider from America, to a particularly stuffy British tailor's shop. Of similar interest are the stories that hang on particular performances, such as the account of one of his rows with the 'Govr' that takes place during a performance of the play Timour the Tartar, and so gives us a vivid picture of circus drama in action. But he is also concerned now to recall his relationships beyond the circus, focused during winter 1854/5 at Portsmouth on the group of officers assembled to embark for the Crimea, during winter 1855/6 in Cheltenham on the local hunt, and during 1856/7 on the contestants in the local election in Chester.*

Conflicts develop between the Hengler's clown and the gentleman in Frowde. He notes his kind reception in several places by the more liberal Christian leaders, who nevertheless deprecate his calling; on the other   hand, he is taken up by the slightly raffish sporting and officer classes, who are willing to mix with an entertainer, practising the kind of bonhomie associated with 'the Fancy'. When he smokes a pipe in the street with a group of 'fellows' who include a lord, Frowde is fined ten shillings for 'disgracing the establishment', that is, falling below the level of petit bourgeois respectability that the Henglers expect. His friend the noble lord, he is told by the 'Govr', 'can afford to be a blackguard, you can't'. This further development of the masculine worlds inside and outside the ring is fascinating, but the story has lost its momentum, and the notebooks become confused, the story ceasing to move steadily onwards, and petering out into desultory memories of individuals. The linear narrative of his circus life is in fact almost at an end, and its last stages would have been very difficult for him to recount, on the evidence of his handling of personal material so far. He brings the story as far as Liverpool in the winter of 1857, and it was in that year that he married out of the circus, his wife a clergyman's daughter. She died in childbirth the next year, and he returned to the circus with his own Cirque Modele. This appears to have been an independent venture, though he uses the Hengler's building in Sheffield, and employs performers who had also worked for the family. It was a much smaller enterprise and probably could not compete with the larger establishments. Frowde made a second respectable marriage in 1861 and was sufficiently well off to purchase estates and live the life of a gentleman thereafter.

We left Exeter and went to the Circus Cooke had vacated.[163] I got a thunderous cheer when I appeared, but welcome and smiles vanished when they discovered they had been deceived, but my foot and knee would stand no knocking about. I was in much pain. My benefit money troubled me, so I invested and for the first time, became the possessor of a watch. I bought a tenting box, a box with a false side to it which lets down so that in dressing you had a flooring to protect your feet. I bought a poncho, hat and box and we started from Plymouth to tent. Our first town was Modbury ...

163. In Plymouth; April–May 1852
(*JT HH*).

Aunt Chas., when with the concern, and I generally travelled together in a light gig, having under our care the cash box, and starting after others had left, we had to pay the gates, which was no mere duty, for often the gate keepers were very rapacious and unjust ... But we had some pleasant times. One inconvenience following the company was that they too often denuded the roadside inn of bread etc., for whilst the horses were being attended, the performers etc were fortifying themselves if possible with rum and milk, bread, etc. Sometimes nothing was left for us.

I must, as tenting things come to mind, recite them irrespective of dates and names of places.[164]

One of the scenes in the Afghan War[165] was a comic one. The man who played it was Moreton, a rider.[166] His character was a drummer boy, there was skirmish, baggage upset, a chest left behind, drummer gets into this, hiding from some natives. In pursuit of them a soldier comes in and a really exciting combat, to set music – in which the British soldier, after several narrow escapes, defeats the several Afghans, the drummer taking occasional peeps at what was going on, and making comic ejaculations. One of the Afghans in his escape makes for the chest, to the horror of the drummer who held the lid down. Soon as the combat was over the hero, the Govr., exhausted, rests upon the chest. The inmate in ignorance fancies the savage is there, till he hears the soldier mention his name. For in one of the escapes, when fighting his enemies the drummer knocks the head out of the drum by an action that ... enclosed the enemy's head and shoulder. A prick from the spear sent the boy howling to his retreat. The soldier remembering the incident, refers to his late assistant. On the drummer hearing his name and his native language, kicks the lid of the chest and shouts for deliverance. The soldier gets up,

164. We are now into part of the journal that bears evidence of considerable revision. Pages are not used consecutively, as Frowde doubles to and fro, and his pale blue pencil changes to black ink, black pencil and red ink. It suggests that his revisions were ongoing and that he was prepared to compromise the chronological narrative. We have attempted to rationalise the order of pages, but can do little about his nonchronological recall and recording.

165. There was a dramatisation by George Almar in 1843, and doubtless many others.

166. Moreton: probably the Mr Morton, equestrian, who was with Hengler's and billed as one of the 'Sons of Olympics' in Exeter in 1852 (*JT VA2*).

opens the lid and drags out the drummer, who thanks to whitening left in the chest, has made himself pale with fear. After some comic dialogue the soldier invites the drummer to assist him to empty his water bottle and devour his sandwiches, and then shouts 'Be done for the enemy is near' in such a hurry, that Jimmy the drummer chokes himself.

Now as the Gov. had to partake of this food, Aunt with her usual devotion to her liege Lord used to cut the sandwiches and make them herself at the hotel, and of course they were very nice, so Jimmy instead of cramming the luxury into his mouth, used to eat with deliberation and enjoying the good food provided till the last mouthful and, John Orderly[167] as you like, Jimmy would take his time. This was a matter of comment. At one dinner Uncle John suggested a remedy or experiment, which was that sandwich should be so arranged that the Govr. should know which to take, the others were to [be] well red pepper[ed]. Before the scene, Jimmy was expostulated with and told to act the part of devouring. This riled him and when the feast time came, he had a good sandwich, he took his time and had a warm injunction and a hot sandwich. He literally jumped with rage, which the audience took for acting and roared accordingly. But Jimmy did not stay long after.

Frowde then recalls touring Wales, where he was impressed by the absence of beggars but could never get enough to eat. He was also duped when he asked someone to teach him a compliment in Welsh to use in the ring, and found, of course, that he had been tricked into saying something that provoked a roar of derision.

I call to mind an eventful journey. Aunt was very unwell and was packed with rags etc – we had not proceeded far when the mare was taken ill and became so weak she could not drag the gig – I gave aunt the reins got out of the trap and pushed behind. I never entered a town in such an ignominious manner – I suggested her walking or getting

167. 'John Audley!' was the boothers' code for 'Cut the performance and get the next house in!' If that is the reference, it means 'tell him to cut to the next business'.

out and waiting till I got a better horse and returning for her – but she was too ill – we got in to Aberavon late – met the governor – the spectacle was an awful shock to him and his language to me was shocking – the poor mare was tucked up in an awful manner. How I got her along I don't know – the vet after examination gave his head an ominous shake – mare however got all right in a few days – was well enough next morning to be walked to the nearest town. Poor old spot Mary (Jno.'s favourite padhorse) took us many hundreds of miles – in all kinds of weather snow hail rain and wind – but we had lots of sunny days and merry hours.

We had in our Band 2 men that took great interest in me. They were Wm Allen,[168] a pronounced teetotaller, in those days it required pluck to be a teetotaller, not only to resist temptation, and he being a thorough musician and a clever man was sorely tried, by his admiring disciples of Apollo who were as musicians generally are votaries of Bacchus, but had to submit to the scorn and impertinence of those who hate others who dare to do better than themselves. The [other] man was Collins, a tall, lean fellow.

Our next winter town was Dover.[169] Adrian was the principal clown, but I did not fear him. Jas. Thorne[170] was the tumbling clown and a very good one. He was also [a] good draughtsman and scene painter of some experience . . .

There follows a tale of Frowde's rescuing a young soldier from bullies, and the consequent support he received at his benefit from the man's officers, producing a good benefit, where 'Adrian was nowhere. Among my newspaper critiques are two very good, entirely or nearly so in my favour, especially as a low comedian and private life.'[171]

---

168. William Allen, bandmaster and musical director. He was still with Hengler's in 1872 (*JT VA2*).

169. 25 October–22 December 1852 (*JT HH*).

170. James Thorne, clown and vaulter. He was a clown at Astley's, then with provincial (but also some London) circuses (*JT VA2*).

171. The *Dover Telegraph* wrote, 'the witty displays of the clowns, Messrs Frowde and Adrian deserve especial notice, and the more so because their effusions are characterised by a total absence of offensive remark at times heard in other establishments' (6 November 1852).

Mr Henry Cooke's[172] benefit was at hand. He as an attraction advertised that, on the tight rope, he would do certain tricks and carry Mr Thorne on his shoulders. On the morning of his benefit, the rope was fixed and a kind of rehearsal or practice was arranged. Cooke did certain things, and then came back to rest to start with Thorne sitting on his shoulders. It was but the work of a moment for Jim to get on the shoulders of Cooke, who prepared to walk the rope and without a balance pole fall. It was but the work of half a moment for him to get down again. 'Poor Cooke,' Jim said. 'Oh it will be alright at night.' Night came and so did Jim but under command. He had a wife he said, to keep, and wasn't going to risk his limbs for the sake of all the people in Ramsgate. I think Jim had a very bad benefit. H. Cooke was in agony – there was a decent house and he was most anxious to keep faith. I felt sorry for him and asked whether I should be too heavy. He was delighted and sitting down I got on his shoulders and received very minute instructions. I was not to look on the ground, nor move, put my hands one on each side of his head and fear nothing, and all would be well. So he finished his first dance, came back for a rest, I climbed up the back of the starting point and got on his shoulders. Henry was a good six foot, I was about 14 feet only above the ground, no great distance, but the sensation was any thing but pleasant. I could hear a confused hum of laughter, knew the ring entrances were full of grinning performers, grooms, etc., but never once did I look at audience or staff, till Cooke halted and stood on the cross piece. Here I drew a breath and looked at the people with an impudent leer and a bow of thanks for the applause Cooke had earned. The by-play pleased the Col. and his party[173] and I just saw a bouquet being manipulated upon. Cooke went backwards to the start, 'Steady,' said for a gag, he pretended to lose his balance, oh how gratefully I slid to terra firma. I left the ring for Cooke to work out his act, got called back and received a bouquet, to which was attached a pencilled note and in which was a Sov. to revive and champagne my nerves. Did

172. Henry Cooke, tightrope walker, later animal trainer (*JT VA2*).

173. Colonel and Mrs Underwood, who are mentioned earlier – no doubt patrons, since Frowde notes that he 'received several marks of approbation' from them.

Cooke thank me? Well yes, but it was evident the bouquet had been intended for him.

I used to walk the rope and do a comic act upon it. One night, I was doing this without a pole, the Govr. was standing at the ring door with others and applauded me, saying 'Well done'. Down I came, looked at him in dumb astonishment, turned to the audience and apologised to it for falling – saying, pointing to the Govr., 'A compliment from him is enough to frighten anyone.' The fellow roared with vengeful satisfaction and the audience with amusement, for the Govr. was chary of praise. We had some words in the dressing room. I often took advantage of Motley[174] and gave him one – that was the cause of a scene behind the scenes notably at Ramsgate when it was near to blows, but for Jim Lee, a skilful boxer, and an eye-closer to many a vindictive joss. We finished up the season with the play of 'Timour the Tartar'. Jno. played the Old Man,[175] a part I thought should have been mine, instead of which I had a small part of no significance and treated it as such. This riled the Govr. who was playing Timour. We were having an altercation during a supposed-to-be night, where everything done is by music, piano and slow time, and standing in the ring doors which by canvas and laths represented an opening of a room of the Castle. Chls. lost his temper and, in a stage whisper, called on Vokes[176] to put me down. (I in like voice told Mr Vokes to do something else.) The consequence was a laugh from such of the audience as were in hearing. That scene was spoilt. Vokes you will find in 'Tenting adventures'.[177] Now he was secretary and mummer. Putting down means noting in the treasury book those who deserved to be fined. Fines were from 20/- to 1/-. Our next town was Norwich.[178] We had a place near the fairground, at the back of a

174. Took advantage of Motley: of being the clown, of having the fool's licence.

175. Oglou, father of Timour, a comic role.

176. Possibly William Vokes, who was with Hengler's in the provinces 1852–4 as agent in advance and acting manager (JT VA1).

177. 'Tenting adventures': there is no trace of these in Frowde's notebooks.

178. 28 February–19 March 1853. According to the *Norwich Mercury*, Tombland Fair that year was a miserable wet affair: 'The only aspect of real life in the circle of the fair, was Mr Hengler's circus, but even in this instance, the lofty and capacious dome of the structure, hanging aloft amid the doubtful lights of hail and snow showers, appeared more suggestive of a mausoleum, in which the masses of the dead might be invoked, than a temple devoted to the vagaries of

public, used as a short cut to the street and drops of shorts.[179] Here was our first Treasury day. I went for my salary and was fined a Sov., just half my screw. I did not say anything, but went home, wrote a note to the Govr. asked for 20/- rise in salary, and got a sharp rejoinder. He thought if he had fined me 10/- instead of 20/- I would only have asked 10/- rise, but I deserved to be fined and was only riled at it being a vindictive fine. I wrote back and gave him a fortnight's notice and by the same post a letter to Cremorne.[180] By return with the letters (all had their letters directed to the Circus) was an official Cremorne letter. Before I had time to answer it, a note was by a groom given me in which the Govr. agreed to give me £3-0-0 a week, subject I think to a month's warning.

At Norwich I joined the Odd Fellows, and got acquainted with the Chief of them, also with a very decent fellow called Drury. Mussels was one of the dishes I could then enjoy. I found a good pearl in one. It must be among some of your mother's muddles with, I think, some loose diamonds. I used much to admire market day,[181] any amount of stalls with different coloured awnings making quite a gay scene. I think Cambridge, on a smaller scale, has the same sort of thing, or had. In these days of expensive building, perhaps those open markets have been sacrificed to the new style. Here butter was sold by the yard. Here I made acquaintance with some actors, Rouseby etc. note – who made names. Just a word for Norfolk dumplings. These are with butter and fruit grand, or with gravy and meat. Jim Franks and his wife joined us. He made no headway.

Frowde describes seeing the great boxer James Mace, then a 22-year-old local lad, beat a much larger professional boxer in a booth at the fair; Mace was to join the booths himself, turning professional in

Apollo and his truant steeds' (*Norwich Mercury*, 26 March 1853).

179. That is, the circus people went through the public house to get to the street, and had a small glass of spirits on the way.

180. Cremorne Gardens: pleasure gardens, opened in 1832 and offering open-air dancing, concerts, circus entertainments, fireworks and balloon

ascents. Like Vauxhall and Ranelagh before it, Cremorne quickly became unfashionable, deteriorated and closed in 1877.

181. Silas Neville wrote in his diary for Saturday 19 October 1777 that Norwich Market was 'one of the largest and best furnished in England'. Quoted in Frank Meeres, *A History of Norwich* (Chichester: Phillimore, 1998), p. 106.

1855. By 1861 he was champion of England, and toured with several circuses, including Pablo Fanque's. Another tenting tour commences, round the south-east of England, in summer 1853. Frowde recalls buying a new outfit and reminisces about the girls he has loved, to whom he now adds one Rebecca Spooke, a member of the new company.

We got to Derby for our first winter town.[182] Here I became acquainted with some nice people. My Church was St Peter's. The clergyman in his sermon made an ungenerous comment upon our circus.[183] People present knew it was as unjust, as uncharitable and eyes were cast towards me. My face was thus incapable of lying, what I felt I showed, but I suppose the elevation of eyebrows amused them. The pastor saw the amused expression of the congregation, but neither his black gown or black looks deadened the smiles on their faces. He had never been to see the place or witnessed the performance, and yet held us up as something awful and, mark, at the time publicans were abusing us because of the injury we did to their public houses. I received sufficient sympathy from the hearers to amend for outraged feeling ...

We had a long continuance of snow, unfortunate for poor Jim Franks. He had issued a ben. bill and for gags, giving away a pig. My pals begged of me not to follow this example but do the swell.[184] I wrote an address to show as I wished my benefit to be one free from

182. Winter quarters November 1853 – January 1854 (*JT HH*).

183. Four years later (19 September 1857), the clergy's hostility was still keen. 'A Watchman of the Church of England' took a boxed advertisement on the front page of the *Derby Mercury* to make the following statement: 'HENGLER'S CIRQUE/ All Ministers of the Christian Religion, Sunday School Teachers, and others, who remember the demoralization caused by the prolonged stay of this circus in the Town of Derby, about two years ago, are earnestly invited to memorialise the Chief Magistrate, and other authorities of the Borough on the subject, in order if possible to prevent a recurrence of such evils; and considering the awful judgments which have fallen upon British India, and the present sufferings of our countrymen, it is to be hoped that all those who fear the wrath of God, and sympathise with their afflicted brethren in the East, will, by way of humiliation, abstain from giving their money and patronage to such vain amusements.'

184. Jim Franks had sent out hand bills and posters for his benefit night announcing that he would give away a pig (a play to attract an audience). Frowde's friends urged him to cut more of a dash.

vulgar display and [not] out of touch with the character of
Mr Hengler's style of catering, I would forego the licence he allowed
a beneficiary, but would, trusting only on the friendship of my bene-
factors, introduce a fresh act and scene for myself, and thus by the
amount of patronage I received, judge as to the number of friends it
would be my proud privilege to call mine. Although my bills did not
appear till after Jim's night, he was much offended. I had an over-
flowing house, poor Jim had had a failure, but this was owing to the
weather. Snow was so deep that most of the shops were closed, traffic
entirely at a standstill. Consequently Franks could not by his benefit
gauge the extent of his popularity. He certainly had many friends and
deservedly. The overflow of my benefit was lucky for some other
showman – an opera troupe. There were in those days 3 kind of
showmen … We were actors or performers. Actors were mummers,
opera people cuckoos, circus people (– and sawdust) clowns (vam-
pos.) Well the cuckoos were doing a starve till my benefit when those
who could not get into our place went to the opera. Dear old
Brocklehurst Barber the tenor has often referred to it and said their
company from that date had luck.

*Incidents in Frowde's love life in Derby follow, and then the
company moves on to Chester,[185] where he joins yet another
convivial society, perhaps of Masons or Oddfellows, with the social
elite of the place, including the Mayor, aldermen and local army
officers. He then continues his account of his successful performance
career.*

Jim Franks worked me hard but I kept up my head. I had a good many
of the militia at my act. I amused them by an accident. I was on the
Rhardee[186] witnessing a drill, 'twas company drill. The men were line,
or should have been, but one man missing the touch was slightly in
advance. The O. C. expostulated with him, saying half an inch is not
much but take it off your nose and some would find it a great deal. He

185. 6 February–8 April 1854 (*JT HH*).

186. Rhardee: actually the Roodee, a
large open space on the west side of

Chester, by the River Dee, and now the
site of Chester Racecourse. It was used
for drills and military displays.

and some others were in the boxes at night. I got grooms and ring door men in line and gave a mock drill, imitating as well as I could the sub in mock authority. It pleased the people. After the laugh came a spontaneous one from the officers. The victim told his comrades of what I meant, and they enjoyed it. We had a good many of the men nearly every night, in the gallery, and I generally managed to get a joke at one of their expenses.[187] One came in with an umbrella. I soon espied the war-like implement, soon was by the side of the warrior, soon obtained the Mrs Gamp [umbrella] and improvised a drill. One was by the side of a female who made some exclamation that a more modest woman would, in the presence of many people, have refrained from. 'I can tell this is one of the rearguard,' I said to the ringmaster, 'How?' inquired he. 'Because he has the baggage with him.' Not very clever. I don't know whether it was original but it got a good laugh. . . .

Our next winter town was Plymouth,[188] at the Theatre Royal. I always enjoyed playing from the stage, it is so much easier if only from having your audience before instead of surrounding you. My favourite part of the audience was however on my right, the box of Mr Newcome, from whence I got many a round and kept the pearlies showing.[189]

187. Lawrence's act includes similar militia gags and interaction with an audience member (see p. 48).

188. October 1854, after a tenting summer in the West Midlands (*JT HH*).

189. The Theatre Royal, Plymouth, was rebuilt in 1811 in neoclassical style, to seat 1,200, and had a rough audience from the dockyards. The manager for forty-two years was John Riley Newcombe, a man despised by the ultra-legitimate Macready, as evidenced by an entry in his *Journal* for 23 November 1846, when he found the company 'most wretched' and Newcombe 'utterly ignorant of his business'. See William Charles Macready, *The Journal of William Charles Macready, 1832–1851*, abr. and ed. J. C. Trewin (London: Longman, 1967). His ignorance cannot have been that damaging, since over forty-two years, he imported stars such as Macready, Taglioni, Charles Kean and John Buckstone. See Harvey Crane, *Playbill: A History of the Theatre in the West Country* (Plymouth: Macdonald and Evans, 1980), pp. 117–19. An advertisement in a local newspaper notes that Newcombe leased the Theatre Royal temporarily to Charles Hengler, who was unable to 'procure a site respectably and conveniently situate whereon he could erect a building (according to his custom)'. It further notes that the theatre 'was found to afford ample room for a Circle to be formed on the stage, as large as that of the London Amphitheatre with facilities for the production of every novelty in the equestrian world . . .' Frowde is billed as 'Mynheer Frowde' (see p. 106) (*Plymouth, Devonport and Stonehouse Herald*, 30 September 1854).

We had a star from the American circus there at Plymouth, Young Hernandez,[190] a rider, and to my idea and experience the most elegant trick rider that ever poised upon a pad. A neat figure, a good face and head and a perfect balance. He could fall, or rather miss, when he liked. There was among many of our patrons a very pretty girl. She, usually with her friends, sat in [a] front seat of the boxes. Said Jimmy [Hernandez] to me, 'I must be introduced to her this eve.' I was clowning to his act. As he started at the conclusion of my wheeze, I ran by his side, got that introduction set. He was on his feet next scene and archly smiling at her. Presently he threw a somersault and came, not on horse, but upon the ring fence. The next moment he was apologising to the lady and her friends. She spoke to him, smiles were exchanged by this section of the Circle. The horse had finished the round. Like magic Jim was on board and the next round he had turned his somersault and ridden as a statue, struck a posture, a perfect Apollo, all this in less time than it takes to write it ... But on – All the London ladies had roseate crushes on the young American ... Hernandez was drawing crowds to Astley's. Hernandez went to one of the clerical shops to be measured for a suit – it was a long low dark solemn-looking place and the attendant with his yellow cadaverous face and white tie looked like a resuscitated skeleton promoted to a higher position in the new existence. He waited for some time only to be rewarded by a hollow glare from the ghostly – James, was becoming impatient – so was I – James, said he, have you got no help or boss to this store – no insult was intended – but you should have seen the horrified look of the ghostly – their establishment a store, they who had clothed divines of all ranks to be spoken of as though they were common measurers of unsanctified humanity ... it was to me irresistibly comic. Another cleric came in and was immediately assisted. Jimmy looked at me frowning. Taking one hand out of his pocket he jammed his hat on the back of his head, threw three back somersaults, turned round, saluted the astonished, almost petrified three at the rear of the shop and left. Not a smile upon H's face nor any allusion to the

190. James Hernandez: born Mickey Kelly in America, 1832, he was the same age as Frowde, which probably accounts for their close friendship. A hugely talented equestrian, of whose debut at Franconi's Circus in Manchester Wallett said that he 'achieved a success unparalleled in the history of equestrianism' (Wallett, *Public Life*, p. 93.) During the 1849–50 season he also appeared at Astley's.

120

event, save that they of the shop were sleepy-headed asses – a rather romantic event.

One night a servant in dark livery accosted me – someone asked to see [me] as to my benefit. I got into the carriage and was driven some distance till some drive gates were opened and outside a mansion. I alighted, but all in the dark, till I was ushered into a beautifully lit and furnished room. On a table was refreshment to which I was invited – two ladies in evening dress came in and ate and chatted for some time; at last the carriage was announced. I arose to take my leave and went. Not a word could I get from the coachman, I got out by the morn and from that time to this am in ignorance of where I went and who the affable ladies were.

Charles was away and Jno. was manager. He used to annoy me by ringing the bell that announced a fresh act during the time I was before the house. I was at times very nervous: tuning a fiddle would take all the fun out of what I was doing. Henderson, who was always good at a practical joke and somewhat indignant at the efforts made to crab me, came from the ring door and saw Jno. was tiring the people with a cocked hat gag, and suggested I should ring the bell. This I did and to effect. Another lark of his: Jno. was [rope-] dancing. Behind the back trestle in the gallery, the bottom section of which came up to the ring fence, a great yaw-mouthed joss had squeezed himself into a place on the seat close by the pulley ropes that tightened the Jiff (professional for the rope danced on). Jno. was performing magnificently, to the admiration of his brother artistes, but the clod with a face expressive of a new crummy quartern loaf, distorted with a chasm, grinned. Henderson came to the dressing room, beckoned me. We went to the curtain, he pointed out the victim of his scorn, said look at that mutton-headed beggar – come. [He] and I crawled till well under the gallery seats, at the rear of the horses stabled in [the] gallery stalls. Here we passed a rope round the legs of the laughing hyena and a beam. Jno. and the whole house were started by noises from our friend, 'what be ye at?' and other exclamations of indignation, embellished with sanguinous and other curdling adjectives, which instead of alarming seemed to delight the audience. The struggles of the poor fellow to get at his imprisoned and bound legs delighted all save J. Hengler. Of course it stopped his performance until the ring men had released our Devonian friend.

Strange but nevertheless true, an audience are ever more ready to laugh at a fellow's misfortunes than wit or humour. See or listen to the delight evinced by spectators at a fat man on a windy day, puffing, perspiring and gasping to capture his hat that Boreas is having a lark with. Hear the audience scream with delight at the clown with a red hot poker, whether he burns [the] policeman, his father or puts the poker into his own pocket, somebody is being served out, let us laugh.

I don't know why, but the audience was under the impression that I was the perpetrator of the practical joke. Jno. was in a rage and it happened that the Gov., just from Portsmouth, came behind and without rhyme or reason commenced to row me. 'Hold on Charles,' said Henderson, 'he has been with me, talking over our parts.' This was true, so the Gov. with this and a threat if he could find out [who] the perpetrator was, he would fine him a week's salary, subsided.

My benefit was good, and the Gov. started me to Portsmouth, putting under my charge Susie Ryan and 2 Brummagems,[191] acrobats. In those early days of trapeze a good many of outsiders were getting into the business and this was galling to the old school born and bred in the business ... The old circus people and their slang and world were very clannish ... We opened to a good house, the Govr. had started a man known in Nottingham and around as Bill Melihil la Geisy,[192] a political orator. He was blessed with a great flow of words and a happy knack of appealing to the feelings and passions of the people. I thought when I heard him that I had more than a rival and for a week I had. Then I found him very stereotyped and as void of humour as a blacking brush.

The Crimean War was on, Portsmouth was full of sailors, soldiers and militia. A great many midshipmen were up for exam for promotion to mates, and mates to lieutenancies. One eve some of the seamen waited for me with an invitation to supper and a dance, got me into one of their cabs and off we went. At the supper was plenty of cheer, food, wine and conversation. After a song Prince Renyden,[193] who then spoke English, while a German play[ed]. I had to sing and

191. Brummagems: natives of Birmingham.

192. He remains a mysterious figure, untraceable in Nottingham archives; we

may have failed to read the MS correctly, but no better guess presents itself.

193. Similarly, we have been unable to trace Prince Renyden.

improvised a verse on Billy Barlow in which I introduced his Highness who with the others were amused. A hearty good night then. 'Twas early morn and I put on my Inverness and was off. I thought there was a heaviness about the pocket and on putting my hands in my pocket was surprised at the number of half-crowns that had found their way there. Night after night this occurred, till I made a strong protest. Invitations for Sundays were strong but I kept my lodging a secret and kept from my friends till after evening service and then to the Parade, Portsmouth or the Nut, Wheatsheaf, Common Hard, Portsea. The Govr. was dead against my capture of a night, declared it was killing me, pointing out that my friends were only at it for a short time, and would be at their County homes or at sea recruiting themselves and I promised to stand clear. But it was no use, there were the cabs and men waiting for me and there was no back exit to get away. Our place, now a church or chapel was in Linforth Road, built up to the shops, filling an angle of the road. The side of the building faced the road, the end of the building a court with but one entrance. The end was the entrance into the stables and cirque, so it was impossible to escape the vigilance of my friends.[194]

There follow some confused accounts of Frowde's involvement with French soldiers and an ex-pugilist, now a landlord, called Harry Bourne. Frowde seems to have been rather dissolute at this point; the drinking stories culminate as follows.

We had much champagne. When I got to the cirque I was not fit for bus[iness], but the audience would have me. At that time 'Vilikins and his Dinah' was a favourite song,[195] and I suppose I used to

194. Linforth Road may be a corruption of Lion Gate Road, in the centre of Portsmouth, on which Hengler's Equestrian Circus had been built, the side of the building facing the road. In 1857 it was acquired by St John's Church, Portsea, as a mission centre for dockyard workers.

195. 'Villikins' is a famous song, a pseudo-tragic ballad couched in elaborate cockney for mock-heroic effect. Its parodic, intertheatrical play suggests familiarity with the gamut of theatrical and street song. Its first printing was in 1853 as sung at the Olympic by Frederick Robson in character as a street singer, in *The Wandering Minstrel* by Henry Mayhew, but it was around from about 1836. Current across the performance culture, it was a hit for Sam Cowell in the rising music hall. It has a valuable malleability, evoking pathos as well as humour in differing degrees, for varying audiences, in the right hands. Frowde had

sing it very well. I dressed for it, made-up my face, the table or platform was taken in ... but my tongue was so dry and I did not know
what to do. Govr. was in a way, 'Charlie my boy, it's no use I must
have a soda and brandy.' 'Go in,' said he, 'and I will bring it.' I got on
the platform; my malady was taken for acting and saw the Govr. and
others grinning at me. 'Where's that soda?' said I. He bit his fingers in
his rage, sent for the stuff, and there all that time were the people
amused. I told them what he had said to me, how insulted I felt and of
his promise to give me a soda and brandy. All were in laughter,
bandsmen. The soda came, I drank good health to the audience and,
I was told, never had the song been so well given. I was quite sober all
at once, what made me bad I can't conceive. The wine was good and
I moderate.

'Well,' said the Govr., 'you had a good rise out of me. I shall
deserve the fine.' The Tiger men[196] came across the ring, after the
performance, and persuaded the Govr. to meet them at Weston's. We
by agreement went together, and Oh, the Govr. got a drop in the eye,
I saw him home. Said I, 'About the fine.' 'All right my boy,' said he,
and maudlinised and advised ...

We were rehearsing a piece called 'The Heights of Alma'.[197]
I was some Russian swell, and in addressing the army, I had to say
'I have received orders from Prince Menchikoff to spare neither
man, woman or child.' The Govr. had gone to some expense in the
production of the piece, having assistance of a detachment of soldiers.
Well, I had recd. an invitation to a 12 am b'fast with Capt Peas–ll
and Commander P –. Whilst so engaged a gentleman was announced.
My friends were in lodgings in St. Geo. Square. 'Show him up.' They
were in a slight fluster. 'Frowde you are Colonel. – ' 'All right.' The
gent, a civilian, came in. I was duly introduced. My opinion was
asked on some war point, I gave it. The intruder left, and my

learnt over the previous few years in the
concert rooms, it seems, the art of
working a song.

196. Seamen from the *Tiger*, a warship
famous during the Crimean War.

197. This Crimean episode was instantly
dramatised at Astley's and across the

country. See J. S. Bratton, 'Theatres of
War: The Crimea on the London Stage
1854–5' in D. Bradby et al., *Performance
and Politics in Popular Drama*
(Cambridge University Press, 1980),
pp. 119–38.

friends threw themselves in convulsions. That afternoon I was talking with some of them outside an hotel, much frequented by naval officers, as the Fountain at High St was by midshipmen. As we were chatting, an officer in uniform passed us, accompanying the visitor of the morn. The men saluted them as they passed and my friend speaking to me passed short remark but called me Colonel. The look of wonder and astonishment, almost alarm, the faces of my friends wore, was a one that set me off laughing. [I had] a very solitary walk home to rest and prepare for night, for as the mysterious [man] passed me I turned to the right saying, in as colonel-like manner as possible 'Good day gentlemen,' not caring to stay to be questioned and chaffed.

Well: a sleep, a look over my part, tea and a wash and off I went to business. First night of the piece and of course with others anxious as to its success. Pit and gallery crowded but boxes nearly empty. Piece seemed to go well, the army has just concluded a fight, as unit of Russian officers were gossiping in a group when [in] I rushed, or galloped, breathless with exertion and gave the first lines of 'spar[e] neither man, woman or child' and then came such a deafening roar of applause from the boxes, a roar in the gallery, of 'Bravo Colonel'. I could not go on with my part. I left the ring and found the Govr. frantic with rage – it nearly spoilt the piece. It was my last appearance in it. It appears those fellows left to themselves were wondering at my being addressed as Col. by the mystery [man] when Capt P – came up. His nickname was Bobby, a kind fellow and great favourite with the men, and they told him of my new rank and he explained the circumstances of the case and then was concocted a scheme the perfection of which I have now related. They went round and enlisted all they could and got some blue jackets in their pay at ½ price, the boxes were worked by these beggars. The Govr. and others were puzzled but next day when I explained the matter he was amused but said, 'You must keep out or the piece will be crabbed.' . . .

At that time smoking short clay pipes was becoming the rage, a Turk's Head was the design. I had several, presentations from my naval patrons, mounted more or less elaborated in silver. They were not sold mounted. The ornamentations were manufactured by local silversmiths and good solid work. Coming from the barracks, in High Street, by the theatre Dickens immortalised in

David Copperfield,[198] with them, I was smoking one of the clays just presented, and passed the Govr. Now smoking in the street was, according to his rules, not allowed by any artist. Next Tuesday, ghost walking day, I presented myself at the Treasury for my sal[ary]. Fined 10/-! What for? 'Disgracing the establishment.' 'What do you mean?' 'Smoking a short pipe in the street, last Wednesday, with some other fellows.' 'Well,' said I, in some temper answering, 'one of those fellows was Lord –.' I had not time to finish my expostulation. He roared out, 'Lord – be d–d, he can afford to be a blaguard, you can't.' The manner in which he said and looked this so struck me that I burst out laughing. I took my dibbs. He came to me soon after and said that he had raised my salary another pound per week and returned the fine.

Spring and fine weather had come. We had finished a successful season. I had a great benefit and made a host of friends. One remarkable incident. Henderson, who had come to bring out the pantomime and star, lived with me. He got up, came to me just after I returned home and said he could not sleep. He had a presentiment that there was something the matter in the cirque, I got a lantern and went in to see, we [h]ad not been there long before I smelt fire and saw smoke, and there in the property room was my dress burning. I played Friar Tuck[199] and my rotundity was formed of wicker work, covered with a calico priest frock. This had, we think, caught a spark and been smouldering with other inflammable matter. Henderson followed me and we quickly had the burning matter into the ring, and doused the flame ...

198. Actually *Nicholas Nickleby*. Having joined Vincent Crummles and his theatrical company at an inn outside Portsmouth, they arrived in the town and 'accompanied the manager up the High Street on their way to the theatre'. This was found by 'turning at length into an entry, in which was a strong smell of orange-peel and lamp-oil, with an undercurrent of sawdust, groped their way through a dark passage and, descending a step or two, threaded a little maze of canvas screens and paint pots, and emerged upon the stage of the Portsmouth Theatre'. See Charles Dickens, *Nicholas Nickleby* (1839; Harmondsworth: Penguin Books, 1986), p. 362.

199. The pantomime of *Bold Robin Hood* was performed by Hengler's in Cheltenham (see below) during Christmas week, and presumably Frowde's clown Friar Tuck role was from the same piece.

After our tenting tour, the first 2 or 3 weeks of early rising and constant occupation had put me in good condition. We arrived at Cheltenham[200] and occupied a cirque built by a Mr Blizard. A brother of his and I became, till his ill health, for many years great chums. We occupied a piece of ground in Claren St., on which is now built [?] Church. Dean Close was Vicar of the old church.[201] I had for a rival a J. Cooke, note no relation to my friends of that name, Mr Henry of equestrian fame. He was a smart little fellow, most particular in his [?] all made in imitation of Wallett. He made a decided hit. I always was very nervous at the commencement of a season and here I was particularly so. Beside Cooke was a clown of London repute named [?] He was a trick clown and very versatile.

We had been there some days, I made no headway, trying to do my best I was stiff. Presently Bill Allen[202] the Leader and Panty, in much solemnity, formed of themselves a Court Censure and gave me to understand unless I attend I should no longer be the Band's jester. 'What would your Portsmouth friends think of you?' said they. 'Tonight just forget fighting and striving. Fancy you are at Portsmouth or tenting, don't pose, but give nature a chance.' It was on a Monday, a crowded house, box filled with the elite, graced with beautiful women and girls. My first was a little by-play on my morning's censure. It got a general smile and from there I walked to the front. Cooke's turn had gone, he soon gave notice. Edwards and tumbling clowns, became stereotyped. It was here I became acquainted with G D Griffith, Bat. L.[203] He was then blessed with sight. One night, a crowded house, I had finished my last turn before the piece, when the property man came, saying a gentleman in the

200. October 1855; they stayed until the following January (*JT HH*).

201. The circus was temporarily erected on the site of the Clarence Boarding House, later to become St Matthew's Church. It was built as a chapel of ease to St Mary's, where the Revd. Francis Close officiated as perpetual curate in 1879.

202. See note 168.

203. One of the Griffiths family of Marle Hill, Cheltenham, 'a stout young gentleman who hunted with the Cotswolds in the fifties.' See Edith Humphris and Douglas Sladen, *Adam Lindsay Gordon and His Friends* (London: Constable, 1912), p. 292. He was afflicted with blindness for many years. The *Cheltenham Looker-On* (15 December 1855) noted that the 'Hengler's Tuesday Evening performance will be under the patronage of E [i.e. Ted] Griffiths, Esq and Gentlemen of the Amateur Steeple Chase'. Bat. L.: probably Batchelor of Law.

drive wanted to see me. 'You ought not to have let him in.' 'Couldn't stop him.' This was against all rule. The Govr. would not then allow anyone behind. I went to him, he requested me to take another act. 'Can't. There is no other, the performance is finished and I cannot, even if it were not, for the Govr. would not allow it.' 'Will you if he consents?' 'Yes, all right.' The Govr. came with him to me and said a party wants you to give an entrée. 'All right, Sir,' and in I went, made some fun and was rewarded with a signet ring Mr Griffith took from his finger and gave, and with many acknowledgements of kindly smiles of approbation from the ladies, from the boxes and often on the promenade. Ted Griffith was a difficult man to put on one side. A daring, good natured, determined fellow, a one in the field and all sports, and a dangerous fellow to cross and withal very quaint.

He, Capt. West MSH,[204] another hunting man, Nicked Finger Davis, with some others were winter quartering at the Fleece. Here I went occasionally of an evening, where in the snuggery they were wont to assemble to drink and smoke, and fight again the battles of the day. I had been singing in character a la Sam Cowell,[205] who was in my opinion the most naturally comic and best acting comic singer of the time. The 'Ratcatcher's Daughter', I did this in character and riding on a milk white donkey,[206] which during the summer did duty as a zebra, it was a beautiful beast with much vigour. Our appearance nearly always was a good ½ minute's roar. I was then not so round in the face, my moustachio was a very mild arrangement, my hair was cropped as is common now,[207] but then to have gone into a place of worship with such a country crop would have been to have awaken[ed] as much mirth or censure as going in with a night cap on would do today. Consequently for common life I used to wear a wig, my little cousin Fanny had a great antipathy to the wig, one morn's

204. The *Cheltenham Looker-On* for November and December 1855 notes the meet of Captain West's stag hounds a number of times.

205. 'The Ratcatcher's Daughter' is another mock-cockney, mock-folksong, sung in character, made famous by Sam Cowell from about 1852.

206. The association of clown and donkey, the two low extremes of artiste and horse, is an ancient one. Wallett writes of singing 'a local song, written by myself, mounted on [a] donkey' (Wallett, *Public Life*, p. 30). See Figure 10.

207. Writing in 1894, Frowde was referring to a very short hairstyle fashionable in the 1850s: curly hair full round the face, with luxuriant whiskers.

Figure 10. James Frowde with a donkey and clown paraphernalia; note the
sketched indication of stage footlights.

performance I was doing a trick on the back of a chair amid solemn silence, whereon a shrill young voice in imperious accent cried 'Chim Chrowde, don't you take your hair off!' Result, a laugh, a lost balance and a fall. My hair being black and short, a painted pair [of] Newgate Knockers – a side lock twisted into a ½ curl[208] a fashion of the then Coster, a black eye, a Bill Sykes make-up, I had only to scowl to my left and right, and bring down the house. One night hearing some incident of the day's hunting rather amusing, I worked it up into a couple of verses and incorporated [it] into the original song of Billy Barlow.[209] It met with a success that surprised me. Among my Chelt. friends was a smart semi-journalist, and sporting young lawyer named Fred Marshall. He was delighted with the song, and was constantly bringing me verses apropos to hunting's daily exploits. The song became all the rage, and I was compelled to sing it every night. It was a line on the bills.

Xmas came 1855 and a new pantomime which the popular Olympic clown had superintended.[210] It was rather long so the Govr. shortened the number of acts preceding the play and to my relief W. Barlow was put on the shelf. This was a relief to me. I was tired of it. Scenes of the Circle were over, the Govr. gave out that after a brief interval, would be the long-advertised panto. He was met with a perfect roar for Billy Barlow. He paid no attention to the call, and

208. Newgate Knocker: a lock of hair like the figure 6, twisted from the temple back towards the ear, fashionable 1840–55.

209. Another Sam Cowell number picked up from the streets: it was published by the broadside printer Catnatch c.1830. The hero Billy Barlow is a street clown and a mountebank, and was, in performance, the commentator on topical matters, hence the useful extendibility of the song. Sam Cowell's 'Billy Barlow' costume became standard: 'the tattered remnants of a workman's dress, the cord of a dressing-gown tied round the waist, a clay pipe in hand, and one eye badly blacked; the whole crowned by the famous brimless hat.' See Harold Scott, *The Early Doors: Origins of the Music Hall* (London: Nicholson & Watson, 1946), p. 121.

210. The *Cheltenham Looker-On* records this as *Bold Robin Hood*. The 'popular Olympic Clown' is the Mons. Edouard of the advertisements, Edward Edwards, who joined them at Halifax in 1851 and rejoined in Cheltenham, December 1856. Charles Keith records an example of Edwards's wit: 'Edwards was playing clown at Astley's Theatre – then under E T Smith's management – and received, I believe, £25 a week. On leaving the treasury one day, with his week's salary in his hand, he heard the remark – "Well, what does he do to get a big salary? What is he clever at?" "Clever enough," replied Edwards turning round to his detractors, "to get £25 per week!"' (Keith, *Circus Life*, p. 12).

was highly indignant. So was the audience. In the end I had to dress and make up, go on and give the song . . . The papers used to give fresh verses and the tune, and song became a nuisance. Copies of the song were printed and sold by someone who used to forward me the receipts . . .

Time came that I had to leave Chelt. and friends of all classes. I had two thumping benefits, one I shared with Jno. Hengler. This happened at the first. The house was crowded before time. When I got to the circus the road in front was impassable, I could not get through and was in a stew, for as usual I never went to Bus. till the last minute and never stayed in it one moment longer than I could. Consequently I was afraid I could not get in in time for dressing. I got on some steps and cried as loud as I could bellow for permission to pass through. In a moment all seemed to turn towards a sea of smiling faces, a passage was made and I got into the building followed by a roar of cheers. I left for the station some weeks after. Outside the Circus about a dozen boys commenced to cheer, others joined them till a crowd gathered. People came to the shop doors to see what was the matter and from a shop and more mouths I received, farewells and good lucks.[211]

1856

Returning to Derby,[212] Frowde discovers that the woman he had wooed there had married in his absence, and he is sent 'a huge wedding favour trimmed with black and sable streamers'. He responds to this 'crusher' by making it public.

No one to advise with, determined to take bull by the horns, went to business, clown to the trick act. Govr. ringmaster, let horse and groom, ring master and artiste proceed. Soon as the rider had done a few tricks, I with lachrymose countenance stept over ring doors and followed the Govr. having pinned the wedding favour to my sugarloaf hat. There was a buzz and then a laugh, Govr. in a rage, said to me,

211. The *Cheltenham Looker-On* records: 'On the occasion of Mr Frowde's – the clown's – benefit, on Thursday the Circus was so full, that hundreds had to turn away, unable to obtain admission' (8 December 1855).

212. 14 January–25 March 1856 (*JT HH*).

'One at a time.' The rider indignant jumped into his fork and pulled up the horse. Govr. in a rage, thought I had been guilty of some by play, could not understand what the people were laughing at, for I stood as if wrapt in serious contemplation whilst all around were conferences and fresh laughter, which ended in a long round of applause, of condolence for all. I said, 'Well this was,' pointing to my hat ornamentation, 'sent to me.' I said, 'This is a Stiggins kind of whimsey.' Band started, the Govr. said, 'Get out, you are crabbing the rider.' So putting my hat under my arm, I leapt the boundary and came back minus the favour. Whilst the Gov. was keeping up the horse, in as few words [as] time would allow me, I gave a preliminary explanation.[213] When the rider stopped for breath he was laughing with as much gusto as the audience, which made them more hilarious than before . . .

There follows an interpolated story about the clown Barry,[214] told to him, he says, by the lawyer Sergeant Adams.

Barry was a witness to some action and adverse to the Sergt's side. He had given his evidence in a firm manner and could not be shaken. Thinking to get him off his balance, the sergt. said, with a sneer, 'You are a clown.' With cross hands a look of resignation and e'en a true resignation, Tom sighed, 'I am.' A laugh from the Bench, and of course the public, etc. Sergt. was baffled and was about to resume his seat when he marked Tom's upper lip. Rising, 'Are you a clown? Clowns don't wear moustaches . . . what's your reason for wearing one?' Tom replied, 'Same reason you have for wearing a wig, to distinguish me from other fools.'

Complicated details of Frowde's love life follow, before he returns to the circus business.

Chester was our next winter town.[215] It was like coming home, a warmer welcome could not be accorded to any son than I received

---

213. Presumably Frowde's 'explanation' was humorous, since the equestrian *and* the audience were laughing.

214. Tom Barry, clown with Hengler's in the late 1840s and Astley's in the 1850s.

He reached the heights of fame and popularity, earning £10 per week at Astley's.

215. 6 October–18 December 1856 (*JT HH*).

from my dear Owens, relative kindness from the Messiners . . . We had a capital opening. I had a glorious reception, but had to contend with a ringmaster too talkative. He went by the name of Henry,[216] he was business manager as well as ring master, also a literary man and dramatist, but he liked circus life. He was an awkward kind of man to jest with, going in for laurels, but if humoured he would lead a man on to many a little joke. I wanted to go on one tack, one night, and ignored his leading, he laughed ironically, I told him to close his mouth. I did not wish to lose myself. 'Do you,' said he, 'infer I could swallow you?' 'What do you think, with such a tunnel-like arrangement which you call a mouth.' Henry was a small man, with a good head, large drooping whiskers and a most pronounced Hebraical nose. Replied he, 'If you were to reverse the order and you swallow me, do you know what sensible people would say?' 'Well, perhaps they would say after that I could stomach anything.' 'No,' said he, 'they would say there goes a man with more brains in his stomach than he has in his head.' 'Oh,' said I joining in the laugher with the people, 'you have brains in your composition.' 'Yes,' said he, 'Of what do you suppose I am composed?' 'Nose and whisker,' said I. This did not please the Govr., but turned the laugh in my favour. As a rule I was most particular in avoided references to gastronomical arrangements. Never for the sake of a laugh, can I remember giving way to vulgarity. I had many letters on leaving towns from Clergy and others complimenting me on this head . . . Henry was riled and 'nose and whiskers' became to an extent an objectionable term, because ill-naturedly used by performers who detested Henry and unjustly so. He was an honest servant and ornament to the profession and a clever fellow, though very sarcastic not a bad sort . . .

There follows an anecdote about a bishop's son 'somehow out rather late at night', and a visit from Frowde's brother George, by this time in the navy. Frowde consults a homoeopath, Dr Joyce, regarding nervous depression; a change in his diet, and quiet, are recommended.

216. A. Henry, circus manager, later proprietor, who also wrote spectacles and pantomimes (*JT VA1*).

At this time, one morn, I met the Govr. Said he, 'Jem your Aunt wants you.' I went to their lodgings, teased the kids and last said to Aunt, 'Did you want me for any particular purpose?' 'Yes,' said she, 'I want you to do me a favour.' 'I wish I could,' was my reply, for she was very kind to me and always on my benefits made up the house for me. 'Well,' said she, 'I told your uncle last that I was sure to please me you would study the part of Mazeppa[217] and play it. Now will you? and I will play Olinska.' I made excuses, pointed out that people would laugh at my passion, or my love passages. All was of no avail! I left the house with my part to study, a miserable funking hypochondria. I had a horror of study. I don't believe I was ever dead letter perfect in a song or a part in my life, save in the part I now had in hand. I had a week to study it. I had the Doctor's advice to keep quiet. So bed being the best place to educate the memory, I used to come soon as business was over usually about 10.30. have my supper a pipe and go to bed, as soon as my cold whisky was consumed ...

The rehearsal of *Mazeppa* had gone well. The last rehearsal was on in the eve. The piece was to be played – box office had been busy and crowded house was anticipated. The wild horse, the fiery untamed steed, was the white horse Firefly, model of a horse whose portrait has been in the *Illustrated London News* more than once. There is a good portrait of the horse bestridden by Mr Hengler in the equestrian picture of Henry their father. At that time it was full of vigour and well depicted a wild horse. On this I was supposed to be fastened with ropes but really holding on to straps firmly fastened to a short surcingle.[218] All this was done to perfection. The horse pursued is seen by a dim light to enter the ring and fall down exhausted. It was necessary for the horse to have some control over him, which was achieved by a whipcord bridle and reins invisible in the low light to the general spectator. Mazeppa also faint and almost lifeless yet cunningly by whip and rein he gave the cue for the horse to fall, then

217. A hippodrama, *Mazeppa* was dramatised many times from 1825 onwards, most famously at Astley's with Ada Isaacs Menken, but then as a regular feature on circus and amphitheatrical programmes. Its notable feature was the lashing of the hero Cassimir/Mazeppa (occasionally played by a woman in fleshings and short trunks) to the back of a bounding horse. Frowde seems to be taking this role.

218. Surcingle: see note 141.

burst of thunder and shout confusion; a group of tartar peasants, terror stricken by the storm, approach and beholding the horse and man, screams in superstitious horror – 'the Volpas!' The lady who did this at the rehearsal probably had an umbrella and in throwing up [her] arm brandished the weapon [and] frightened the horse. I hung on, he reared and came down on the toe of my damaged foot. It finished my part of the rehearsal. Off I went to Mr Joyce.

'Well,' said he, 'this will give you [what you] want: you want rest.' 'Can't,' said I, 'I must go this eve.' 'Your toe is so swollen,' said he, 'that I cannot say to what extent it is damaged.' He wrote the Govr. with a result that riled him, kept me in his private rooms with Buttons in constant attendance with arnica and hot water. Night came and I [was] found in the dressing room. After much difficulty and pain I got on my fleshings[219] and with plenty of help, dress and attendance, I was ready. Scene was early twilight, I had to cross the ring to serenade . . . dear Olinska: 'Ere yet the envious daylight robs my soul of drinking deep draughts of liquid fire from those eyes. Appear dear life and raise Cassimir . . . to a throne of glory, monarchs might envy me.' I made Bus. crossing the ring, halting to listen (and thus easing my raging toe) whether spies or guards were about. Some changes had to be made as regards the wild horse. Altogether things went well, Aunt gave me thanks and the papers gave on the whole good critiques. One Mrs Hengler reminds me of, for I have had to write her for help and reminders, and she has give[n] me good help. She says one paper speaking of my acting gave me double credit in as much as I had to make my audiences forget the hero of the spectacle was their favourite clown and had to contend in chamber scene with the fantastical acting of Count Premislas. The Count was Henry, you will find in scrap books[220] some newspaper cuttings of my Chester doings and notices of *Mazeppa*. Under the careful nursery of old Mrs Onslow, my foot, or rather toe, daily became less troublesome. Among anonymous correspondents, and I had several, some conveying compliments, hints or jokes, was one whose notes, verses, or handwriting I had a kind of

---

219. Flesh-coloured tights, or a body-suit. The helpless rider, an exiled prince, is supposedly naked during this ordeal; this was one of the reasons for the huge success of the piece.

220. One of several tantalising references to cuttings books that have not apparently survived with the diaries.

fascination for. I often wondered whether she was present on the show. She must have been lately for some of the verses were of my Mazeppa.

Frowde goes into detail again here about his tentative encounters with ladies: he is self-conscious about compromising his genteel female acquaintances, but they and their families reassure him about his acceptability in polite society.

Jno. son of Alderman Peacock was a capital in keeping [me] posted on things of local consequence. In Nov. [the local political] parties were so equally balanced that some arrangement or agreement should be made as to who should be the Mayor for the ensuing year. The favourites were Peter Eaton, a brewer, and Potts, a lawyer. I was anxious to know for the sake of snap shot, but the council had not decided till after our doors were open. Peacock however was on the lookout, for he came to property room and left word that the council had only then decided and left the name. I was just going to the front, I spoke of Chester ancient, of its wall speaking witness and of past history and gallant deeds and then with broken voice deplored that her glory and her story was passing in a few months all would be passed. 'What are you trying to assert' growled out the rum cull. 'What,' said I, 'is it possible you a politician and a lover of this ancient city have not heard the news . . .' 'No, what is it?' 'Why, sir, Chester is to be Potted this year and Eaton the next.'[221] This awoke the excitement, Potts' partisans cheered, Eaton's growled disgust. The band was playing, the rider was riding. 'Do something sir,' said the Govr. 'I'll fine you for your so and so politics.' The rider took his seat and all sides with a good humoured laugh gave me a cheer. Govr. was pleased when I gave explanation and pronounced it a good wheeze. Next morn, passing Minshull and Hughes library[222] and gossip shop, much frequented by

221. Topical and local references were commonplace in the clown's performance. See Numbers 1, 29 etc. in Part IV, Thomas Lawrence's Gagbook. In this case, the subject is the Chester Mayoral election of November 1856, which caused some local excitement. The two candidates were Charles Potts, a Justice of the Peace, who had been Mayor in 1844–5, and Peter Eaton, the underdog, who had the popular vote – and won. The Marquis of Westminster (see p. 137) surprisingly attended the ceremony.

222. On Eastgate Row, which boasted booksellers, stationers, bookbinders and a circulating library.

clergy and others, I was called in. Said Peter Eaton, 'You're a bad prophet, Frowde. You put the cart before the horse.' 'Yes,' said I, 'for the sake of poetry.' 'Oh' and a laugh as I beat my retreat.

Study and bad toes got my nerves tight. Jno. Peacock nearly capsized them. He invited me, with some wine tasters, to the cellars and I sipped and sometimes drank, discussed in sobriety and good will to everybody and everything. But presently we left the stores of Bacchus, the sawdust and cob-webby warm nooks and corners of lustrous drinks and solitude for the fresh air and noisy street and then as Caudle[223] said, 'All became oblivion' as far as sense of feeling and perceptions were concerned. Outside of one of the old established, old fashioned drapers shops were, on either side of the door, rolls of carpet rested [on] each other. I am told I stood between them, declaring myself Sampson, pulled down the pillars of carpets to roll into the street. Then I went to the City Sheriffs, made impassioned speeches to Mrs Sheriff and made her a present of a packet of tickets, for it was my benefit night, but I knew nothing of this till the next day. My re-awakening to my responsibilities discovered me under the manipulation of my landlady and her son-in-law. I was getting an awful wigging from the old girl and some sobering decoction. I had a hard night's work set: a performance of equilibrium etc. on champagne bottles.[224] I went to vapour baths and was parboiled, had cold drench baths to my head, and at last started for work, wishing port wine had never been invented. The house was crowded. I had received a letter from Mr –, the Marquis of Westminster (see Scrapbook). Where all the clergy came from I don't know. I know where they would have gone to had Edward's imperious wishes been attended to. But allowance must be made for harsh words of a passionate man under the insanity of jealousy. His benefit had taken place the previous eve. and the public had not accorded to him the favour his talent deserved. I was invited to a quiet feed. 3 clergymen, Revd. W A O'Connor, J E Thurland, and G Chamberlain, presented me with a Bible, with an inscription.[225] Afterwards some citizens gave me an

223. Douglas Jerrold's *Mrs Caudle's Curtain Lectures* appeared in *Punch* during 1845.

224. See Figure 8.

225. All three clergymen had curacies in and around Chester at this time.

illustrated Charles Knight's *Shakespeare*[226] with an address, in which is this paragraph: 'It will suffice for us to say; – that we greatly admire your talents, no one could more admire them and further we believe that with those endowments it was intended that you should occupy a wider and more honourable field.'

December 1856

Their next stop is Bradford.[227] *Frowde writes wittily about Yorkshire pudding and bottles of stout before continuing with the narrative.*

There was a very favourable notice in *Punch* concerning me, I think Dickens[228] must have been the suggester, I never spoke to him in my life but knew from friends he was kindly disposed towards [me]. When on his travels his agent, Mr [blank in original], who lived near Ross was one informant. A great commotion in Bradford was made when Kossuth[229] came. I saw but did not hear him. I felt very flat whilst first in Bradford and anything but happy, could not, for a long time, get in touch with the people or myself till Wallett came. Was an immense favourite with the people and drew crowded houses – I think at the Sun Hotel.[230] He much interested me, there was a good company in the smoke room. Wallett was there and was giving some conversational history of things Yankee that had come under his observation, to the pleasure and sometimes the amusement of the listeners, if laughing is a test of being amused they were, but as is often the case, some narrow minded nobody felt annoyed and would have turned the conversation had he the power. I saw Wallett's eyes twinkle and thought that cove

226. Charles Knight's edition of Shakespeare's plays published between 1838 and 1843 was lavishly illustrated.

227. On 20 December 1856. A circus was erected, once again under the supervision of Mr O'Hara, opposite the railway station.

228. Although Dickens contributed very little to *Punch*, its staff were among his closest friends, particularly Mark Lemon and Douglas Jerrold. This

complementary notice, however, has not been traced.

229. Lajos Kossuth (1802–94), Hungarian statesman and one of the leaders of the Hungarian Revolution of 1848. He was exiled in August 1849 and lived in Turkey and Italy, as well as England.

230. The Sun Hotel, Ivegate, one of the leading inns in Bradford.

will get a oner presently. He did. For after a time speaking through a laugh he contradicted Wallett, he turned and looked at the man and asked on what ground he disputed his assertion.

'Why,' said the fellow, getting big with words, 'I never in my life saw –' 'Oh,' was the scornful interruption, '*You* never saw. How could you? Who never was far enough of[f] his leading strings to see the Atlantic. Because *you* have never seen Vesuvius, by the same rule is sufficient to say the mount does not exist.' Then with a look of contempt at culprit he sipped his toddy whilst our companions were laughing and then resumed the conversation as though his disputer had no reality. 'Twas not what Wallett said so much as the voice and acting that influenced people. He took a large sum from the Govr. for his short stay, but he brought in more first. Wallett was always good luck to me: he left and I got on better.

There was a man in the pit one night who gave, now and again, such a laugh as made all laugh, a cachinnation for which he was famous. His name was North, a kind of second Tim Bobbin.[231] There was a man in Derby had like risible power – Tommy Faulkner,[232] a printer. This man had not a tooth in his head but marvellously flexible lip, a smile of his was a most comical, more was a most wondrous performance, would last with various contortions for about a minute and then explode in short falsetto

231. Tim or Tom Bobbin: a North country clown or fool.

232. Tommy Faulkner:

'His appearance was suggestive of "Punch" – nose and chin almost meeting over a wide mouth, from which all the teeth had vanished, leaving a cavern behind them; short, squat figure, and a shuffling mode of progression. But his laugh! never to be dissociated from his personality by those who once heard and saw it! A sudden strident guffaw, that rung out without previous warning, that dominated even the hum of a crowd, and ended as abruptly as it began, not leaving a trace of mirth upon his face. "Old Tommy Faulkner's laugh" was dreaded by managers of public entertainments, for none could be certain when, or from what part of the audience it would break forth, and the effect of that unearthly explosion was instantly fatal to any unlucky performer of a sentimental part. Charles Dickens himself was one of his victims when giving a reading at the Lecture Hall in 1858.'

See Alfred Wallis, *Some Reminiscences of Old Derby. No.17* (Bound volume of Newspaper Cuttings, Derby Local Studies Library).

cracklings. Both were good properties for me and both were friendly with me ...

[Nowadays in Bradford] there is a new Theatre,[233] the one I knew was a wooden shack affair, the gallery was faced by iron bars. Bradford was a bad theatrical town, a noisy gallery and scant pit. It paid boothers. John Wild,[234] father of Mrs Hughes, made seasons here, J. Skerret[235] manager and actor ... Wallett was one of the mumming fraternity,[236] so was Nelson the clown, the innocent cause of the sad tragedy at Yarmouth.[237] Anderson, Wizard of the North,[238] was another. I became acquainted with J. Hoyle a rising and growing actor but as a Stationary. Also, with Mr and Mrs Nunn,[239] both favourites of the Bradford playgoers, she was the daughter of a navy Captain, name Boyle and commanded H. M. S. Arab, which was wrecked off the coast of Rio De Janeiro. They were keeping an Inn, well patronised by their friends.[240]

Memories of first-footing at the inn, and an anecdote about William Allen, the leader of the band, getting married in a hurry follow. Frowde also mentions his depressive illness again.

233. This may be the Royal Alexandra Theatre in Manningham Lane, built in 1864.

234. John Wild: the original 'Old Wild', actually James Wild, born 1771, and owner of Wild's Theatre, a portable theatre, and father of Sam Wild (see note 72). Mrs Hughes: Sarah Ann Wild, his daughter. She married Edwin Hughes, equestrian, working in Batty's Circus.

235. A Mr Skerritt hired the large upper room of the Oddfellows' Hall in Thornton Road (1840–1970) for theatrical performances for some years. See Mellor, *Bradford & District Theatres and Music Halls.*

236. See note 50.

237. Arthur Nelson, clown, originally with Parrish's theatrical booth, In May 1845 he was with Cooke's Circus at Yarmouth, where, in imitation of the famous clown Dicky Usher, he apparently drove four geese, pulling him in a bathtub, down the River Bure. It was a hoax but, in the crush, a suspension bridge collapsed and almost a hundred people died (*JT VA2*).

238. John Henry Anderson, the self-proclaimed 'Wizard of the North', magician and showman.

239. Jack Nunn and his wife Ann Boyle, members of the stock company in the old Liver Theatre, who managed Bradford's London Music Hall (previously the Bermondsey Hotel), Broadstones, from 1863. See Mellor, *Bradford & District Theatres and Music Halls.*

240. Frowde's point seems to be that a few successful circus performers began their careers as actors, either in portable or permanent theatres.

And now for foggy Liverpool, our building was in Dale St. the first of its kind known in that town.[241] I stayed with P. S., an old musician who kept a public house in a street leading, I think, into Castle St. He had a daily ordinary[242] for a few professional men and very jolly our meetings were. Peter was ancient, his better half was the largest portion, fair to look upon and withal buxom, about 25 years junior to P. and 15 senior to me.

A section here crossed out, which seems to imply Frowde's potential (though probably not actual) involvement with his landlord's attractive younger wife, alias 'Mrs Potiphar' (in Genesis 39 Potiphar's wife tried to seduce Joseph).

I wanted a quieter lodgings where I could have an opportunity of reading etc. so I gave Peter, my landlord pal, notice. The old boy was wrath but I would not listen to his arguments or give explanation, for he knew. I got a very good lodging at [?] nicely furnished and capital attendance. I think single men always do – as far as my own experience goes, I know they do. In the same house were Mr and Mrs A Bridges;[243] soon after Mr B Webster, Ned Wright and Paul Bedford,[244] who came to star at the Amphi became brother lodgers. Wright was an old sweetheart of Aunt Fanny's, a good natured fellow, a splendid low comedian. Some time after his death, Toole[245] came to the fore, I went to hear and see him. Facial action has a great deal to do with the popularity of a comedian. Ned, by the power of facial expression, would convey a meaning to his words and sentences far in advance of his utterance, so much so that people would express surprise that the audience should get so excited at almost meaningless

241. Hengler's Grand Cirque Variete in Dale Street had been built in 1857 by Charles Hengler.

242. Ordinary: a meal provided at a fixed charge.

243. Probably Mr and Mrs Anthony O'Neil Bridges. Bridges was an equestrian and scene act rider and worked with Hengler's Circus from around 1854 until his death in 1879 (JT VA1).

244. Ben Webster (1797–1882) was manager of, among others, the Haymarket (1837–53) and the Adelphi theatres (1844–76). Edward Wright (1813–59) and Paul Bedford (1792–1871) were noted comic actors. See George Taylor, *Players and Performances in the Victorian Theatre* (Manchester University Press, 1989), pp. 68–9.

245. J. L. Toole (1832–1906).

expressions. Toole riled me at what I considered his clumsy imitation of the illustrious Ted, who by the bye was a favourite of our Gracious Monarch. Mr Webster, after the run of the piece, he was here [for], left for Town. Bedford and Wright stayed to play in their farces and they invited me to dinner and with me 2 of Mr Copeland's Company,[246] viz. H Nevill and Jno. Laurie, one then playing light comedy and respectable utility, the other a clever pantomimist.[247] Both achieved a big position, though then not much thought of in Liverpool. Yet as clever then as ever. The Amphi and Royal were the only principal theatres of L'pool and Copeland to the fullest the autocrat of both. They were not far apart so the same actor at the Royal in the first piece would often be seen in the 2nd at the Amphi. It was a good school for a young actor. Old Bath,[248] as the Gov'nor was irreverently called, was always about and very exacting, very little on the stage or in the house escaped his scrutiny.

Well, we had a nice little party, a very nice little dinner and some friendly repartee, 'til 'Horrors!', the hour struck time for our theatrical friends to depart for their dressing rooms at the Amphi. 'Our sawdust friend has a sweet hour and half to the good,' said Wright, 'and him we leave the decanter', apropos of sawdust, a name that in the profession points out the circus actors, riders, etc., who in like spirit designate the legitimate profession as size rubbers or mummers. The late Douglas Jerrold was uncle to the Misses Copeland, who on a visit to them gave vent to a sneering sarcasm, the ladies ... were speaking in egotism of their family, spoke of the blood of the Copelands. 'Yes,' interrupted D. J., having in his mind the Amphitheatre (which you know is a theatre and circus). 'Yes,' said the great satirist, 'grand blood – a mixture of size and sawdust.' I wish I had been there. I hear it took the breath out of the cousins through whose veins the blood of the Copelands coursed. Yes, said he, wonderful good blood, a mixture [of] size and sawdust, poor girls, cynical

246. Already the manager of the Amphitheatre since 1843, William Robert Copeland became manager of the Theatre Royal, Liverpool, in 1850. Wallett writes of him that he was 'one of the most honourable and kind-hearted of his class' (Wallett, *Public Life*, p. 72).

247. Henry Neville was playing Cromwell in *Henry VIII* at the Theatre Royal, Liverpool, in October 1858. Jno. Lauri was one of the famous Lauri family of pantomimists (six in number), all of whom were employed by Copeland.

248. A nickname for Copeland, origin unknown.

uncle, cruel Douglas. Well, soon as my friends left I had a wash and smoke and started for Dale St., but halted at the Amphi and made for the pit, persuaded the man to let me pass, saying I only wanted to have a look at the house. Now Copeland always gave us the entrée to the Theatre but would not allow a pro free to the pit. Boxes were free to our people, we were always free an hour ere the theatre was over. Well, I was standing by the pit entrance obliquely opposite Paul Bedford, who was seated at a tea table on the left. He noticed me and with tea cup pantomimed, Bath saw the action, I happened to look up at side boxes and saw the autocrats eye skimming the pitites. Presently he was pointing me out to Shuttleworth, in a moment I was at the money box and paid, took my ticket and warned the ticket collector and not a moment too soon for the factotum of the front was at him, I saved his and my own bacon. Built almost into the theatre, by the stage entrance was a Pub kept by Mr and Mrs Bibb, a resort for all pros and many journalists and other bohemians, lawyers, &c., showmen in the term profession only include themselves.

He moves into a catalogue of the frequenters of this pub, and the reminiscences break down into miscellaneous recollections, in no particular order, of people he has known, including Charles Sloman, the Jewish improvisator, whose liking for sucking pig Frowde considers comical, and at odds with his ability to compose beautiful verses. The memoirs come to a stop after a few further anecdotes, obviously not wound up, but perhaps not susceptible of closure without more self-revelation, or even self-questioning, than he was prepared for.

❖

Part III

❖

Thomas Lawrence's repertoire: popular humour unmediated

❖

The clown in the ring

There is every possibility that what follows is a unique survival: a Victorian clown's gagbook. Whether or not Thomas Lawrence's notebooks were a working tool, they are certainly something he wrote for himself alone. In our annotation, and in this introduction, we have attempted some sort of mediation of the book we have transcribed; but the document remains difficult to interpret. Perhaps further research will answer some of the basic questions – such as how and why this material is funny – by putting it into practice. Despite its challenges, the material demonstrates vividly the particular relationships within which a professional comedian of the 1860s and 1870s, working chiefly for lower-class audiences, actually operated. Here we have Victorian popular performance, unmediated by a class-removed observer or the artistic or moral intentions of a writer.

The book begins with very old jokes, of the kind that many commentators complained about when they said (and indeed still say) that circus clowns tend to boring repetition of a few old gags. Such chestnuts have their own appeal – the listener enjoys a sense of superiority and familiarity, and no doubt the clown working to the horse or to the rope, needing always to have an instant interjection ready for any hitch or emergency in the main act, found them useful. Reviews[1]

---

1. See *Era*, 15 May 1870: 'The parade in Alford of Messrs Powell, Foottit and Clarke's Circus Company, on Saturday, May 7th, was a great attraction . . . The tent was erected in the Windmill Inn paddock and will evidently accommodate three or four thousand people . . . An unusual feature in this entertainment was

speak of Lawrence as witty and original; but he was still a professional circus clown, required to follow the ringmaster as he followed the horse, ready with the impromptu distractions required. Like his modern American equivalents working in the dust and danger of the rodeo, the clown in the physically stressful, animal-rich nineteenth-century circus had distinct and important tasks to fulfil. As well as rushing in to cover hitches, his structural function was to provide a variety of verbal and physical comedy to fill in long gaps or short rests throughout the bill. On stage, too, clowns would be used as fillers, to do a few minutes 'front cloth' to cover the building of a spectacular set; but in the ring the linking task was continual, merging seamlessly in and out of other people's performances. 'Peter Paterson' offers a clear description of the method of working with the ringmaster alongside and around an equestrian act:

> In the scenes in which I act as clown, I arrange my little patter with the ring-master. If I go in with Miss Caroline, I tell him first that I will do the streets; he takes his cue from that, and asks me some trifling questions which bring out the names of all the principal streets in the town. Thus I say a desponding person ought to live in *Hope* Street, sir ... A good portion of what is said, however, is arranged on the spur of the moment; the clown gives the ring-master his cue as they walk round following the horse, and at the next pause – there are at least two pauses in an act of horsemanship, for each scene, allow me to say, is divided into an exordium, an argument, and a peroration – the clown flies off into a verse of poetry about
>> What are lovely woman's sparkling eyes
>> Compared with Bagot's mutton-pies?[2]

Lawrence's book offers instances of many of these interactions with the ringmaster, and records several such punning lists and bathetic couplets. Paterson shows how they were used, while incidentally taking the opportunity for a sly clownish assertion of his superiority

that the Clowns selected uncommon jokes, facetiously causing the most enjoyable laughter on all sides.'

2. Paterson, *Glimpses of Real Life*, p. 131. Compare with No. 15, ''Tis Sweet', for the antithetical use of mutton in romantic gags.

to the horse-rider by dignifying the act with a Latinate rhetorical structure. Lawrence sets down his material complete with lead-ins from the contiguous act, praising the grace or bravery of the equestrian or apologising for running into someone on entrance. Sometimes he indicates responses from the ringmaster acting as his stooge, though for some reason few of the numbers include the get-out or link back to the main performance; when he inserted a line of this kind in 'Children', (p. 226), he subsequently deleted it.

The wheeze

As well as working with the equestrians, established clowns had their own acts. Unlike the twentieth-century clown entrée, these were not entirely physical, and the 'classic' pattern, in which the whiteface clown and the auguste use slapstick, whether crude or subtle, to explore dominance and insubordination, order and chaos, had not yet been set. Many Victorian clowns worked alone or with the ringmaster as stooge. Their individual acts might be musical or dramatic, and were of adjustable length, made up of units they called 'wheezes' (spelt 'weaze' by Lawrence). These could include sketches and songs, and often employed parody of the other performers or of 'high art', like the clown Dewhurst's Taglioni dance.[3] Most comics, now as then, make some of their material out of the burlesquing of other performances, but the circus dimension added to the challenge. Stage burlesque requires only a nodding acquaintance with Shakespeare, a few 'classics', and current plays and songs; a circus clown also needed real ability in the physical skills he parodied. The book records two such parodies of performance: a comic tightrope routine with a second clown, and a scenario for a burlesque dog drama complete with basic set and props. One can deduce what the skills behind the parodies were. Lawrence advertised himself as able to act in circus plays; Frowde was a contortionist and an equilibrist – balancing on bottles is a kind of parody of the graceful Hengler rope-dancing. Frowde failed to learn to ride well,

3. See Thomas Frost, *Circus Life and Circus Celebrities* (London: Chatto & Windus, 1881), pp. 105–6, where he quotes the bill for Dewhurst's benefit night at Batty's Olympic in 1841, to include burlesque dancing, 'in a style nothing like Madame Taglioni'.

coming to the ring late, but his clown role model Wallett and many others were equestrians who moved on to clowning when they failed to achieve distinction in physical performance. They could still be very good: some equestrian acts refused to have clowns in the ring with them, fearing the undermining of their solemn exertions by skilled and insouciant parody.

The surprise and challenge of the gagbook lies in its revelation of how far Lawrence's act goes beyond what one might have imagined would serve circus purposes. The repertoire it suggests seems to us more like that of a stand-up comedian or a television comic. The scope of its parody, for example, extends far beyond the physical act, to all kinds of popular verse and oratory; and the implied or explicit interactions with the audience bespeak comic skills that would be useful in a comedy club today. A modern stand-up would share audience familiarity with a wide range of song and especially television performance; Lawrence's audience can recognise stage drama including not only Shakespeare but also a version of the drama of *Jane Shore*, as well as contemporary melodramatic conventions, and he sings and/or parodies songs from the broadside tradition of the streets, the song and supper room, the black-face minstrel show and the polite amateur evening round the piano. The book alerts us to the versatility of the Victorian professional comic, and reminds us that this was a time of great opportunity in show business. The 1860s saw the coming of age of a new entertainment form, the music hall. By Lawrence's time the halls were proliferating daily, taking off into dominance of the British entertainment scene, and sucking in all available professional talent. We have surviving song books from that period of development, some sold cheaply at the venues where they were performed, so representing good evidence, at least, for what the proprietors were prepared to see in print; but we have almost no evidence of what a music hall comic actually sang, nor what he said on stage, that is as unmediated as Lawrence's book.

Popular comedy: puns, wordplay and misogyny

Perhaps the most striking thing about Lawrence's material is its apparent unfunny verbosity. The game of words is relished at a pace and length that seems in cold print the reverse of humorous. But the same could probably be said of the material of many twentieth-century stand-ups: imagine the unfunniness of Ken Dodd's constant reiteration of invented words and nonsense questions without his bizarre but compelling presence. Lawrence's verbal jokes are of types still very recognisable. Comics still use his favourite structure, the elaborated conceit, in which he takes an intrinsically grotesque idea – people are like potatoes, for example – and builds more and more tortuous and wire-drawn variations upon it. Or he will move on from the single word to exploit rhymes and aural coincidence: 'soldiers want their bounty money. Musicians like harmony, Frenchmen like ceremony, the Englishman likes ready money. The Irishman likes anybody's money ... young ladies they want matrimony'. The pun, which lies at the heart of such verbal riffs, is a central element in English humour; it comes alive only in the delivery, and will get across if there is sufficient life in the working of the wheeze, 'lots of gag in telling it', as 'Peter Paterson' says – 'by a little physical exertion an immense deal of fun may be made out of nothing'.[4] He might have added that the audience's complicity is also essential: we relish the way the joke is made to work upon us, and cooperate in making it amusing. Another characteristic technique still employed today is undercutting: the deliberately banal, bathetic or indeed rude anticlimax to an apparently bland or sentimental remark. This is common in Victorian clowning, as in Paterson's couplet, above; Lawrence uses it over and over again, as he builds up a wild quasi-dramatic description and lets it down with a thump ('Shaving', p. 196) or trowels on saccharine praise of a girl and then prefers a meat pie ('Sweethearts', p. 178). Again, what seems laboured on the page could be vividly worked round the ring, acted out with melodramatic pantomime or imposed by false smiles and petting upon women in the audience.

One of the most obvious ways in which Lawrence exemplifies old popular comedy is in his attitude to sexuality, and to women. Surviving Victorian printed matter is almost invariably censored; but here close scrutiny, digging behind the now-forgotten slang, reveals

4. Paterson, *Glimpses of Real Life*, p. 115.

that Lawrence's humour, free from that constraint, is at least as 'blue' as the jokes of the twentieth-century music hall, of Max Miller and Nellie Wallace. Moreover, the most cursory glance shows us that the majority of the wheezes express unremitting hostility towards women, in their repeated trashing of sentimental attitudes, their portrayal of women as oppressors and harridans, deceitful temptresses who trap a man by their sexual promise and then turn into grotesque, hated bodies and predatory money-grubbers. They share this characteristic not only with music hall in general, but specifically with the imported black-face minstrel tradition, where extremely sentimental song was weirdly counterbalanced by grotesque physical humour demeaning black people in general, and women in particular. John Towsen notes the link between clowning and minstrelsy,[5] and slapstick physical humour is a feature of black-face acts on the British halls.

Victorian popular song

Lawrence's rhymes and song lyrics reveal demotic song culture in a period of rapid development and change. They relate to broadsides sold on the streets, to recitation pieces and to music hall songs, exemplifying how the rapidly developing professional music industry profited from materials emerging from within informal and even oral culture. Such transactions could involve the repeated passing to and fro of verses and characters: Frowde records his utilisation of songs that belonged to famous performers, notably Sam Cowell. Cowell had found the song 'Billy Barlow', for example, on a Catnach broadside and fixed its persona and costume by his own performances. Frowde used it to respond to his audiences, adding new verses that local people wrote for him day by day. Lawrence records various songs in the early 1870s that were to surface in print over the next fifteen years, claimed, on publication, by writers who may have originated them, arranged them or, simply heard them sung. In one instance, 'The Fellow That Looks Like Me' (p. 243), two songs were published in the same month of 1876 with this title, neither of which is identical to Lawrence's version of five years before – transparently a case of writers or singers

5. John Towsen, *Clowns* (New York: Hawthorn Books, 1976), p. 187.

picking up a good piece and making it over for their own use. Lawrence even records three verses of 'Cockles and Mussels', a song claimed in Dublin today as belonging to ancient tradition but actually only traceable in print to the early 1880s; it was sent to Lawrence from Cheltenham ten years earlier. The popular music business is still full of rival claims and disputes about the origin and ownership of individual songs, and while the sums of money involved have escalated, the underlying truth remains the same: that popular song is the currency of a culture, appropriated by all, and the richer the mixture of reference and allusion, the more vital and productive the entertainment. Lawrence's gagbook is a unique demonstration of the way that circus, street entertainment, music hall and stage shared a foundational stratum of comic taste and form.

The clown and his Victorian audience

Lawrence's text is therefore full of suggestions about the audiences as well as the performers of the travelling circus in the 1860s and 1870s: what attitudes they shared, and what cultural coinage they had in common. Here is a concrete guide to a certain structure of feeling, all the more important for its rare preservation. Here we have evidence of taste largely unmediated by the usual commercial imperatives that show up in, for example, printed music hall songs. Paterson records that he was advised to look in *Punch* and the *Morning Herald* to augment his stock of jokes,[6] but such sources show up only rarely in Lawrence's material. He uses literary parody freely, but in a debunking, materialist manner that is quite unlike the middle-class self-reflexive fun of *Punch* or of educated entertainers like W. S. Gilbert. There are a few wheezes in which he can be seen to adopt a clown persona that 'others' him: in some of his links, and pieces such as 'Love' (p. 216), he is the clown in the sense of 'simpleton', the country clod or childish 'Silly Billy'; occasionally he speaks consciously as a member of the exotic circus group, talking about his strolling life; he even has one passage, the disquisition on being a fool, which self-consciously claims kin with the Shakespearean clown – Wallett and other Victorian

6. Paterson, *Glimpses of Real Life*, p. 113.

'Shakespearean' clowns used a similar monologue. But most of Lawrence's material adopts no separate, alienated or acted persona, and is a direct exchange of beliefs and prejudices with its sixpenny audience. On a political level, Lawrence expects his auditors to admire Gladstone, and to support the English working man against the world. His favourite butt is the policeman. Where he points a moral, it is that he, like everyone else, looks after himself first because no one else will do it for him; and that snobbery is an evil, the poorest having a right to respect. His patriotic material is largely limited to praise of soldiers and sailors – those in the ranks – and rarely passes up the opportunity to condemn such class oppression as army flogging. There is often an aside that qualifies praise of the brave volunteer or the redcoat by a little dig at his just slightly ridiculous vanity, or at his lack of proper pride in having allowed himself to be purchased for a shilling. The subtle range of Lawrence's jokes on this subject suggests his need for alternatives: each moment in the ring must be carefully calculated upon a reading of the audience in front of him, at each specific performance.

Theatre and circus historians have followed the lead of nineteenth-century writers and cartoonists in middle-class periodicals, who turned the baggy-trousered clown with the red nose into an easy cliché of harmless fun for children, cocooning the circus in a haze of safe nostalgia and belittlement. But Lawrence's gagbooks challenge that reification. They are specific, concrete, resistant to generalisation or sentimentality. Their unmediated class commentary, their capturing of a moment in the history of popular song, their exemplification of the grotesque and intensely verbally self-conscious Victorian sensibility, their constant recurrence to gender hostility, make them one axis of a uniquely valuable microhistory. Frowde's retrospective account of his experiences gives us a time-based account *in extensio*; Lawrence's materials dive deep into the moment.

✤

Part IV

✤

The 1871 gagbook of
Thomas Lawrence

✤

Figure 11. Photograph of Thomas Lawrence with his wife and three of their children. Date unknown.

No. 1[1]

ABC

This first piece in the book is one of the most antique. The linking material, in which the clown comments to the ringmaster on the number of legs on a horse, is cited by Mayhew in 1851 as an example of the 'venerable' jests of the lowest clown he interviewed, who worked the streets. The following trick account of divisions of the year is probably as old and stale.

The main body of the wheeze is a topical ABC, a form that is as conventional as the old jokes. It is interesting to note what topical platitudes were acceptable to the 1870 audience of a travelling show: independence, freedom of speech and fair elections are approved, patriotism is conceived 'from below', in terms of the soldier and sailor, coupled with the inevitable protest about flogging. Praise of the volunteers might have been ironic – the cliché 'useful body of men' sounds very tongue in cheek. Disapproval of mock auctions and of the notion of 'kleptomania' would seem to be topical. In Middlemarch, published in 1872, George Eliot mentions the latter as an excuse for theft by young noblemen. It is interesting to see 130-year-old complaints about dangerously missed signals and unintelligible timetables on the prenationalised railways.

A clown's gagbook was a piece of equipment, quite as important as his mock trumpet or red hot poker. It would have been carefully placed inside the ring curtains where he could consult it each time he left the ring, an *aide memoir* containing the accumulated gags and wisdom of his clowning career. We can picture Tom Lawrence after his exertions in the ring, clowning to Young Hernandez's horse or Mons Rivers' strongman act, out of breath, and quickly turning the pages of his trusty book to find that particular gag, and knowing exactly where to find it. He made this a simple exercise, by placing each gag on its separate page, eschewing economy of paper out of professional necessity. In this present volume we had not been able to follow Tom's example. The constraints of modern publication methods have required us put more than one gag onto a page and to use artificial means – ♣ – to separate them. But having retained so much of the original content, we hope that these minor intrusions will not detract too much.

1. We reproduce the original numbers that Lawrence gave to his wheezes, written large at the head of the page; they are by no means consistent or consecutive.

That's a nice horse. What a number of legs he has got?

4

I say he has got 10: two front legs and two 4 legs – well – 2 fours are 8 and 2 hind legs are 10.

Did you ever go to school?

Yes

So have I, I went twice, once we had no candle, and the second time the master was not at home. How many months was there in the year where you went to school?

12

And how many weeks?

52

So there were at our school – and how many days were there?

365

There wasn't at ours.

How many?

325. The other 40 was Lent and the man never paid them back. Still I learned a little – I learnt to spell C A T dog D O G cat and mud and there I stuck . . .
Oh yes I learnt my A B C and I have put a different construction on the letters to what they did some years ago, I remember it used to be A for Apple, B for bread, C for cat, D for dunce, E for Edward, but I have altered it all together – would you like to hear it?

Yes

> A stands for our Brave army
> With all the World spare
> B our British Bull Dogs
> To guard old ENGLAND'S share

2. The answers written in for the interlocutor are distinguished by bold italics.

C stands for CAT o'nine tails
With which they often flay
D stands for disgust
That with flogging we don't do away[3]
E stands for election
No bribery we employ
F stands for franchise that
All subjects should enjoy
G stands for Gladstone
To unseat him many have tried in vain
H the Honours that he's won
And ever will retain[4]
I stands for independence
That's felt by Great and Small
J for country justices
That's seldom good at all
K stands for kleptomania
Or theft in modern dress
L for looseness of law
And liberty of press
M stands for mock auctions
A swindle I do declare
N stands for noodles
Who purchase their goods there
O! stands for opinions
In country and town
P for perseverance
That tries to put it down
V stands before Queen Victoria
A good Queen all aver
R for railway accidents
That often do occur

3. Flogging was abolished in the British Army in 1881 but had been a cause of liberal and working-class complaint for decades; branding for some offences was abolished only in 1871.

4. Gladstone entered into his triumphant first ministry in 1869, with strong popular support.

S stand for signals
That drivers seldom heed
T stands for time tables
Not one in ten can read
U stands for unions
With inquiry now and then[5]
V stands for volunteers
A useful body of men
W stand for Wimbledon
Where often they do repair[6]
X we'll say X, stands for exercise
That they obtain when there
Y is yourselves my friends
That I have tried to amuse
Z the zeal with which I have used
Some wisdom to infuse
And if I gain your kind applause, delighted I shall be
And some other night I will recite, my comic A B C.

❖

No. 2

Wants Money

The wheeze begins with a link to the departing act, in which the clown creates a tremendous build-up of mock-admiration and undercuts it

5. He would seem to refer not to the union workhouses – a longstanding grievance of the poor – but to trades unions, at that time finding their institutional base in Britain: the first Trades Union Congress met in 1868, after a Royal Commission of Inquiry in February 1867.

6. In 1859 France launched the first steam-powered iron-clad battleship, and the British Navy was rendered no longer invincible. This event inspired a fear of invasion that overcame the longstanding aversion of the British Parliament to the dangers of arming civilians – who might turn their guns on the civil power – and the first Volunteer corps were founded. They were endowed with a tract of land on Wimbledon Common by the landowner, Earl Spencer, and there set up an annual camp and shooting match. In the early years the fears of creating an armed mob were assuaged by confining the Volunteers to those who could buy expensive uniforms, and the social cachet of the Wimbledon meeting was ensured by high entrance fees and the participation of royalty; but by 1868 when nearly 199,000 men enlisted, 'the rank and file were drawn from amongst the ranks of urban artisans' with an eye to respectability. See David French, *The British Way in Warfare 1688–2000* (London: Unwin Hyman, 1990), p. 136.

by finding that he has empty pockets. He asks the ringmaster to help him out with what he intended to give – a very small sum – only to discover that the artiste he is offering to reward does not want his money. This affords a springboard into a call-and-response rhyme, with 'money' as its refrain, moving on to a riff that piles up stereotype jokes and puns and culminates in two quatrains that sound like 'motto song' pieties but actually deliver a clearsighted view of the oppression of capitalism.

That's a very clever boy. I should like to reward him. I will do something for him that will hand our names down to posterity something that will be talked of in all parts of the world. Something that will be heard of read of and seen in East or West, North or South, from pole to pole, I will do something that will immortalise his name and mine something that will cause our names to be written on the blazing scroll of fame: and handed down to posterity till time is no more, and here in the presence of these ladies and gentlemen now present I offer to give to him the great sum of – have you got 3 halfpence – don't he want money – he is the only being in this world that don't then. Everybody is looking for money, what will men *not* do for money, some cry for it, some sigh for it, some lie for it, and some die for it.

What cheers the miser's heart? Money.

What who makes the ladies dressed so smart? Why money.

What gains promotion some times in our army? Money.[7]

What will make men tip their Barney?[8] Money.

What will make many drunk and kick up a riot? Money.

What will keep your wife's tongue quiet? Why money.

7. The purchase of army posts was a longstanding scandal that Gladstone tackled with the Army Enlistment and Regulation Acts of 1870 and 1871.

8. Make men tip their Barney: a barney is a sporting competition, a fight or a race, and especially one that is unfair or fixed to make money from unwary gamblers. The sense here, therefore, is that men will 'tip', i.e. give away, the barney in which they are competing, for money – they can be paid to lose a race or a fight.

If you only go home on a Saturday night without money and see how soon you will get your hair curled with a 3 legged stool, why we all want money. The child wants its cake money, when it gets older he wants his school money. Girls want their pin money, sailors want their prize-money, soldiers want their bounty money. Musicians like harmony, Frenchmen like ceremony, the Englishman likes ready money. The Irishman likes anybody's money, and a Scotchman wants everybody's money. There is another class of people that want money just as bad as any I have named – young ladies they want matrimony. But that is the worst kind of money you can get hold of. If it should be bad you can't change it, and it's a very bad thing to let the world know that you want money, for if they know that you want money, they will very kindly let you want. Then you take my advice

> And it's the best of advice in existence
> It's rare on the world's kindness to call
> And if ever you claim its assistance
> Make the world think you don't want it at all
> No doubt you may think it surprising
> But it is true though I speak like a clown
> The world will help all those who are rising
> But they will trample on those who are down.

❧

No. 3
Man   Woman

Just as melodrama works on the alternation of heroics and low humour, so this mode of Victorian comedy is based on juxtaposition and inversion – both faces of which, the romantic and the bathetic, are simultaneously felt to be true. His starting point in each section here is an accepted platitude on the subject he gives as title – 'man/woman'. First he undercuts the cliché of the parlour love-song – the exotic 'sweet rose of Kashmir' drinks beer and becomes that other Other, 'a young Blackymoor'. Then he makes an apparently irreproachable claim to participation in middle-class moralising – a contented mind is a continual feast, he says, and dares you to laugh. The original proverbial saying was about a good conscience, rather than contentment; Lawrence's version reflects the falling-off from Protestant high-mindedness to bourgeois self-congratulation. Faux-innocently, he goes on to offer the usual hegemonic platitudes about happy married life – and then comes the let-down – the single have no one to make them – pause – miserable. But he immediately retreats from the laugh into the language of the conduct book, deprecating 'perpetual jars' and taking the high moral ground to explain how his audience should understand Domestic Love; this was the theme of Coventry Patmore's verse novel Angel in the House, *published in 1863. Lawrence's redaction of the poem's sentiments is interestingly precise, in that it deprecates the ideological appropriation that moved rapidly from glorifying married love as an Angel to imposing that elevation upon the wife. His conclusion, however, is to revert to the working-class male perspective of his time – the real point about women, and especially wives, is that they cost you money.*

In performance the wheeze depends on the carefully timed play of repetition and irony. Like the more obvious verbal riffs of 'Wants Money' (see p. 160) this piece, too, works on the links between words and ideas from the outset, building up a complex pattern of echoes of sound and theme, intercut with admonitions, direct appeals to the audience, and pauses. The timing is crucial. Built into the repetitions is an insistent tempo, pacey but not rushed. The pauses then allow the audience, (rather than the performer) to draw breath, but they cannot be too long, otherwise the links will be lost. He is working on the audience throughout, playing with common knowledge, accepted subjects for jokes, irony. He addresses them directly, works on their complicity, understanding and sympathy.

Begin

Song
Oh I love her I love her sweet rose of Kashmir
I love her because – she is fond of strong beer
The first time I met her she was scrubbing a floor
And her face was as white as a young Blackymoor.

I feel very happy this evening. I suppose 'tis because I have a contented mind. They do say that a contented mind is continual feast, and I think every body ought to be happy.

Married men ought to be happy because they have loving wives to make them so. Married ladies ought to be happy because they have loving husbands to help them. And single men ought to be the happiest creatures in the world: because they have no one to make them miserable.

I don't know how it is that married people are so miserable, it may be because they don't begin in the right way. They should avoid perpetual jars and sharp abradings, be lenient with each other's faults and above all avoid falsehood, for once deceive a wife and she finds it out, she can never trust you again.

Now look here, this is just the reason there is so much uncomfort in a married life. When a young man meets with the object of his affection, no matter how fair the lady is, no matter how brilliant her eyes, no matter how luxuriant the hair, no matter how small her feet or how large her heart, she is only a woman; and not an angel. Do you see?

And by the same rule when a young woman meets the object of her affection, no matter how strong his mind, no matter how noble his form, no matter how wealthy he is, no matter how moral his principles he is only a man; and not a god.

Well then it stands – one is a woman the other a man: man and woman are mortals and mortals are imperfect creatures, and that one is the most imperfect that expects to find perfections in the other.

Man, if I had my will do you know what I would have? – a sign board painted and hung over the door of every married couple in the civilised world. It should have on these few words

A world of care without
A world of strife shut out
A world of Love shut in

You know I'm very fond of the ladies –

I say bless those wives that fill our lives
With little bees and honey,

They ease life's shocks they mend our socks,
But can't they spend the money.

❖

Matrimony

This short piece follows on, perhaps, from Lawrence's thoughts about marriage in the preceding wheeze; it seems to be a collection of somewhat mysogynist platitudes, which he begins by the typical stand-up comedian's manoeuvre of accosting an audience member as butt. On the whole it works again the joke in which the clown offers sage advice, sending up hegemonic attempts to influence the working man. Its most interesting aspect is probably the several levels on which it could be understood, via double entendre: in the denouement, for example, he asserts that he married 'judiciously', a 'big' word (added in the later version of the wheeze) that works in the cod-advice-manual framework but also, especially since he spells it 'Judishusly', reminds the knowing that a 'Judische complement' meant a large penis but no money. Whether in performance he merely left this suggestion latent, to be picked up by some of the men in the audience, or underlined it by a gesture (his hand in the pocket of his baggy trousers?) would no doubt vary according to his nightly judgement of the house.

Are you a married man? Though I can see that you are – there is serenity in every feature, while a single man has a face as long as a fiddle. How often have I recommended matrimony to some of my bachelor friends! But they are frightened at the very name of marriage, and I am sure there's nothing to be frightened at – surely it is only like bathing in cold water: give one plunge and it's all over.

Then they say that times are too hard and provisions too dear to get married; besides, they say we can't do as we like when we are married – we should have to sit moping in the house and nurse the baby, but now we can do as we like, go where we like and stop as long as we like, but if we were married we should lose all these privileges and not only that – we should lose our *liberty*. But that's all nonsense. A man never loses his liberty, not if he marries judiciously: do as

I did – marry a woman with a wooden leg, and when you want a spree, steal the leg – she can't run after you.

❖

No. 3½

Dogs

This is not a full-blown wheeze, a section of the clown's solo performance, so much as a note of another string of puns that, as clown to the horse or rope, he might use at a break in the main performance. He begins by engaging with the ringmaster by deliberately walking into him; one imagines an uppity clown dancing round the smartly dressed figure – often in a military or huntsman's costume – nudging him, either literally or verbally, until he accepts the role of stooge and replies 'Which the Dog?' and is drawn in; when his butt retreats again into silence, the clown has to goad him – 'You're no dog!' – repeated twice. Two versions of this material appear in the earlier book.

Now then Spooney mind were you are pushing, don't you take such a liberty! Remember there is a difference between you and me. I have heard say there is a difference between an officer and a soldier – the only difference is, one is a *bloater* the other is a *red herring*[9] – but there is a difference between you and me. There is as much difference between you and me as there is between the *Shepherd* and his *Dog*.

Which the Dog?

I don't know which is the Dog, but I consider myself the Shepherd.

Me the dog!

You don't look like a *Dog*, you don't walk like a *Dog*, and I am sure you don't act like a *Dog*. You are *not a Dog* – a *Dog* is the faithful friend of man.

9. In other words, no difference, merely more pretensions: both terms mean a preserved herring, but the bloater has been only lightly salted and then smoked, while the red herring is steeped longer in salt, so is tougher and drier. The throw-away sneer at the military or rather, perhaps, the militia officer (as opposed to the other ranks) seems typical of his attitude (see pp. 233ff.).

So he is.

A *Dog* will stick to his master in the hour of adversity.

You're no *Dog*.

A *Dog* would die by the side of his master's sick couch.

You are no *Dog*. No – your ears are not long enough.

You are only a *Puppy*.

> A soldier is a *fighting Dog*,
>
> A sailor is a *water Dog*,
>
> Policeman are *watch Dogs*,
>
> Young Ladies are *pet Dogs*,
>
> Children are *lap Dogs*,
>
> Those who discover unknown countries are *new-foundland dogs*.
>
> Those who go up in air balloons are *Sky terriers*[10]

And your dandy fops are *Puppys* because they wear more collar than shirt.[11]

❧

No. 4

This wheeze is structured very like No. 3 above, 'Man/Woman', and is on the same subject. It begins with a burlesqued love-song, taking off Henry Carey's 'Sally in our Alley,' itself an eighteenth-century exercise in the faux-pastoral that substituted the city poor for shepherds

10. Lawrence spells this 'tariers', which makes the pun work (they tarry in the sky) and may suggest that he pronounced the word in that way.

11. The dig at 'dandy fops' as puppies – untrained and arrogant – as indicated by the wearing of a large showy collar while being unable to afford a whole shirt – is very reminiscent of music hall representations of the fashionable (pseudo) gentleman and his swagger.

and shepherdesses; its class condescension was often parodied. Lawrence's clownish persona throws down the gauntlet by reducing the sentimental to gross physical greed. Harry Sydney's music hall version of 1873, also sung in blackface by Mackney, adopts the opposite burlesque strategy and elevates the simple language of the original to a ludicrous degree.[12] Both inversions mock the high art song for trespass on the territory of humble life. Turning next, as he does in 'Man/Woman', to introducing himself and asserting his happiness – so that his audience will be happy, too – Lawrence interpolates a classic, indeed a 'Shakespearean' fool's, jest, teasing the audience with an incomprehensible wish to see them hung drawn and quartered, which he proceeds to make good (compare Feste's dialogue with Maria about being well hung in Twelfth Night I.5). Then he picks up his mockery of sentimental speeches about love, using the reductive physicality of language that was set up in his opening gambit, both grotesquely – love is like being up in the clouds between two large pancakes – and by means of double entendre – the single man will find the fire out, the husband has not enough to throw into his wife's lap. Through several twists and interactions with the stooge and with the men in the audience, the literary glorification of love and romance is variously juggled against both sexual and domestic realities, and the enticements and the entrapments of women and the insecurities of men are glanced at from several directions, always coming back to the most cynically down-to-earth position.

Begin

Sings
Oh of all the girls that Dress so smart there's none like Pretty Sally
She makes the tarts so very nice for to Put in my Belly.

I am so extremely happy tonight, I feel as happy as if I was hung drawn and quartered – I should like to see you hung drawn and quartered; in fact I should like to see everybody in the circus hung drawn and quartered – I should like to see them hung beyond the reach of

12. Published by D'Alcorn, London. It begins 'Of all the feminine specimens of humanity who indulge in neat and becoming attire / There's none like pretty Sally.'

adversity, I should like to see them drawn in their own carriage, and quartered in the arms of those they love best. That's what I would call capital punishment.[13]

Was you ever in Love? There! You have felt the tender passion!

They told me it was a tender passion, but when I was in love I was doubled all up in a heap. Love is like a potato it shoots from the eye, and when you are love sick, you are like a cabbage gone to seed: you have lost your heart entirely. I remember once being so deeply in Love that the heat of my body set my shirt front on fire.

Love! O! Love is like being up in the clouds between two large pancakes and all the little angels pouring treacle down your back … though some say love is like fishing – the lady is the rod, her voice the line, her eyes are the hooks, her lips the bait, and matrimony is the frying pan in which he is cooked when she catches him.

I thought you was caught last night – I saw you walking with a young lady, it would not have been well for you if your old woman had caught you,

What sort of a bonnet had she on?

It wasn't a bonnet at all, it was a hat – and a feather in it as long as my arm.

What was the colour of her shawl?

It wasn't a shawl it was one of them little (*bags with pockets*)

What do you mean?

What do I mean, you ought to know you was there I heard what you said.

What did I say?

Why you took her hand in yours and you said: 'O! Maria there is not a breeze that does not whisper thy sweet name: there is not a star in the bright arch above that does not remind me of thy love beaming eyes,

13. Capital punishment was considered by Parliamentary Select Committee in 1868, and public execution was abolished, though not the death penalty. Perhaps newspaper reports of parliamentary debate had familiarised the general public with the legal term. There is a suggestion of poking fun at a circumlocution in Lawrence's pun on the other current use of 'capital' as a slang term of approval.

there is not a flower that throws its perfumes that does not remind me of thy sweet breath!! Oh Maria!!!'

Allow me to tell you that that Lady was my sister.

Oh Gammon – people don't say 'O! Maria!!!!' to sisters! Well, it's only natural; it's just as natural for a man to fall in Love as a puppydog to have the distemper. I love!!

You!

Yes me.

> For love is a thing we all must feel
> As we travel through this life,
> Show me the man that love can feel
> That does not want a wife.
> Man you have a wife and that without a doubt
> When a single man comes home he'll often find the fire out
> But if a nice little wife you've got,
> You live as snug as a bug in a rug in some nice pretty cot
> You bring home your wages, your wife comes out without a call
> You throw it in her lap and she exclaims 'What Jack is this all?'

❖

No. 5

Another brief verbal riff for use as a filler, like 'Dogs' above, and similarly opened by the business of barging into the ringmaster, which gives him his cue – the idea of liberty. From there he builds his word games and rhyming mouth-music, through the common association of ideas of his time: the liberty proclaimed by the people of America, desired by the Irish and claimed by Old England. Which is all very fine – but only for the rich.

Begin

Buss.: Run against Ringmaster
Now then stupid mind where you are running will you and don't take such a liberty.

Don't you take a liberty with me

I shall if I like and I shall if I don't like, if I like, I have a right to take a liberty! This is the land of liberty. We have the same liberty here as they have in the free state of America – why if you haven't got a dinner you are at liberty to go without it. Ireland is the country for eating and drinking, rivers of whisky and mountains of praties –

> So if you wish to be merry and frisky
> And never die when you are in bed
> Go to old Ireland and tipple the whisky
> And you'll live ten years after you're dead.

But there's nothing like old England, as the song says, there is no place like home, for England is a famous country it is famous for exhibitions, politicians, musicians and physicians, for Galvinism, mechanism, and any amount of rheumatism; for donkey racing and steeple chasing, for cricket playing and wager laying, for smelling gin palaces that brings poor people to the gallowses, for lawyers who cheat men and lots of policemen, for handsome females and ugly Hemales – in fact

> Old England is the glory and pride of the world,
> Where the banner of freedom is ever unfurled,
> Where the rich can live in sweet communion,
> And the poor that can't can go to the Union!!

❖

No. 5$\frac{1}{2}$

Cutler's Shop

The elaboration of a comparison between categories of some sort and different people is a repeated structure in Lawrence's jokes, a conceit that he works out in many forms. Here the most striking aspect of

*his comparison of people to various kinds of knife is the
performance technique it suggests: he is clearly, from his first question
about 'our circus', asking for audience response, and he goes on to
engage with a series of individuals, eventually putting in a stage
direction to clarify whom he is to address. It is notable that he arrives,
via digs at lawyers and policemen, who are traditionally butts of
working-class resentment and scorn, at a rather serious-looking
declaration of hostility to the rich factory owner. Then, perhaps
in retreat from this quasi-melodramatic claptrap, he finishes on
an old joke.*

Don't you think our circus has a very strange appearance this evening?
Why does it resemble a cutler's shop? – because we have human
cutlery of every description.
Now here we have a few rough blades, but who knows in the course
of time they will become smooth and bright, polished by the hands of
some young lovely woman.
Now here's a more useful blade – this was manufactured for pruning
and cutting, cabbage cutting, and broad bean eating.
(*to boxes*) Here we have more polished blades, set in pearl and ivory
handles. Ladies they are fish knives, because they are always fishing
for compliments at some mercer's or draper's window; fathers they
are table knives, lawyers are lances because they bleed their clients,
policemen they are dull blades and often want grinding to make them
sharp and there are some men who are not blades at all: they are
nothing more than rasps and files who are continually rasping down
the wages of the poor working man who turns the wheel that keeps the
mill in motion and fills his master's pockets with the grains of human
industry.

Did you hear of that accident today – three men run over by a railway
train?

Killed?

No, they were saved by a miracle – the train was going over the bridge
and they were going under it.

❖

No. 19

Catching Fleas

A mock-gothic verse depending on bathos for its punchline, as many of Lawrence's jokes do, and presumably also reliant on delivery in a recognisable parody of heroic/melodramatic acting style, with exaggerated large gestures and declamatory tones.

It was all last night by candle light
And the light of the moon dimly shone –
A figure in white gave me such a fright
As it stood in my bedroom alone.
It rattled no chains to scare my brains
Nor was it ghastly to the sight,
Yet what it could be so strange to see
I could not tell for the fright.
It rolled[14] its fierce eyes as it hoarsely cries
'I'll crush the body and bones',
Then threw itself down on the cold, cold ground
Amidst horrible yells and groans.
I knew my belief it could not be a thief
Yet the sight of it made my blood freeze
And turning again I found out then –
It was only my wife catching fleas.

❖

No. 6

The link here is the same used to preface several other wheezes – a reference to the departing equestrian act, which gives Lawrence a hook on which to hang a rather simple, noncomic declaration of solidarity with the poor; there is an air rather of the melodramatic claptrap than of the drawing-room motto song about his moralising, here and else-where. It leads into a set of verses that are similarly pitched at heartfelt egalitarianism rather than fun, and which may well have been a song;

14. He spells this 'roald', which suggests
stagey pronunciation.

he prefaces them with reference to a 'good old song' that sounds as if it belongs to the street or oral tradition. 'Fustian Jacket' surfaced in print in 1874, in a collection published by John Guest, and he claims to have written it, but there are at least two others on the same theme in print also claimed as original. Guest's text is not the same as Lawrence's, but it does mention 'the coarse fustian coat' that covers the heart of gold. In his earlier gagbook, however, Lawrence carefully credited this song to 'F. Allen / Worcester Sept 16 1866'. For a discussion of the fertile singing culture out of which these texts seem to be bubbling up, see pp. 152–53.

Begin

That's the way to get through the world – that's the way to travel.

Now I have discovered there are two ways to get through the world: if you want to get through the world easy you must dress well, have a suit of black, a Paris top hat and patent boots. Only appear respectable and the world will bow and scrape to you. A man needs no gold in his pocket if he has got plenty of brass in his face. But if you appear in society with your coat out at the elbows, your toes out of your boots, the world would pass you by in scorn, and wonder that you have the impudence to walk on the same side of the road that they do. But I am happy to say that's not the way with me, I respect *all* my fellow men, no matter whether he has got a ragged coat on, or one just home from the tailor's goose. I never forget that good old song: 'Never despise a man because he wears a ragged coat.'

> Fustian Jacket[15]
> For though I am a simple fool
> And live by honest labour,
> Of fortune's share I have some to spare
> To assist a needy neighbour.
> Content and health is a poor man's wealth,
> With honesty to back it –
> My meaning's pure and of this be sure
> I respect a fustian jacket.

15. Fustian: a cheap fabric used for working men's clothes. Lawrence spells it 'fustin', which perhaps was how he pronounced it.

Let people say what ere they may
About fustian and its wearers –   10
It's not the coat that makes the man
But the deeds through life which bear us.
Then I will help my fellow man,
If contentment should he lack it
And do him all the good I can –
Though he wears a fustian jacket.

All men were equal born at first
In this and every nation,
The rich among the poor would be
But for wealth and education   20
And when we are laid beneath the stones
And a hundred years to back it,
There's none can tell which are the bones
That were[16] the fustian jacket.

It grieves me as I walk the streets,
Through this and other cities,
So many sadder hearts to meet
So few that help[s] and pities.
Men of noble minds despair
As through the streets they track it   30
Were I a prince with him I'd share
His simple fustian jacket.

As through this life we sail along
Its seas though rough and stormy,
If with a friendly breeze you'd go
I am willing to inform ye –
Enter a ship called number one[17]

16. This may be a pun – Lawrence's spelling does not allow us to be sure whether he means 'were' or 'wore' or both. The earlier gagbook has 'wore'.

17. This appears to mean 'look after yourself', an interesting motto in view of the preceding sentiments about helping those worse off, but possibly intended as a rebuttal to the demands of middle-class moralisers that the working classes should selflessly serve their betters. 'Number ones' are also the seaman's best uniform.

175

It's the safest sailing packet
It's the ship that I sailed on
In a simple fustian jacket.   40

Then God bless every working man
That fears no tyrant's frowns:
May his beef and beer increase each year
And his wages ne'er go down.
May his dear little wife be the joy of his life
And never kick up a racket
But do all she can to please the old man
And love his dear old fustian jacket.

❖

No. 6
Pack of Cards

Another short piece for filling in moments in the ring; the conceit about card games is comparable to others such as 'Cutler's Shop', (p. 171).

How many things has this world been compared to! Do you know what I think this resembles?

No

A pack of cards – simply because we are all playing different games.[18] Now if a man is drunk and rolling about in the street, he is playing at *all fours*. If you see a knave picking a gentleman's pocket, he is playing at *Cribb* and if the police catch him they'll take him back a peg or two. The magistrate he plays at *Put* – because he puts them on the mill.[19] Poor people are *low game*, rich people are *high game*. But her Majesty is the Queen of *trumps* and long may she reign to keep the game in her own hands, and *take* any Foreign King or Queen that dare to come *against her*.

❖

No. 9

Once again Lawrence begins with reference to the act with which he is working, this time a female equestrian. He refers to her as he takes over, exchanges a gag – of variable length – with the ringmaster, as she gets her breath, and then refers to her again, praising her and commenting

18. The games named: All Fours is the ancestor of Seven Up and other current games and involved a deal of six cards each, scored by taking tricks and for holding particular cards; Cribb is the old English game cribbage, which originated in court circles more than 250 years ago. It is still a popular two-handed game in which cards are scored individually and added up to make a winning total by the use of a pierced wooden scoreboard that lies on the table and is marked with movable pegs – hence Lawrence's reference to being taken back a peg or two. 'To cribb' is also thieves' cant for to steal. It is already a joke to say the magistrate plays at Put, since it is an old game confined to the lowest social levels consisting 'of tricks, bluff and highly organized cheating' (p. 170), a means of stripping the unwary of their money. 'Low game' and 'high game' may be general references to the stakes in card-playing, or refer to variations of poker. Information from David Partlett, *The Oxford Book of Card Games* (Oxford University Press, 1990).

19. The treadmill, a hated innovation in prison discipline.

on her foot as she rides by him, to begin the main section of his wheeze,
which is another of his mysogynist attacks on romantic illusions.

Sweethearts

Begin

They may well say that woman is the pride of our hearts, the joy of our
lives – and the ruin of our pockets. That's the way to travel, did you
ever travel much? Have you been to France?

Yes

Been to Germany?

Yes

Been to Spain?

Yes

England?

Yes

Ireland?

Yes

Been in Wales?

Yes

Was you ever in jail?[20]

This is a very clever young lady and what a nice little foot that is –
what the young gentleman [call] 'tadsey putsey wutsey' when they are
courting[21] the young ladies and taking them out for a walk. If the
weather is wet and the footpath damp they will say 'Now Sarah mind
where you put your pretty little tootsey putsey', but they don't say
'tootsey putsey' after they are married – they say 'Now Sal mind where
you put your great *stratipers*'.

20. And the automatic answer would be
'yes' again – to the discomfiture of the
ringmaster: a very old schoolboy trick.

21. Spelt 'carting' – could be pronounced
thus, antiquely.

You never saw my sweetheart –

> She was a Pastry-cook's daughter
> She loved me for the tales I told
> And I loved her for the tarts she sold[22]

Oh she used to make such nice mutton pies! I shall never forget one evening, me and my sweetheart was taking a walk, she had hold on my arm and I had hold of her hand she squeezed my arm[23] and I squeezed her hand, and she looked up in to my face and said 'do you love me?' and I said yes! And she believed me!

With that she put her hand in to her pocket and pulled out such a nice mutton pie. Well, we were walking and talking about pigs and politicks and a lot of things we didn't understand,[24] when just as I was about to imprint a kiss upon her ruby lip, her foot slipped and down she went into the river that flowed beneath us. There I stood upon the bank amazed. My knees shook beneath me. I was undecided. Presently I took courage, when I thought of . . .

What?

. . . the other mutton pie she had got in her pocket. I plunged into the foaming torrent, seized her by the hair and dragged her ashore. I pressed her to my throbbing heart. But judge my horror and surprise when I found – no, worse[25] – the water had got in to her pocket and spoiled the other mutton pie.

♣

22. The faint echo of *Othello* I.3.166–7 ('She loved me for the dangers I had passed, / And I loved her that she did pity them') would probably not be lost on Lawrence's audience.

23. Spelt harm, in both instances here – either Lawrence normally used this lower-class extra aspirant, or it is part of his characterisation of the soft-hearted (and soft-headed) lover.

24. Interestingly reminiscent of Lewis Carroll's 'The Walrus and the Carpenter' in *Through The Looking-Glass and What Alice Found There*, 1872: '"The time has come," the Walrus said, / "To talk of many things: / Of shoes – and ships – and sealing wax – / Of cabbages – and Kings."'

25. The stooge presumably indicates that he thinks the clown means she was dead; or perhaps Lawrence 'found' that response in the audience.

Buss.[26] For Tight Rope

This is the only silent clown routine included in the notebook. It is an example of the deployment by clowns of the skills of the other circus performers – and just as Les Dawson really could play the piano, and Tommy Cooper would finish his cod magician act with a dazzling sleight of hand, these clowns would need to be able to walk the wire in order to present this parodic story about tightrope walking, complete with characters and plot.

It is interesting that 'Joe' has been acting as clown to the rope during the real act that precedes this, and is then joined in the ring by 'Tom'. The business is divided equally between them.

After the performer has left the rope Joe makes his bow and is about to leave the ring. Tom turns him round and wants to know where he is going. Joe tells him he is sleepy and wants to go to bed. Tom tells him that he has got to dance the rope. Joe goes up to the rope, very unwilling. Tom calls him back and mocks the lazy way in which he was going and at the same time shows him in a lively manner how to make his bow to the audience and then runs to the Cross Poles as if to get on the rope, but in doing so his foot slips off the Cross Pole and he strikes his face.[27]

This makes Joe laugh. Tom turns round to see, picks up a handful of sawdust, walks up to Joe and looks him in the face two or three times; but finding he is not laughing at him he slides the sawdust down by his leg, takes Joe by the hand and presents him to the audience. Joe gets one foot on the Cross Pole and as he lifts up the other gives Tom the slap. When Joe is on the rope Tom picks up a cane, draws a line in the ring to represent the Rope and shows Joe how to skip and forms a picture, then hands the cane up to Joe but in so

26. 'Buss.' is the standard abbreviation for 'business' – anything in a performance done without words.

27. The usual equipment for such acts in the ring was a rope stretched tight at up to three metres from the ground with wooden supports, the cross poles, at each end. Highwire walking and balancing, at much greater heights from the ground and using various props but often without a balance-pole, gradually replaced rope-dancing from the mid-century. Lawrence clearly has the older act, with the emphasis on graceful dance, in mind; his two clowns can just about reach each other when one is on the rope.

doing strikes him on the feet, Joe then takes the cane and gives Tom the knap. Joe takes one step on the rope, passes the cane under his feet then makes a bow and stands in position holding the top of the Cross Pole all the time.

(If no cane, begin with pole)

Tom then tells him that he must dance with the Pole and shows him how to do it on the line in the ring then struggles with the Pole till he gives it to Joe then stoops to pick up something from the ring and Joe strikes him on the behind with end of Pole. Joe gets the Pole right and commences to dance the rope, gets half way and is dreadfully frightened, puts the end of Pole on ground. After many attempts gets back to [the] Cross Poles, then tells Tom that he must have his feet chalked. When Tom tries to chalk his feet he dodges it from one side to the other; at last Tom threatens to throw the chalk at him, returns and catches hold of Joe's foot and in doing so drops the chalk. Tom is in a fix – don't know how to hold the foot and pick up the chalk at the same time. At last Tom pulls Joe into almost a sitting position. By so doing Joe's leg is far below the rope which enables Tom to pick up chalk.

Joe then tells Tom that he had better come on the rope and hold him; Tom does so, and after a little *Buss.* they both get in middle of the rope. Both get frightened; Tom jumps off rope and runs and holds the bottom of the Pole until Joe gets back to Cross Poles after *Buss.* Tom tells Joe that he will take the end of Pole on his shoulder whilst Joe dances the rope. He does so and when Joe gets in the middle of rope gets frightened and falls into the funny pose. Tom takes him from that position and carries him out.

The whole of the above is done in ballet.[28] *The two clowns can whistle to each other as though talking.*[29]

❧

28. 'In ballet' here means 'in silence', rather than necessarily implying dance, just as as in the music hall '*ballet d'action*' is normally double-talk for a dramatic sketch, carried out, supposedly, without speaking, to avoid licensing restrictions.

29. A practice that survived: cf. Harpo Marx's mute clown, who communicates by whistling.

No. 9
Policemen

This wheeze is interesting in its complex – or perhaps merely lax – construction; it may simply be a note of several 'policemen' jokes, from which he would select in performance. Taking off from his usual comment on the departing act, he begins with a parody of literary hyperbole, building a string of oxymorons reminiscent of Shakespeare (compare Bolingbroke's farewell to his homeland in Richard II, *1.3.257–62, 'Oh who can hold a fire in his hand / By thinking on the frosty Caucasus . . .') The references – sliding from fire and ice to a cobbler's awl, a gnat and a brickbat – become less lofty and broader, if still extravagant and faintly biblical, until they inevitably climax in slang and an antiwoman joke, before he fixes upon the actual subject: the policeman. Lawrence then runs through the antipolice jokes of the time, which were very widespread from* Punch *to music hall. They are cowards, he suggests, and avoid trouble; they are chiefly interested in food, which servant girls give them in exchange for kisses. This characterisation is not unlike the reputation of the soldier, but exacerbated by daily familiarity and scorn for the jack-in-office.*

The most interesting aspect of this section is the shifting point of view. The clown first engages the audience present in the circus in a joke against the individual policeman who is also actually there. He would be standing at the back to keep order, which gives an opportunity for innuendo – the policeman is 'always behind'. Then Lawrence has a brief exchange with the ringmaster in which he claims, as a stand-up comedian might, to have been in the force himself once, before abruptly slipping into a piece from his earlier notebook in the persona of a householder of a very middle-class cast, whose servants steal his luxury goods to give away, before reverting to working-class mockery of the uniformed man with round shoulders – who has not even a soldier's excuse for kissing the girls. He winds up with a rather weak link via 'his brother' to another verbal stunt dependent on overstatement and bathos, and a final mysgoynist punchline to get him off on an easy laugh.

Begin

Wonderful, most wonderful is it not? Why, some years ago it would have been thought quite an impossibility but bless you those things that were thought impossible have been discovered to be only improbable. Why, it's possible to seek fire in ice, constancy in the winds, darkness in the blaze of sunshine. You may whistle against thunder, with your repelling breath blow back the Northern blasts, silence a full mouth battery with snowballs, quench fire with oil, you may drain the sea dry with a cobbler's awl, you can knock a gnat's eye out with a brickbat, you can actually stop a woman's tongue when the steam's up, all these things you may do but there is one thing you can never do – find a policeman when you want him.

I beg pardon – I did not see that gentleman, he stands so far behind. Though that's generally the case with policemen, they are *always behind*. I am very glad to see him here – it is a sure sign of peace and quietness – they never go where there is a *row*. Policemen are like rainbows – they never appear till the *storm* is *over*.

I was in the force once.

They turned you out?

No they did not. They *kicked me out*.

Why?

The sergeant complained to the superintendent – he said I spoiled too many new uniforms by putting the cold fat mutton in my pockets.

Are you a married man? Before you go into housekeeping, I should advise you to kill all the cats on the premises, for according to our servants' account, last week a cat stole out of our pantry no less than one pigeon pie, two veal cutlets, a roast fowl, half a leg of mutton, two bottles of wine, and a dozen cigars and then made its escape up the area steps as the housemaid was just in time to see it and it was dressed – just like a policeman.

Never mind they are a useful body of men and it's just my opinion that were it not for the police our wives and sisters could never walk quietly in the streets and I am sure they are a fine body of men in this town. There is only one fault I have to find with them – they are all a little round shouldered – that is easily to be accounted for – why stooping down to kiss the short girls.

> Did you ever see my brother Bill – he was a policeman.
> I shall never forget the last time I saw him.
> I went into his room, his feet were fast to the ground,
> His face was buried in his hands, the tears came trickling down
> And with one despairing yell from his soul he cries –
> I can't find the towel, and the soap's got in my eyes.[30]

Man is strong and powerful, woman beautiful and unassuming, nature made the man the strongest

And woman's tongues the longest.

❖

30. This passage about 'brother Bill' occurs in the first notebook, detached from 'Policemen'.

No. 10

God Bless Those Poor Souls

It's difficult to know whether this piece, which also occurs in the earlier gagbook, is meant to be sung or recited, but it bears some relationship to the 'motto song' as popularised by Lawrence's contemporary performer, the 'drawing-room singer' Harry Clifton. The striking difference is that while Clifton's songs are rigidly lower-middle-class in their advice and their construction of morality, Lawrence has quite a different class point of view. He begins in a strain Clifton might have used, invoking blessings on the honest man who tries to 'fight fair', but the form the benediction is to take – may he have enough to eat – has quite different suggestions about the rank and aspirations of the subject. As the verse goes on, it focuses in on ideas about survival and generosity at the basic level of food and drink. Lines 17–28 are additions in the second book. They suggest the drinking culture of the free and easy: two quatrains patronise the total abstainer, and lines 25–8 are a toast or convivial catch. He returns to his first theme in the final couplet, defiantly praising the working man's pride and self-belief.

<blockquote>

God bless those poor souls who are striving
By means that are honest and true,
For something to keep them alive in
This world that we're all struggling through.
For the life of a man is full of fighting
And he that wants to fight fair,
Should never be robbed of his eating
For the hardest of battle's his share.
And he that feels it a pleasure
To lighten misfortune and pain,   10
May his pantry be always full measure
To cut at and come to again.
May God bless his cup and his cupboard
A thousand for one that he gives,
And his heart be a bumper of comfort
To the very last moment he lives,
And he that scorns ale to his victuals
Is welcome to leave it alone

</blockquote>

For some can be wise with a little
And others be foolish with none.   20
And some are so queer in their nature
That nought with their stomachs agree,
But he that would rather drink water
Shall never be stinted by me.
Good cooks are the best of all doctors
Good livers my parsons shall be,
And any poor man that is hungry
Shall have a good dinner with me.
Old time is a troublesome codger
Keeps nudging us on to decay,   30
And whispers you're only a lodger
Get ready for moving away.
So let's have no skulking or snivelling
Whatever misfortune befall:
May God bless him that works for his living
And holds up his head through it all.

❖

Fools

*This is Lawrence's version of the famous speech on which
W. F. Wallett's reputation as 'Shakespearean Clown' was partly
founded. It is indeed very close in content, though not in order, to
extant versions of Wallett's oration.[31] Self-consciously literary, it is in
some ways the talking clown's 'masterpiece' or self-justification,
setting out, through high-flown quotation and wise saws, his claim to
consequence. There is a briefer version in the earlier gagbook, which
does not include the list of contrasting fools near the opening, nor the
sub-Shakespearean conceit about principle and interest. It begins with
a tag that links to the departing act – another clown or the ringmaster.
'Run against' is a performance direction, used in No. 5 (p. 170).*

31. See *Nottingham Guardian*, 23 April 1927, and a cutting in the Nottingham Local Studies Collection, call mark L98 WALLETT, attributed '?Nottingham Guardian c.1920'. This printed version is decidedly less egalitarian, omitting the claim that fools 'stood up for the great human family'.

There never mind don't make any apology, that's been my misfortune through life do as I will, go where I will, I am sure to run against some fool or the other, and though there are a many kinds of fools, and a many unkind fools; there are tall fools, and small fools, lean fools and fat fools, witty fools and pretty fools, old fools and young fools, and there are drunken fools! And drunken fools are the worst of fools – except teetotal fools, they are fools in their own right and fools in their own wrong. Though right often works for a shilling and wrong lives on it. Right is right, but wrong is by no means right. Then we have fools of pretension,

> And fools of pretence
> And fools that don't understand other fools' sense

Now I am like the man that had the snuffles, I was born so, yes I was born a fool but the knife of adversity has so cut the wood of my wit to a point that I am wiser by snatches, than when I cried in my cradle for Cardal.[32] Shakespeare says – let me play the fool.[33] With mirth and laughter let old wrinkles come, and rather my liver heat with wines – than my heart cool with mortifying groans – Thompson says a feeling fool is better than a stubborn sceptic.[34]

But you say you are no fool – then give me your hand – they say that *two* of a *trade* never agree so as you are right opposite to me we shall agree exactly well – you and I may represent the two great masses of society – Rogues and Fools – oh yes, you must be one or the other and you said you are not a fool – so you must be the other, and if you're the other it's ten to one that you are both – because you can never prove a man a rogue until he is fool enough to be found out in his roguery.

Now I am a fool, and I glory in it – because I have an interest in it, so being a fool and having an interest – I must be an interesting fool. At the same time I must be a fool of principle for if I had no principle

32. Cardal: i.e., caudle, thin gruel fed to babies. The earlier version has 'cordial', suggestive of the Victorian child medication Godfrey's Cordial.

33. The Shakespearean reference is probably a vague echo of Feste in *Twelfth Night*, where the nearest line is Viola's musing about him in III.1.60–2: 'This fellow is wise enough to play the fool, / And to do that well craves a kind of wit.'

34. Benjamin Thompson's *The Stranger*, a translation from Kotzebue, I.1: 'A feeling fool is better than a cold sceptic.' The play was first seen at Drury Lane in 1801, but remained popular, and was an especial favourite in booth and portable theatres in the mid-century and after, so most of Lawrence's audience could have known it.

I should have no interest – for interest is derived from principle, so being a fool and having a principle I must be an interesting prin-ciple fool.

But there is no character so misunderstood as the character of the fool. The people of the present day imagine the fool of the olden time was a man that dressed in rags, and loved to distort his features and put his body in a thousand different shapes. No such thing. The fool of the olden times was the wittiest man of his hour, the fool of the olden times stood up for the great human family, the fool of the olden times was the pioneer to civilisation. The fool of the olden times stood up for the rights and privileges of his fellow man, for under the guise of laughter he dare tell such truths to the teeth of tyrants that other men would have lost their lives for. Kings kept fools and royal jesters, then they were well fed and well paid, but now there is so many making fools of themselves for nothing that the trade is hardly worth the calling. In the olden times fools were great men, now great men are fools.

❖

No. 12
Rash Man

This is the first of several brief pieces that burlesque tragic performance – whether play-acting or recitation – and which were, presumably, used for laughter-enhancing shock moments in the ring, either on their own or in the midst of more conventional clowning. It is reported that in the 1850s James Boswell, Shakespearean clown at Astley's, 'would sometimes pause in the middle of his fooling as if yielding to some macabre fantasy, and draping some piece of tawdry finery over his costume, assume a tragic expression upon his white-painted face and run round the ring declaiming the most frightening lines from Shakespeare in a shrill and raucous voice'.[35]

> I saw him bare his throat and seize
> The blue cold glittering steel
> And grimly try the tempered edge
> He was so soon to feel.

35. Speaight, *A History of the Circus*, p. 92.

He raised on high the glittering blade
Then first I found a tongue
'Hold madman, stay thy frantic arm'
I cried and forth I sprung.
He heard me but he heeded not –
One look around he gave,
But ere I could arrest his arm –
Why he'd begun to shave.

❖

No. 14
Welcome Little Stranger

A brief verse, on the lines of sentimental recitation, which is attributed to the leading clown Wallett. It would presumably be pursued in all seriousness until the final rather deflationary and slangy couplet, delivered in quite a different tone; the mixture of the pompous and the slightly heartless is reminiscent of what we know of Wallett himself (see pp. 54–55).

Thou art welcome little stranger
How you stare! And well you may
For not one hour yet has past
Since you beheld the light of day
Kings, and Queens, and Lords, and Ladies
Once was just the same as thee
The midnight murderer who decks the gibbet
Once was born as pure as thee.
You little think, you darling poppet,
How I shall have to toil for thee
But when I am old and forced to drop it
You'll maybe do a bit for me.

Wallett Bath Jan 15th

The above is spoken to a child among the Pit.[36]

---

36. 'Peter Paterson' says that the clown often 'dives without introduction among the people in the pit' (*Glimpses of Real Life*, p. 134) and today comedians in small venues will do the same, to the embarrassment of those singled out.

❖

A mere note, without a heading, of a gag to be worked with the ringmaster, presumably in a short break. The slightly nagging, or maybe childlike, tone of repetition seems to be characteristic, either of Lawrence's personal style or ring clowning in general. The punchline is a surprisingly obvious double entendre.

Walking down the street the other day I got a very curious sign. This is what was on it. 'Licensed to sell tea, coffee, tobacco and snuff.' Now I ask you if that was right?

   Yes

You think so?

   Yes

Well so did I. Well, then it said, 'Foreign and British wines sold here.' Now do you think that was right?

   Yes

You do?

   Yes

Well so did I. Well, then again it said, 'Families supplied.' Now do you think that was right?

   Yes

Well so did I – for the moment I read it I went in and ordered a wife and 13 children. But the man said he had got no children on hand – but he would make me some by tomorrow.

❖

Poetry[37]

These are probably three tags or fragments noted down together but to be used separately as required. The first verse uses the usual anti-romantic bathos, the second by contrast is an apparently sincere sentimental invocation of married bliss (though it could be tongue in cheek – 'roll right over'?) and the third is a set of political slogans, incorporating a very old-fashioned quatrain, resembling something by Hannah Moore, followed by the Harry Clifton motto 'work boys work' but capping them with a much punchier catchphrase that looks like something from contemporary politics – 1870 saw the First Education Act, introducing compulsory schooling for all.

A young maiden stands beside the brook
Her hair in ringlets flowing;
Now down the stream she turns to look,
Her cheek with blushes glowing.
With swan like form see how she bends
Until her fingers meet
The rippling stream where she intends
To wash her little feet.

I wish I had a little wife
A little stove and fire
I'd hug her like a lump of gold
And let no one come nigh her
I'd spend my days in happiness
I'd vegetate in clover
And when I dies I'd shut my eyes
Lay down and roll right over.

Crave not for wealth.
Nor to labour think it a shame:
He is most blessed that lives by his labour
And teaches his children the same.

37. Lawrence has various shots at
spelling this word; here it is 'pautry',
perhaps reflecting his pronunciation.

Work lads work, work while you can,
Better build schools for children, than gibbets for men.

❖

No. 15

'Tis Sweet

*The link from the previous act (presumably imagined to be a woman,
since he says 'brava') is gracious, this time, but only so as to introduce
the theme of 'sweetness' as the foundation of his characteristic rhetorical
game: a mounting series of romantic platitudes overset by deflationary
physical references. Like music hall comedians, he seems to regard
mutton as a particularly anti-romantic, comical kind of food; and he
enjoys childish words and rhymes – mutton chop/flipperty flop. We
have punctuated this set as verse, because of the rhymes, but Lawrence
has not taken much trouble to make it scan, and he wrote it out
run-on; we can only guess how he used the rhymes in performance.
His punchline is the characteristic turn he makes many times from
the shared dreams of courtship to the conflicting desires of marriage –
an emphasis also central to the music hall analysis of relations
between the sexes.*

Brava that was sweetly done, and I like to see things sweetly done –
why, it's sweet to hear the linnet sing in the bush it fills the heart with
rapture, the soul with delight, but it's dreadful to hear two tom cats
fighting in the middle of the night.

> Why, it's sweet to see a maiden's dark blue eye moisten
>   with a tear,
> It's sweet to hear her sigh her soul within thine ear,
> 'Tis sweet to hear her say she'll share thy fate,
> But sweeter than all these is – a mutton chop upon a plate.
>
> A beef steak or a mutton chop
> Will make your mouth go flipperty flop
>
> But talk about sweet things I'll tell you what they are –
> It's sweet on a summer's night to roam,

To speak of love and constancy and dream of future homes;
'Tis sweet to hear the parson say let none be parted
That have been joined today;[38]
'Tis sweet to see a child upon its mother's cheek,
'Tis sweet to hear its tiny lips trying for to speak.
'Tis sweet to see a wife into the ale-house come
And say to her husband sweetly
'I'll warm your devil when I get thee home.'[39]

❖

No. 16
Tragedy

This is a full-on burlesque upon high art – high-flown speeches and tragic acting. Lawrence's audience would have included people familiar with theatrical performance, including both Shakespeare and contemporary melodrama. The first section draws on rapidly touched-in scenes from gothic melodramas: the one in which the hero finally challenges the villain; that between the abducted maiden and her captor, who has imprisoned her father (probably in a dungeon, decades before); and the denouement of many plays in which someone supposed lost is brought back to life from a trance or from apparently being turned into a statue.

The windy idea of the voice of the storm is the object of the bathos in each of the other two sections, which are really versions of the same joke, and would not, presumably, have been used together. Each includes Shakspearean echoes, most obviously of the opening of The Tempest *in the second version, but also suggests innumerable sub-Shakespearean costume dramas. The inflated language of the serious Victorian stage in general is sent up by the vulgar modernity of the catchphrase in which each culminates.*

38. This plural version of the formula is suggestive of the mass weddings conducted in city churches as part of Christian campaigns to get the poor to marry rather than live together 'in sin'. The cost of the individual ceremony was often cited as an excuse, so parsons would assign a day when they would unite all couples who presented themselves at once.

39. Spelt 'whome', as if he spoke it in a northern dialect.

Wretch, come forth and meet me like a man. O! Don Alfonso, my first and best of friends, restore to me my parent dear restore to me that peace of mind I once possessed and I will be thy slave . . .
Still as thou art thine eye moves,
Art thou void of all feeling? I'll try – *bites finger*

Thou rememberest well, the night was dark and tempestuous, when a sudden and terrific storm [broke] o'er our heads, the rain fell in torrents, the forked lightning flashed through the murky skies, the horrid artillery of heaven rolled[40] as if it were about to burst the fiery element, all nature seemed as though chaos was come again – when a voice, a giant's voice, was heard above the roaring of the waters, a voice that sounded from East to West, from North to South, from hill to hill, from cataract to cavern, a voice proclaimed aloud to the affrighted world: 'Have you got a clean shirt for Sunday?'

From yonder lofty tower I espied a shivering barque
Combating with the waves, the affrighted mariners in horror
Stood, some prayed, whilst others wept aloud,
Whilst by the repeated lightning's flash and amid the thunder's roar
I heard a voice say – 'How's your poor feet?'

♣

No. 19
Wishing

This wheeze starts with one of the less common of Lawrence's links to the departing act – a wish that he had money to reward its excellence (cf. 'Wants Money', p. 160.) His chain of examples and associations built upon the initial idea, 'wishing', leads, unusually, to a climax instead of a bathetic anticlimax: he wishes his children were 'honest working men', a clear signal that most of his audience regarded themselves as exactly that. The piece seems broken-backed: it comes

---

40. He gives the antique spelling 'rowled'.

to an end in the middle, with the line 'Your humble servant wishes for your kind applause', after which, and the inevitable applause, he could not easily start up again unless he made the second part appear as an encore. The wishes in the first part are for innocuous universal benefits such as health and wealth, with only a mild dig at lawyers and a slightly unusual reversal of his normal comments upon marriage – this time it is the woman who soon regrets it. But the additional section is topical and jingoistic, an attack on warmongering and an assertion that the people always suffer. The foreign kings who loosed 'the dogs of war' in 1870 were Napoleon III and William of Prussia; British public opinion was very severe in condemnation of the bloody conflict.

Wonderful! Would you believe that I never sighed for wealth before or riches until this present moment and now I wish that I was someone of affluence, I wish I was a King or a Duke or a Lord – a linen draper, or lamp lighter, or something of that sort – then I could reward that person as he richly deserves! I wish! But what's the use of me wishing – I am only a fool. But I suppose I am like the generality of the world: high, or low, rich or poor we're all wishing ...

> [41]For many things they cannot get
> Mankind are ever wishing,
> And with a most attractive bait
> Continually are fishing.
> Some wish for this, some wish for that,
> And wish that they were wealthy.
> Others only wish that they
> Were hearty, strong and healthy.
> John Thomson has a haunted house
> He wishes he could let it
> You wish you had ten thousand pounds
> I wish that you may get it
> Miss wishes for a sweetheart
> And wishes to be wed –

41. The next 16 lines (to 'wishes she was dead') are an insertion, written out at the end of the wheeze with indications that they should occur where we have placed them. The earlier book has nothing before the following line, 'The sick man ...'

And oft ere many weeks have passed
Wishes she was dead.
The sick man wishes he was healthy,
The poor man wishes he was wealthy,
The ugly man wishes he was pretty,
The stupid man wishes he was witty.
Drunkards wish canals were made of gin,
Lawyers wish that cheating was no sin,
The roguish man wishes there was no laws –
Yours humble servant wishes for your kind applause.

Ladies wish that they were married
Married men wished they had longer tarried,
There are kings who wish for war:
To tax the people's bread,
To stop our trade and commerce
And strew battlefields with dead,
But I wish that king who first the dogs of war let loose
That a ball would reach him first
And cook his royal goose.
Then turn which way you will, wishes beset us sore:
Some people, though [they] much possess,
Still greedy wish for more;
But while other nations wish, Christians Jews or Turks,
The Briton boldly bares his arms and for his wishes works.
And though I'm but a simple fool, were I a father, then
I'd only wish my children should
Be honest working men.

♣

No. 18
Shaving

The wordplay in the rhyme with which he begins works rather heavily around the commercial transactions on which he asserts the world is founded, pointing out that we all profit from other people, but soon arrives at his favourite topic – women's tongues. In a long section, added in the later notebook, he then twists this in a novel direction by admitting that it is a stale joke that he makes too often, and moving into a much more fluid and interesting disquisition on women and motherhood, in which not only his focus, but also both his persona and his position, change several times. He moves from nudging innuendo to childish simplicity to insulting a butt (either the ringmaster/stooge or someone in the audience) to sentimentality to scandalised self-righteousness over sensational stories in the papers about neglectful mothers – which takes him back, of course, to attacking women.

What do you think of that old shaver? Yes of course I did.[42]

    We're all shavers in this world, though in ways shapes and places:

> The barber shaves with polished blades,
> The mercer shaves when ladies trade
> The publican shaves in pints and gills,
> The doctor shaves in draughts and pills,
> The broker shaves for twelve per cent,
> The landlord shaves by raising your rent,
> The pedlar shaves where e'er he goes,
> The lawyer shaves both friend and foes,
> The wily merchant shaves his brother,
> In fact this world is shaving one another.

There is but one class of beings in the world that I know of that never use razors and [that is] the ladies! They never shave.

> Because he who ordained all things below
> Said on woman's chin no beard should grow,
> To shave [them] is impossible however great the barber's skill
> For their tongues won't let their jaws be still.
> Man you know is strong and powerful,

42. Old shaver: a man. Not clear to what this is a response; presumably something the ringmaster says to him.

Woman beautiful and unassuming –
Nature made man the strongest,
But she made women's tongue the longest.

How we do go on about the ladies tongues – why, it is their *only weapon* of defence and they never let it grow rusty for the want of using; but though I speak of the ladies as I do, I have a great respect for them. Not only do I respect them, but I can assure you I love them, I admire them, I honour them! I love them for their[43] I honour them for their virtue! I admire them for their beauty and I love them because – my mother was a woman and that is enough to make a man love anything that wears a pettycoat. My mother was much older than me. Did you ever have a mother – (then she ought to have been ashamed of her self – for rearing such a creature) then I have been misinformed – I was told that you was run up by contract, and the man died before he'd time to finish you. I know I had a mother, but I didn't think every fool had one – I don't think all children have mothers – haven't you read in the daily and weekly papers that children have been left in dark passages, under hedges and in ditches – it was but the other day I read an account of a child being left at the railway station in a hamper, with a direction on it, 'to be left till called for'. Do you think that child ever had a mother? No! There might have been a woman bearing that form, but she could never have been a mother to have deserted the child and left it to the cold frowns of the unfeeling world.

❧

No. 19

Fun Fun

The link here is a more generalised one, and could help him follow any act, even other clowns. He then goes into a primitive version of one of

43. There is apparently a word missing; the MS suggests that he might have made a false start in the stream of semirepetitions he was writing down and abandoned it without striking it through; alternatively, however, there might be a gesture here that he did not need to specify in writing: the emphasis on virtue that follows immediately is suggestive.

the classic British joke structures, playing off the national stereotypes within the British Isles. The ending turns towards the relationship between himself, his audience and his employer, the manager of the circus, somewhat sycophantically asking for reassurance that his act is fun for all. The wheeze has a rather third-rate feeling, not helped by his scribbling down unrelated material – two feebly suggestive similes and a very poor pun – at the foot of the page.

That's rare fun – you may say what you like but I say it's fun, though the world will differ in opinion respecting fun. Some will say it's fun to play at cricket, others will say it's fun to get drunk and have the head ache for two or three days. Some would say it's fun to ride, others to walk, some to talk and so on. Go into what country you will you'll find they're all at different opinions respecting fun. At least so I have found it –

> The Englishman smokes when he's drinking,
> The Scotchman takes snuff when he's thinking,
> The Welchman goes down when he's sinking,
> And the Irishman shuts one eye when he's winking.
> *The Englishman* says in his belief
> There's nothing like pudding and lots of roast beef,
> For he never imagines that things can be right
> Unless he is drinking and smoking his pipe.
> *Now the Scotchman says*
> The best of the fun is to take care of number one
> But that's all stuff without plenty of snuff,
> And the dish he would choose before either of those
> Is a whacking blow out of good Barley Brouse[44]
> *Now the Welchman says*
> Of the Rose and the Thistle you've often heard speak
> But before either of these why give him the leek.
> For smoking and drinking are shocking bad habits
> Now his fun consists in eating Welsh rabbits.
> *Then the Irishman says*

44. Barley Brouse: ale.

The best of all fun, that's under the sun,
Is to sit by the fire, till the praties are done,
And when they are done, and you feel yourself frisky,
There's no fun so great, as cracking of heads and drinking
   of whiskey.
Now what I call fun and I think I am right
Is to see such a number of friends here tonight,
There's another gentleman whom I can name
Would like to see it every night the same,
Mr – he's the one would think it's the essence of fun
As for me, my cause no further extends
Than to gain for my share [of] fun, the applause of my friends.

Bad husbands are like bad coals, they smoke, they go out, and they don't keep the pot boiling.

The best way to look sharp, is to stick a needle into the point of your nose and squint through the eye of it.

Women are like sealing wax, only melt them and they will take what form you please.

♣

No. 20
Work Boys Work

Harry Clifton's famous motto song of this title[45] was published in 1867. Lawrence's material has sometimes an equivocal relationship to the lower-middle-class aspirational moralising in which Clifton specialised, but here he is clearly sending it up. The callously platitudinous insistence by the better-off that all the working man need do to become like them is to work with unremitting dedication as a wage-slave is comprehensively mocked by the clown, who begins by asserting that he himself would not dream of working. Having implicated his laughing audience in admiring a faux-naïf man whose cleverness is in getting away with idleness, he repeats the slogans of the copybook imposed upon the schoolboy – ironised by their repetition in this place dedicated to amusement and leisure – and plunges into verses of the epic-heroic kind praising the working man in terms of archaic manual labour. The bourgeois William Morris's glorification of mattock and shuttle (The Earthly Paradise *was published 1868–70) seems to lurk in the background as Lawrence stomps through the poses of idealised physicality – no doubt very comic in one who has never done a hand's turn – before he goes in for the kill, in the final quatrain. The man who works hard in this life will find, he proclaims, that he is starving. He ends – apparently in a separate entry, but one clearly suggested by the train of thought he has been following – with a return from abstractions about work to the workplace in which he began the wheeze, the job he and his fellows are actually doing in the circus. The comparison of the audience to busy bees – harking right back to wise maxims for the nursery – is flipped into a much less comfortable place by Lawrence's reminder to them that they have paid out their hard-earned cash to laugh at him. It is interesting that this twist replaces a much more anodyne conclusion in the previous gagbook, where the final six lines from 'Poetry' (pp. 191–2) appear here instead.*

---

45. It used a very long-lived tune originating in G. F. Root's American Civil War anthem and the Christie Minstrel song 'Tramp, Tramp, Tramp, the boys are marching'. See Michael Kilgarriff, *Sing Us One of the Old Songs: A Guide to Popular Song 1860–1920* (Oxford University Press, 1998), p. 105.

That must be very hard work. Though I don't know why I should say so, because I don't understand hard work from the very fact that I don't do any – I can lay my hand upon my heart and honestly say I never robbed a poor man of a hard day's work in all my life – though work is a fine thing for the rising generation, they do say that work is the youth's best presentative [*sic*] from evil, as idleness is the worst of snares

> So I say work lads work, and be not afraid,
> Look labour boldly in the face
> Take up your mattock or your spade
> Nor blush not at your humble place
> There's music in the shuttle song
> There's triumph in the anvil stroke
> There's merit to the brave and strong
> Who dig the mine or fell the oak
> And those who are not afraid [to] try
> Will find as through this world they go
> Provisions are a deal too high
> And poor men's wages much too low.

Why does this circus resemble a beehive?

Don't know

Because there's so many industrious bees in it.

But they've not brought much honey to the hive

No, but they were forced to drop their sugar at the door.

❧

No. 21
Sayings

A note of a handful of comic remarks useful to fill or cover – an indication of the vital role of the clown in the ring in keeping the audience relaxed and amused during a hitch or a break. The third, which to a modern eye is really very unfunny, had already been noted (p. 200); perhaps its importance is that it is a response to the order to 'look sharp!', which might be addressed to him as a demand for cover in a moment of stress in the ring. He included a similar group in the earlier gagbook.

Do you understand astronomy? This is just how we stand at the present time (*to rider*) the first blush of morn (*to clown*) the noon of manhood, rather late in the evening (*the last to old man in pit*).

That's the way to jump, but she can't jump like me, I once jumped so high that I couldn't put sixpence between my head and the moon, I hadn't sixpence to put there.

The best way to look sharp is to stick a needle in the point of your nose and squint through the eye of it.

> Two ducks behind a duck, to ducks before a duck
> Two ducks looking on, and a duck in the middle
> How many ducks is that?
> 9
> No, it's only 3.

The girls are the boys for jumping, they'll jump into a poor fellow's heart before he's got time to button up his waistcoat. I know it was the case with me for the heat of my love was so great that it burnt all the front of my shirt away.

❧

No. 22
Blacksmith's Daughter

The recurrent mysogyny of the stand-up comedian is evident in this kind of material; here the inversion of saccharine love songs turns the woman into a grotesque monster as well as an idiot and a burden to the man. Her pairing with the fool persona is perhaps the excuse for the release of gender hostility – he is a simpleton, a clown, so a grotesque woman is his match. In the verse, comparing parts of the blacksmith's daughter's body to various hard and hideous items from the smithy, there are further overtones. It recalls traditional rural

*songs like 'The Derby Ram', where the aspects of the totemic beast are
inflated by comparison with ever-larger everyday objects – so his tail is
used to pull the church bells, his horns stretch up to the moon. In a less
magical, more aggressive frame of reference, it is reminiscent of the
demonising of the black (female) body in minstrel songs that trumpet
the huge size of lips or buttocks or feet.[46] Inverted love songs making
verbal games by mocking the body of the beloved are a staple of
comedy right down to the 'herring boxes without topses [which]
sandals were for darling Clementine'; but the playfulness of the
language does not disguise the violence of the feelings, and Lawrence
ends this piece so excited by giving his girl black eyes that he offers to
fight the ringmaster.*

Brava, brava! That lady puts [me] so much in mind of my sweetheart –
you saw my sweetheart – such a beautiful creature –
Eyes of diamond brightness, teeth of pearly whiteness,
Skin of alabaster smoothness and her mouth –
Crammed full of ginger bread.

In fact she had so many wrinkles in the face that you could not tell
which was a mouth till she opened it and when she did open it, her
head was half off. Talk about a mouth being from ear to ear, hers was
from here to over yonder, but she used to call me such sweet names.
She called me her moss rose, her lily, her tulip, her daffydowndilly, her
sweet william, her rosebud. One day she called me her pickle cabbage,
I didn't like that. Then she called me her barley sugar, her sugar candy,
her bullseyes, her almond hardcake, her peppermint drops, her sugar
and treacle, she would have called me honey only she couldn't think of
it. But she called me something very near to it – why she said come here
old beeswax.[47] But she was a nice girl –

> She was a Blacksmith's daughter mild and meek
> With tinpot head and flat iron teeth

46. An instance from the famous 'Sally Come up': 'Dar was dat lubly gal, Miss Fan, / Wid a face as broad as a frying pan; / But Sally's is as broad again – / Dar's not a face like Sally's! / She's go a foot / To full out de boot, / So broad, so long, as a gum-tree root.' See Dailey Paskman, *'Gentlemen, be seated!'* (New York: Potter, 1976), p. 204.

47. Old beeswax: a bore.

She'd fiery eyes and rasp-like tongue
And the hair on her head like horsenails hung.
She'd a mouth like a vice and cold chisel teeth
Compass legs and sledgehammer feet
Her hands were like pincers she'd hobnail toes
A blow bellows face and an anvil nose.

She was an uncommon sort of girl – there was a neatness in her style of dress. Did you notice her bonnet – wasn't it a little duck – *I gave her that*; then her boots did you see them – *I gave her them*; and her jacket did you take notice of that: – wasn't it a beauty – *I gave her that*; and her eyes: you must have noticed them.

Yes they were black.
I gave her them!
Buss: squares at ringmaster

♣

No. 23
Shakespeare

Three of the next-four pieces are noticeably different from Lawrence's usual style. He attributes them to fellow performers, either appearing with him at Foottit's Circus in November 1871 at Liverpool, or sending them to him there.

    Verses or stories created from titles of Shakespeare's plays (or of popular songs or catchphrases of other kinds) are an instance of the games with words and literary puzzles that seem to fascinate English humorists at all levels. This example has some interest as a performance piece – a clown reciter would have had plenty to do, as he declaimed it in the ring – but it is low-pressure and monotonous compared with Lawrence's best wheezes. It has some moments of interest in terms of the popular perception of Shakespeare: the quoted line from Richard III *is from Cibber's version; the* Merchant of Venice *is thought of as an old clothes man, therefore a Jew, eliding Antonio and Shylock; a large range of titles are mentioned.*

To be or not to be, that's the question,
One day while walking between Manchester and Preston,
I saw a dog I thought I'd strike it, but how:
When a voice cried out, How You Like It,
My arm was up I could not rule it
And before my eyes stood, Romeo and Juliet,
Othello too who I thought looked as pale as death,
With his trusty friend Iago, and the Scottish King Macbeth,
Whose clothes were old and shabby, and so I told him,
It was a suit that the Merchant of Venice had sold him.
That crooked back tyrant Richard was also near,
Who cried off with his head, so much for King Lear,
But they all stood listening, to some uncommon din sir,
For Hamlet was larking with the Merry Wives of Windsor
The Two Gentlemen of Verona, cried out for a dentist
For they got wringing wet through being out in the Tempest
King John up and told them, paltry figures they were cutting,
For a small drop of rain, they made Much Do About Nothing
So he told them A Winter's Tale, to disperse their terrors,
Thus making you see, quite a Comedy of Errors,
I awoke from my slumbers, amidst a piercing loud scream
And I found it was only A Midsummer's Night's Dream.

> Given to me by Mr Coleman, equestrian
> Foottits Circus Liverpool November 21/71[48]

❖

48. In July 1871 the circus partnership of Powell, Foottit and Clarke was dissolved, the general consensus being that this was due to George Foottit's persistent drunkenness. Powell and Clarke went to Ireland tenting. Lawrence seems to have remained faithful to Foottit, who immediately started to rebuild his business as Foottit's Allied Circus. Lawrence remained with him until October 1872, when he advertised in the *Era* for a new clowning engagement, and it seems fairly certain that he was planning the move to the portable at this time. It could be that in assembling the notebook material while he was thinking that he needed to get out of Foottit's circus he was hedging his bets. Foottit's opened in Liverpool on Monday 6 November 1871 in the circus building formerly occupied by Quaglieni; Mr Coleman is listed in the company's advertisements, and on 26 November Lawrence is listed as one of three 'excellent' clowns.

No. 24

Erin Dear Erin

This lyric is another instance of the rich proto-professional song culture from which the early music halls drew their materials and performers. The exchange of musical and lyrical ideas created several related songs, and only sometimes resulted in publication and the claiming of copyrights (see pp. 152–53).

The vexed relationship between England and Ireland was often the subject of sentimental as well as mocking or outraged Victorian comment, and at this point the issue of Home Rule for Ireland was very lively. Gladstone's first Land Act had become law in August 1870; 1871 saw Fenian activity in Canada and a law placed on the statute book to allow detention without trial in Ireland for agrarian offences. On the other hand, the first Irish music hall, the Alhambra, opened in Belfast, and the Gaiety Theatre in Dublin. Complicated and contradictory attitudes are evident in this song, which seems to share its sentimental title with an earlier song by Charles S. Clarke and George Crouch, published by D'Almaine and Co. in 1843, in which an Irishman says farewell to the old country. It also shares the same first words and, perhaps significantly, a stanza form, with 'The Dear Emerald Isle' sung by Harry Collard, published in 1875 by Duff and Stewart as being composed by W. C. Levey, musical director at Drury Lane, with words by L. Blanchard.[49]

> Oh Erin dear Erin, thy wrongs are unnumbered
> Thy trials are more than thy temper can bear
> And justice too long has o'er villainy slumbered
> But now she's aroused, and the past will repair.
> But Erin sweet sister, arouse thee to labour,
> Remember thou hast friends still over the sea
> Shake hands with John Bull and be a kind neighbour
> And his sons will see justice is done unto thee.

49. It runs thus:

Erin dear Erin no isle so enchanting
Was ever yet set in the frame of the sea,
A bright emerald gem, in which nothing is wanting,
To show what a jewel of her earth ought to be.
Wherever we wander thy memory we cherish
When e'er from our vision thy shores may depart;
There is not a tint of thy verdure can perish,
So deeply each hue is engraved in our heart.

❖

No. 25
A Game of Cards

Another set of verses attributed to a friend, this time having little about it to suggest performance in the ring; it reads like hundreds of penny recitations of the period. Lawrence's comparisons and conceits are normally much more bizarre than this rather plodding string of metaphorical maxims. There was a vogue for songs based on the analogy of life and a game of cards in 1860, but this is like neither of the surviving published instances, which were by J. Carpenter and Harry Diamond.[50] In his (unpublished) account of Lawrence's life, Paul Newman, his great-grandson, recalled his mother reciting this verse to him as she tucked him into bed as a child. 'The last few lines always caused a shiver, but being one of those little childhood rituals [it] seemed as natural and comforting as a nursery rhyme. Although I didn't know it at the time, I was listening to my great-grandfather speaking from more than 80 years before ... my mother never knew where the poem came from other than her father had recited it to her as a child.'

This life is but a game of cards
Which mortals have to learn,
Each shuffle, cut, and deal the pack
And each a trump doth turn.
Sometimes a high card [comes] to the top
Others turn a low,
Some hold a hand quite full of trumps
While others none can show.
In playing, some throw out the ace
Their winning card to save,
Some play the ten, some the deuce
But many play the knave.
When hearts are trumps we play for love
And pleasure rules the hour,

50. 'Mankind is like a pack of cards', written and sung by J. Carpenter, Duncombe, London, 1860; 'What's Trumps?', written and sung by Harry Diamond, Robert Locks, London, 1860.

No thought of sorrow checks our joys
In beauty's rosy bower.
We laugh and sing, sweet verses write
Our cards at random play,
And while that trump remains on top
Our game's a holiday.
When diamonds chance to rule the pack
Then players stake their gold
And heavy sums are lost and won
By gamblers young and old
Intent on winning each his game
Doth watch with eager eye
So he may see his neighbour's cards
And cheat him on the sly.
When clubs are trumps look out for war
On ocean or on land,
For dreadful horrors always come
When clubs are held in hand;
Then lives are staked instead of gold,
The dogs of war are freed
The Continent fared very bad
When clubs had got the lead.[51]
But the spade! The spade is the last of all
When turned by the hand of time –
It waits upon each player's game
In every age and clime.
No matter how much each one wins
No matter how much each one *saves*
The spade will finish up the game
And dig the player's grave.

> Given by Mr George Nice
> Cork Ireland November. 24/71
> And sent to me at Foottit's Circus Liverpool.[52]

51. A vague reference, but probably the allusion is to the Franco-Prussian War, 1870–1.

52. See note 48 for Foottit's Allied Circus. Lawrence had been in Quaglieni's Circus in Dundee with George Nice in September 1868. Nice appears to have been a strongman who tossed cannon-balls about.

❖

Railway Alphabet

No. 26

*This example of the ABC poem (a more traditional and more comical
example of which genre opens the notebook, p. 157) offers savage
criticisms of the management of railways that seem quite startlingly
familiar at the beginning of the next century but one, after the
reprivatisation of the national rail network. At the time Lawrence was
writing, the most recent serious rail accident was that of 1868 in
North Wales, when the Irish Mail ploughed into goods wagons
carrying drums of oil and caused a huge fire in which thirty-three
people died, and there were many similarly terrible collisions and
derailments. Since the beginning, rail travel had inspired fear through
its potential for severe accidents, beyond those arising from natural
causes, and jokes about this terror, as well as those about complicated
timetables and minor travel irritations of all kinds, were a Victorian
staple.*

A stands for accidents frequent alas
B for the bunglers that bring them to pass
C the confusion that leads to the same
D the directors who are never to blame
E's an excursion too crowded by half
F are the fools that indulge in low chaff
G a goods train with but one man to mind it
H a high pressure locomotive behind it
I is an incline where the train stops too long
J for a junction with points all turned wrong
K is a knowledge of danger ahead
L for the lamps turned too late on to red
M is the mystery how it took place
N the nobody to blame in the case
O for the officers – sleepy, perhaps drunk
P for the permanent way that has sunk
Q for the quagmire in which it stuck fast

No. 28

Watches

This wheeze is a clever example of Lawrence's favoured device of the extended analogy, in this case carried out with a degree of social comment that goes beyond the obvious word games. He begins with scarcely veiled criticism of the expensiveness of Queen Victoria's household, including aspersions upon Prince Albert, who had died in 1861,[55] and moves on to sneer at smart young men and sympathise with poverty. The commonplace joke about policemen keeping away from trouble is reinforced by a suggestion that they are violent (see the more open accusation in 'Poetry', p. 214–6). He ends by covering all his sharp comments in a moment of physical comedy, collapsing or stopping dead like a clockwork toy because his spring has run down.

> The Queen's a watch of sterling worth
> The best finished watch of any –
> One guard for her is not enough
> So of course she has a many:
> Her horse guards, her foot guards,
> Her Life Guards so bold.
> Prince Albert was a German watch
> But gilt with British gold.
> Young swells so stylish dressed,
> So gay, so smart, so spruce,
> Like many other watches
> More fit for ornament than use.
> The tallyman a hunting watch
> To hunt his debtors ever quick;
> His customers are watches too,
> Because they go on tick,
> Magistrates are watches
> With many different cases;
> Young ladies they are watches too,

---

55. This was an issue debated in Parliament in the 1871 session. See

A. N. Wilson, *The Victorians* (London: Arrow, 2003), p. 360.

And some with pretty little faces,
Policemen they are watches
When wanted can't be found –
They are regular stop watches,
They stop at every round.
They're often found a deal too fast
They work by day and night
And like many patent watches
Not only go but strike,
When we get old, like watches
We find it difficult to go;
Our works get out of order
And we're often found too slow.
Our days are numbered like the watch –
It's true as I'm a clown –
And like the watch I now must stop,
For my main spring has run down.

❖

No. 29

Poetry

Another collection of brief interjections to fill moments in the ring, notable for their variety of tone. Presumably the working clown to the horse had to judge what would distract and please an audience moment by moment, and needed materials that would have many different starting points and effects. The collection here begins with two bits of clown's stock-in-trade: mockery of romantic language, culminating in a local joke (he would have filled in the name of a street in the town where they were playing) and an explicit attack on a favourite butt, the police-man. Two very brief and conventional quatrains about love are put in the shade by the following verses, which are about the realities of childbirth rather than the fantasy of courtship, one an oddly fervent plea for the battered mother of the sick child, and the other a delightful use of mock-heroic language to celebrate 'Our Sal' having another baby. He winds up with two noncomic statements, effectively claptraps, about hard financial straits and his admiration of the labouring man.

'Do'st thou live in a coral cave
Or is thy home near the rolling wave?
Or do'st thou dwell where the gentle zephyrs sigh
And the tear falls gently from a maiden's eye?'
She answered me in words so sweet
'I live down here in – street.'

This town is paraded with policemen in blue
They carry a mighty big staff and make use of it too.
They batter your sconce in for pleasure,
In the station house poke you for fun,
They take all your money and treasure
And fine you five bob when they've done.

'Oh give me a kiss my blue eyed Sal,'
The sailor said unto his gal
'I shalln't,' said she, 'you lazy elf
Screw up your mouth and help yourself.'

In war they use swords
       In love they use darts –
In war they break heads
In love they break hearts.

God bless those women with children, be they rich or poor,
For no one knows what they have to endure:
They are hours in the night tending the wailing in pain –
If a man was a woman a fortnight he'd never
strike a woman again.

Sound trumpets beat the drums
       And let the world all know,
Sound it to the furthest point
       Even unto Mexico!
Seize the pens ye dreaming poets

And in lines as fair as maybe,
Tell it now to all the world –
Our Sal's got another baby.

To lend or to spend or to give in,
This is the best world to live in;
But to beg or to borrow or get back your own,
It's the very worst world that ever was known,

God bless that man be [he] friend or a neighbour
That works by the spade the loom or the plough
That gains his diploma by manhood's labour
And earns independence by the sweat of his brow.

❖

No. 30
Love

This is an unusual wheeze in that it seems to be in the character of a 'fool' in the archaic sense of simpleton. He begins by stating that he is a child (a necessary setting of the stage, since he may have no change of costume to indicate that he is in role) and one imagines him skipping about expressing his childishness in everything from truanting and toys to patriotism. The second stanza begins to twist away from vacant innocence, asserting his 'love' for 'the ladies', and eventually coming down to the 'childish' assertion that he – and all of us – love others only insofar as they love us and contribute to our ruling passion, which is self-love. A great deal of the meaning here would depend on performance.

I love my boyish day
And from my school I love to stray
I love my marbles and my tops
I love to pass the sweetmeat shops
I love the days when I had sense
I love all those who gave me pence

I love the tall the short
I love the fat the lean
But above them all
I love my country and my Queen

I love old people
I love young babies
But my greatest love
Is for the ladies
From East to West
From North to South
I'd kiss them all had they one mouth
I love father I love my mother
I love my sister I love my brother
I love the blacks the whites and all the rest
I love them that do love me
But I love myself the best.

❧

No. 31

Love Letters

Another unusual piece, this time in the persona of a man who has left a girl pregnant. He has a letter from a woman – one may imagine him coming into the ring with paper in hand, reading the envelope and/or possibly assuming the voice and manner of the girl, whose message begins very sweetly but changes gear for the punning ninth line. Then the format changes completely and the joke appears to be just playing with long words; but his correspondent is no longer a sweetly girlish voice, and as her portentous words accumulate one can imagine dread gathering in his voice, until he realises that he is about to be forced into marriage and responsibility.

Mr Postman haste away to – Town[56] without delay
To – Circus and there you'll find

56. Another local reference (see No. 29).

Lawrence the clown both[57] good and kind
And as I cannot direct you better
Knock at the door and give him the letter

Dearest Lawrence do not grieve
I'll tell you all about it
I stole your shirt to make a shift
And you must make a shift without

After a long *consideration*[58]
And great *deliberation*
I have come to the *determination*
To remove my *habitation*
To a nearer *situation*
That we may have a *consultation*
Without any *altercation*
I'll see you at the railway *station*
Then we'll have our *conversation*
Respecting the marriage laws of *our nation*
If it meets with your *approbation*
And I become any near *relation*
It will be the sure *foundation*
Of – a rising *generation*.

✣

No. 32
Poetry

*The pages thus headed are normally collections of unrelated verses;
these two are only vaguely linked by being both about women. The first
might be regarded simply as an example of Lawrence's common
technique of the bathetic deflation of high-flown language. But there is
also something of his equally customary misogyny in the way it
contrasts a (somewhat incoherent) invocation of sainted motherhood*

---

57. He spells it 'boath', suggesting a Midland (north Notts) accent.

58. In the earlier gagbook a joke word is used, 'conflabberation'.

with a girl's frivolous concern for dress. The second verse mocks not the girl, but the persona the clown is adopting. The comic rejected lover, falling or being forcibly inserted into the water butt, is a commonplace of early music hall song. Often the story is of his fall into the barrel while climbing to his beloved's high window – which links back in a possibly subliminal way to the first verse here.

> As a fair maid looked from her window high,
> All hope, all joy her fair breast foresaken,
> Soft tears, deep heart rending sighs,
> Declared her tortured heart was breaking
> But no! It was grief,
> More deep than fevered love for chiding mother
> For Ah! Last night her bustle burst
> And she'd no bran to stuff another

> For once I courted as pretty a lass
> As e'er my eyes did see
> But now it's got to such a pitch
> She cares no more for me
> She invited me to her father's house
> I'd never been there before
> She kicked me in to the water butt
> I shan't go there any more

♣

No. 31
Nothing

A short and perhaps rapidly delivered piece, with a link to the act with which the clown is working, suggesting a moment when the horseman or acrobat has come to a stop in the course of his performance. The clown asks him (possibly with real concern) if he needs anything, and is told that he does not. Such a pause needs cover, and Lawrence would pick up the cue and go into this routine. It enables him to direct the attention of the audience away from the stalled performer – 'follow me as I go to fetch, look up there, shut your eyes, answer my string of questions, listen to my rapid-fire patter, give me a round of applause for my cynical maxim: your relatives will give you nothing'.

He says he wants nothing. I'll go and fetch it for him – did you ever see nothing: – then I'll show you it: look up there – what do you see? Now shut your eyes – now what can you see? Why nothing, that's it. Well, now you have seen nothing, what is it? There, I'll tell you, nothing is a footless stocking without a leg. Do you know where to get nothing? Then I'll tell you, in the first place if you want to be healthy rise early, if you want to be wealthy you must be industrious, if you want to be happy get married, if you want a noise have a large family of children or live next door to a boiler yard, if you want advice go and ask a stranger, if you want a friend that will stick to you in the hour of adversity keep him in your pocket. But if you want nothing . . . go to your relations! And they will give [it to] you directly.

❖

No. 34
Brave Men

Another brief interjection, beginning with a compliment to the performer with whom he is working and culminating in another dig at the policeman. The longer version in the earlier gagbook included masons who 'erect stupendous buildings' and averred that soldiers not only fight our battles abroad but also 'keep us from incendiaries at home'.

That's a brave youth. But you can't wonder at that when we have had so many brave men in the world. We have men that descend into the bowels of the earth – those brave men are called miners. We have men that plough the mighty ocean and discover unknown countries – those brave men are called sailors. We have men who study the stars, the moon, the sun, the earth – those brave men are called astrologers.[59] We have men that fight our battles abroad – those brave men are called

---

59. Spelled 'astraligers'. Presumably Lawrence means astronomers; the modern distinction between the two words had been in use since the end of the seventeenth century.

soldiers. We have men that walk into gentleman's kitchens smoke their cigars, drink their wine, kiss the cooks and walk out with a lot of cold mutton in their pockets, and those brave men are called – Bobbies.

❖

No. 35

Ladies Like Sugar

Another of the extended conceits, this one teased out neatly and rapidly. The link at the opening, in which he speaks to a woman and is warned off by someone from touching her, could be either worked with the departing or resting performer and the ringmaster or, possibly, addressed to a girl sitting in the front row of the audience and her escort.

Angels were painted fair to look like you. There's a lump of smudge on your nose – I was only giving her a bit of Romeo! Bless her little heart! She is a perfect Angel! But all women are angels before marriage: that's why their husbands wish them in heaven so soon after. But they are sweet creatures: in fact they are so sweet that I have compared them all to sugar – why a lady that is highly educated would be refined sugar, a very ignorant woman would be coarse sugar, a lady bedecked with gold and jewels would be crystallised sugar, a lady with highly coloured auburn hair would be sandy sugar,[60] a lady in tears would be moist sugar, a baker's wife is loaf sugar, a very stout woman is lump sugar, and if everybody had the misfortune to fall upon her – why then she would be crushed lump!

❖

No. 36

A loyal speech, occasioned, according to Lawrence's note below, by the illness of the Prince of Wales, who contracted typhoid fever in November 1871. It is interesting that this event caused an outburst of

---

60. Sandy sugar: moist sugar (*c.*1810–50), presumably similar in colour to auburn hair.

loyal speechmaking even in Lawrence, whose material is on the whole very nondeferential and champions the poor working man and includes some fairly sceptical comment on the royal family (see p. 213). We have here, perhaps, an instance of our capacity to hold conflicting opinions simultaneously on matters that do not concern us very personally. (See 'Old England', the next piece in the gagbook, for a similar double vision.)

As we have met for *relaxation*, or *gratification* I claim your polite *attention*, to a few words I'm to *mention* and should my oration meet your *approbation*, it will raise me greatly in my own *estimation*, and prove the *foundation*, of a new *association*, or *combination*. May our Queen live long to rule this loyal *nation*, may the Royal Family long hold their present lofty *station*, without *cessation*, for many a *generation*. May Republican Dilke[61] receive just *condemnation*, may public opinion put down such dirty *defamation*, and may the Prince of Wales recover from his great *prostration*

> God bless the Queen, God bless the Prince.
> Thus ends my *proclamation*.

On Prince of Wales' illness
Liverpool

❖

No. 37

Old England

This patriotic effusion has a distinct sting in its tail. It is really a matter of reception whether or not the sudden undercutting of the vaunted superiority of England is as complete a bathetic deflation as Lawrence's frequent attacks on romantic fantasy. In performance he might anticipate routine applause for the nationalist sentiments, but then add the punchline to provoke a heartier roar for its unexpected hard edge of reality.

61. Sir Charles Dilke, 1843–1911, elected MP for Chelsea in 1871 and an avowed Radical republican.

But England is the country for me (as the song says, there is no place like home)

> 'Tis the pride and the boast of all Englishmen brave
> No one lives in bondage, not one man a slave,
> With its army so great that is always victorious
> Its iron-clad fleet and seamen so glorious,
> Bold hearts of oak that never knew fear,
> That have fought, bled and died for their country so dear;
> Its commerce and wealth is equalled by none,
> 'Tis the most prosperous nation under the sun.
> Who is not proud of an Englishman's name
> What country [h]as ever achieved such great fame
> Where peace and plenty for ever abound
> Where the clamour of war shall never resound
> Old England's the glory and pride of the world
> Where the banner of freedom is for ever unfurled
> Where those who have wealth live in sweet communion
> But those who have none – may go to the union.[62]

♣

No. 38
Jane and Walter

A set of verses on Lawrence's common topic – the opposition between the fantasy and the reality of love and marriage, between courtship and childrearing. Its interest is in its formal qualities: the use of wordplay – the transformation of the final rhyme, [h]alter – and the fleeting reminiscence of traditional song burdens in the final stanza, with the use of 'oh' at the end of the first two lines.

Two lovers sat beneath a bower, their hearts were filled with bliss
He placed her lovely hair aside, and gave her brow a kiss

62. Here 'union' means the union workhouse, dreaded destination of the destitute since the 1834 changes in social provision had decreed that a harsh deterrent regime should be adopted.

And oh to see this darling pair, her name was Jane and his was Walter
He swore by all the stars above his love should never alter

The next time I saw this darling pair, 'twas on their bridal morn
The orange blossom did her lovely brow adorn
And he! He looked the god of love and didn't seem to falter
And swore his love should never change, as he led her to the altar

When next I saw this darling pair, the scene alas was changed, oh
Jane at Walter daggers looked, and Walter looked deranged, oh
Laid on her knees the little girl, 'twas Jane, and he had little Walter
He swore he would go and hang himself, if he could find a halter.

♣

No. 39
Almanack

A rapid-fire string of puns and jokes without much structure, relying on venerable popular assumptions and tiny vignettes of common life – women cannot keep secrets, married couples fight, drinkers have red noses. The material could no doubt be cut to fit whatever length of time Lawrence needed to fill. Such a series of pictures hung on a catchphrase or chorus is the basis of the music hall song, which tells a story of this kind in each verse, and illustrates them in little scenes in lurid colour on the front of the sheet music.

Are you weather wise, are you other wise? I can always tell what sort of weather [we] are going to have the moment I come down stairs – why if I see our cat's tail turned towards the fire it's a sure sign of wet but if our cat has got her nose in a bowl of milk it's a sure sign it's dry – and there are many other indications by which you may tell the state of the weather. Now if you see a man pitted with the small pox that's frosty; if you see a brewer's dray standing at a public house door that's a sign of ale; if a woman knows a secret, and keeps it, that is uncommon close; if you see two men fighting and they knock each other down, that [is] very fair; if a child falls down and breaks its nose you may expect a squall; if a man and his wife is quarrelling and she pulls all the hair of his head and he is forced to wear a wig that's change of hair; if a man wears his shirt five weeks without being washed that's very foggy;[63] if a married man is talking to a single lady and his wife catches him that's a sure sign of a storm; if a young man courts a lady for three years then marries another that's changeable; if a gentleman goes into bad company with a gold watch in his pocket you may expect lightning; but if you see a man with a red nose that's a sign of heavy wet.[64] Then you see we have so many sorts of weather: sometimes it's rainy weather, sometimes we have blowy weather, sometimes there's snowy weather, sometimes it's misty weather, sometimes we have foggy weather, sometimes it's frosty weather, sometimes we have dry weather, sometimes we have wet weather sometimes the weather is cold and sometimes it's hot but we must weather it whether or not.

♣

No. 40

Children

Lawrence's favoured trick of the unexpected substitution of a more down-to-earth ending to a moral commonplace is used to begin this wheeze, which then develops into a comic/grotesque vision of himself as a monstrous child. One of its most interesting aspects is that, uniquely in the notebook, he begins at the end to write in a link outwards from his own material back to the act he is allowing to rest; he then crossed it out.

Train up a child in the way it should go, and when it gets old it will whop its father – you are right, train up a child in the way it should go and when it gets old it will not depart from it: they trained me up with a spoon, and I have been a spooney ever since. You didn't know me

---

63. Most slang dictionaries record 'foggy' as meaning 'drunk', but the sense is 'smelly' – perhaps an unrecorded usage derived from 'fogo', mentioned by Hotten in *A Dictionary of Modern Slang, Cant, and Vulgar Words* (London: John Camden Hotten, 1859), p. 41, as meaning a stench.

64. 'Heavy wet' is nineteenth-century slang for malt liquor, specifically porter or stout.

when I was a child. I was a beautiful child when I was born. People came hundreds of miles to see me,

they came in railway trains, they came in coaches,
they came in steam packets, they came in cabs,
they came in open landaus, they came in closed landaus,
they came in horse carts, they came in dog carts,
they came in trucks, they actually came in wheelbarrows to see me!

And one old woman declared she never never did at any time or any place or under any circumstances ever see a larger child of the same size in all her life. Then I was such a forward child for before I could either walk or talk I used to run all over the town asking people for halfpence. Then I was such a clever child: for I remember once going into a Blacksmith's shop, laying hold of a piece of red hot iron and I put it down again, and nobody told me. Then I was so fat that my mother used to wrap me up in sand paper to keep me from falling out of bed: and such a lovely child, O! so handsome, I was so handsome that every body said that I ought to have been born a girl.

Ringmaster says **Handsome children always grow up to be ugly men –**

Then you must have been very handsome when you was born.
　　　[But this is a very clever youth and I should think his mother must be a very clever woman – because I never]

❖

No. 41
Leg of Mutton

An interesting set of verses in a popular mode, telling the tale of the Sunday roast – the working family's only meat of the week. Despite the mythic nature of such an account, this version is remarkably realistic in its detail: one may trace recipes in popular Victorian cookery books for everything here, just as it is described.

On Sunday, being a feast day boasted,
We'd have a leg of mutton roasted.
On Monday, when your taste you'd tickle
Have part cold with Indian pickle.[65]
On Tuesday [h]ashed, with gravy made
First round the table let supits[66] be laid,
On Wednesday make a season pie
If not enough some slices fry[67]
On Thursday broiled with due care
Mashed potatoes too prepare[68]
And the longer it may last
On Friday I announce a fast.
On Saturday when the cash gets narrow,
Crack the bone and eat the marrow.[69]

♣

No. 42

Travelling

This short piece is tied to an equestrienne's performance. It is interesting in the way it frames a short string of comic remarks about travelling and exploration – masculine topics of the day – with a not-very-subtle joke about the proper limits of female experience and a downright attack upon women who leave their appointed domestic sphere. His framing of the performing woman works to put females in general firmly in their place.

65. A very hot pickle, combining ginger, mustard and garlic with spoils of Empire like chillies and cayenne pepper.

66. Thin slices of roast meat reheated in gravy; sippets are triangles of toast with which the dish was garnished.

67. 'If not enough' is a recipe-book phrase meaning 'if the meat is not sufficiently cooked'. Underdone mutton would be sliced and devilled, i.e., fried, as Lawrence says.

68. Mrs Beeton's *Everyday Cookery* gives a recipe for broiled mutton with mashed potatoes; to broil is to griddle already-cooked meat over a clear fire.

69. This is perhaps the only fanciful recommendation, or it may be a move in the direction of Lawrence's bathetic ending, since mutton bones are not large enough to serve as the Victorian delicacy stewed marrowbones, made with the much bigger bones of the ox.

That's the way to travel, but then you know ladies are the quickest travellers in the world! At a certain time of their lives – that is one hour before they are married, and one hour afterwards – one hour before they are married they are in the Cape of Good Hope one hour afterwards they are in the United States. But we have had some great travellers before this lady, there was Sir John Franklin[70] he was a great traveller. Then there was Columbus, he was a great traveller, he discovered America though there's not a deal of credit due to him for that because America is a very large country and if he had not found it somebody else would. And there was Captain Cook he was a wonderful traveller he sailed three times around the world I wish I could persuade some of our mechanics' wives just to follow Captain Cook's example – no not to sail three times around the world, but to sail three times round their own kitchens and take half as much trouble to dress their husband's dinner as they do to dress themselves. There would be fewer drunkards less starving children and more happy homes in good old England.

♣

No. 43
Bottles

Another example of the extended comparison or conceit. This one might perhaps link to a balancing or juggling act, such as Frowde performed with champagne bottles (see Figure 8, p. 102). It culminates in another familiar ploy, the joke against the police.

Shakespeare says that all the world's a stage, and men and women are nothing more than players: now I say that all the world's a shop and men and women are nothing more than – bottles.

> Rich men are full bottles,
> Poor men are empty bottles,
> Fat men are stout bottles,
> Thin men are pale ale bottles,

70. Sir John Franklin, 1786–1847, who made four Arctic voyages in search of the North-West Passage, from the last of which no one returned.

Masons are stone bottles,
Carpenters are wooden bottles,
Shoemakers leather bottles,
Drunkards are gin bottles,
Teetotallers are water bottles,
Musicians are sound bottles,
Lunatics are cracked [bottles],
Dandies are essence bottles,
Ladies fainting are champagne bottles,
Clowns are rum[71] bottles,
Doctors are physic bottles,
Sweeps are blacking bottles,[72]
Scolding wives are vinegar bottles,
Washerwomen are soda water bottles[73] and
Policemen they are only blue bottles.[74]

♣

No. 44
Horses

There is something of the simpleton clown persona in play here, with the weak jokes at the opening about the grey – that is, white – horse getting old and the one who kept changing his spots, and then the sly faux-innocence of the parting shot. In between come games with long words and simple puns of a pantomime kind, the clown's verbal equivalent, perhaps, of the equestrian games of the circus.

That's a very nice horse. He's very old is he not – I thought he was because he's getting grey. I had a very nice horse. But mine was a spot horse, and he used to change his spots 20 or 30 times a day – why when I put him in the field to graze, when he was done eating at one spot he'd

---

71. Rum: cant for odd.

72. Bottles containing the black polish for shoes or kitchen ranges.

73. Soda was used in washing.

74. Because of their uniform. Blue bottles contained medicines and poisons, but the bluebottle is a fly.

change to another, and so he'd keep on all day changing his spots. When I bought him, they called him Graphy, when I paid for him it was tip-o-graphy,[75] when I got on his back it was top-o-graphy when I wanted him to go it was you ought-o-graphy[76] when I wanted him to make haste it was tel-o-graphy, and when I had his likeness taken it was phot-o-graphy, but he was the largest horse I ever saw, he wouldn't pull up hill and he wouldn't back down and when he came to level road he'd stand stock still, he wouldn't pull a coach or a cart and as for a truck, he'd have no truck with that at all and when he died – he was so lazy that he wouldn't pull his last breath – I was forced to engage two post horses to draw it for him. I nearly had a horse given me today, there was only one word that stopped it: I asked the owner of it if he would give it me, and he said no. If he'd have said yes I should have had it directly.

✤

No. 45

Potatoes

A full-blown wheeze, built from a punning link into a set of verses and then on to an extended comparison; it amalgamates three pieces presented separately in the earlier gagbook. It ends yet again with a joke against the police. Lawrence draws his conceit out at almost excruciating length, perhaps working it slowly, teasing the audience with how far he might be able to make it stretch. He sets it out across the page, as we have it here, perhaps to suggest its long-drawn-out pattern. Some indication of audience participation is there, in the 'potato chorus'.

Bravo! That's capital! That's well done and that's what I like to see – I like to see everything well done, if it's only potatoes – talking about potatoes,

> That noble root Sir Walter Raleigh found
> And planted it in Paddy's ground,
> He called it Irish fruit,

75. Tip: to pay.   76. Orthography.

Because it bore its apples at the root.[77]
Ranged on a dish, or seeking a retreat
Under the cover of a joint of meat,
Or on a more pro- bon-o plan
Feeding the public from a 'tater can
Getting a standing dinner from a brown
To those that can't afford one sitting down[78]

Now through this busy world I'll scan
And show you the simlie[79] of a 'tater to a man

Potatoes sprang from the earth	so did man
Potatoes are buried in the earth	so is man
Potatoes have skins	so have men
Potatoes have eyes	so have men
Potatoes are often put into stews	so are men

So you see humanity resembles potatoes

Soldiers	are red-hot	potatoes
Sailors	are watery	potatoes
Bakers	are [floury]	potatoes
Shoemakers	are waxy	potatoes
Drummers	are thumping	potatoes
Fiddlers	are scraped	potatoes
Young people	are early	potatoes
Old people	are late	potatoes
Banks	are smashed	potatoes
Young ladies	are blooming	potatoes

And I hope they will never be nipped in bud

| Policemen they | are blue | potatoes |

And very often turn out bad peelers.

♣

77. The suggestion is that all things Irish are upside down, inside out.

78. The reference is to the provision of baked potatoes at a penny (a 'brown') out of charity to the poor in towns and cities; in 1871 there was an investigation into the various forms of subsidised food by the Charity Organisation Society, which was by no means convinced of the propriety of such 'pro bono' interference with the market economy, which tended, they thought, to 'pauperise' the recipients.

79. Lawrence's intention here is clearly to indicate similarity.

Hard Times

A brief wheeze elaborating not the single conceit –'people are like x' – but a set of puns based on the jargon of various trades. The initial idea, of 'hard times', was a recurring lament; Dickens's novel of that name was published in 1854. The fragment ends once more with a dig at the police.

Times are very hard and money very scarce; I have had a little conversation with a few of the princip[al] tradesmen of the town and they positively assert that if times don't alter there will be no change. The watchmaker says he's wound up, the main spring of his business gone, and his customers like his watches all go on tick. The shoemaker says he can't keep body and sole together, though he has bristled up and stuck to his work like wax but he can't make both ends meet. The bailiffs are in his house. They have taken his awl and that's the last thing they can leather him out of. The carpenter says it's very plane that things are getting a deal worse than he ever saw them so he'll have to cut it for he can't live on the square so he'll be compelled to chisel them. Then the police complain more than all the others. They say through the scarcity of money and the high price of provisions the servant girls can't afford to give them the same amount of kitchen stuff that they used to do!

❖

Boots

A filler to be used in interaction with the ringmaster, who would wear polished high boots as part of his smart costume, conventionally a military or hunting uniform. The grotesquerie of Lawrence's ideas is evident here as elsewhere, and his preoccupation with women talking too much.

Those are nice boots: they say the man that's up to his knees in leather is up to his neck in debt. I hope that's not the case with you. Why don't you have your boots made of tripe, so when you have worn out the bottoms, you can eat the tops. I gave him that pair, they are top boots – they are all tops, they got no bottoms, they'll keep his feet dry for as fast as the rain runs in at the top it's sure to run out at the bottom. I think of starting [in] the boot and shoe line. If I do I shall make my boots and shoes out of a new material – I shall make the tops of the skin of a drunkard's throat and make the soles of old women's tongues – because the skin of a drunkard's throat will never admit water, and an old woman's tongue will never wear out.

✤

No. 48
Rifles

This is the first of three consecutive pieces, not found in the earlier gagbook, that play with the idea of being a soldier – either a regular (uniformed in 'scarlet') or a volunteer or member of the yeomanry (dressed as Lawrence suggests in 'grey, or green'). There is a continuous thread of comedic thinking going on in, for example, the puns about 'arms', but the tone and the apparent attitude to the army varies very much between pieces, presumably because he would need to judge his audience and pick what would go down best at each different venue, indeed each night, according to the makeup of the (very close and visible) audience. There are taunting references to soldiers as well as to police and other working-class persons doing the work of authority throughout the book. These three pieces illustrate the range of attitudes available to him in dealing with such material. It is worth comparing Lawrence's pragmatic but essentially sceptical, working-class attitude to the army with Frowde's eagerness to spend time with officers and gentlemen, and his willingness to develop his material to suit them. The first of Lawrence's pieces is a lengthy wheeze, a sly parody of the lower-middle-class persona adopted in the set-up. Here is the socially aspiring married man, a clerk perhaps, who is unsure about his ability to afford the Volunteer uniform but keen to 'give the word of command' and censure loose behaviour. This moves into an acted-out version of the parody of arms drill that is a common device in the nineteenth-century comic press, where it was a vehicle for all sorts of social comment. Lawrence's wise saws suggest such an origin in the popular prints; their respectable tone and disapproval of raffishness of all kinds fits the character he is acting out.

I see we have some of the rifle Corps here to night. Do you know that I had some idea of entering that Corps myself – in fact my wife's strongly advised it. Only I thought I could not support the expense of new clothing and arms – but my wife assures me that the government finds arms. That's very strange – I saw one of the rifles coming down the street with arm around a young woman's waist and don't think government finds arms for that purpose. Besides, if I entered the rifles I should want to be a sergeant or a captain so that I could give the word of command. Then I should introduce a new drill, indeed I should like to introduce it right through the army – this would be it:

> *Attention* that means mind your own business and don't blow your nose into other people's.
>
> *Eyes right* if you are a married man don't look after the single women. If you're a single man don't look after the married.
>
> *Dress* neither like a sloven or a fop, and be sure you pay your tailor's bills before you wear his clothes.
>
> *Carry arms* never be ashamed or afraid to nurse your own children.
>
> *Secure arms* marry the woman you love, and prevent a man striking his own father.
>
> *Load* your head with judgement, your heart with feeling and your hand with liberality.
>
> *Fix bayonets* stick a knife into a good round of beef and a bad argument.
>
> *Fire* belong to a coal club to distribute coals in the winter and make the poor as warm and comfortable as yourself.
>
> *Charge* charge no man with faults he has not committed, or for more than he has a just right to pay: and I charge any military gentlemen present, whether in scarlet, grey, or green, to be ready with his rifle, for his country and his Queen.

❖

No. 49

Soldiers

This and the next brief piece play with the traditional and deep-seated scorn that the British working class held for the army: the strong sense that no man sober enough to look after himself would be so foolish as to take the king's shilling, and so lose his independence and probably his life. The distrust of footloose troops on leave, and discharged and unemployable ex-soldiers, was still strong enough twenty years later to inspire sentiments very similar to those apparently expressed here in Kipling's Barrack-Room Ballads. *These two pieces differ, however. In this piece Lawrence claims to have great respect for the soldiers, who are welcomed and their taste for female companionship flattered; the verse is apparently speaking up for the 'poor soldier', just as Kipling was to do. It is only in the implications of the apparently generous welcoming of 'a Friend and a Brother' that irony enters: the phrase is taken from the antislavery campaigns, and implies that the soldiers are no better than slaves. The second piece, set up as a hazing of the 'spooney' clown, has the same implication in a much less disguised form. The soldier in the pit 'was sold for a bob' (a shilling) – however brave he is proclaimed to be, this can only make him twelve times less self-respecting and worth while than the clown-butt of the joke. Perhaps Lawrence would use one or other of these pieces depending on the strength of the military presence in the audience, and whether he was seeking to amuse soldiers or the more sensible people who avoided and distrusted them.*

I see we are patronised by the military to night. I like to see the military in the circus, because where you see the military there you generally find the *millinery* – not only that I have a great respect for the Soldiery, because I have been in the army myself – yes I have been a soldier all my life ever since I was so old (*Buss.*)– when I was a child I was an *infant in arms*, when I grew older and had a sweetheart and we embraced each other I was a *man in arms*, then I got married and had got a family of my own, I was captain of the *light infantry* and on a Sunday when I pulled them about in the perambulator I belonged to the *Heavy Dragoons*!

Besides – When war is proclaimed, and danger nigh,
God and our soldiers, is the people's cry
But when war is ended and all things righted,
God is forgotten and the poor soldier slighted.

But they are not slighted by me: I think the men who fight our battles abroad and keep us from incendiaries at home ought to be treated as a friend and brother.

❖

No. 50
Raffle

See the discussion of No. 49. This little piece is also unusual in the notebook in that it is necessarily worked with another clown, rather than the ringmaster; Lawrence also works with a partner in the more extended wheeze below (p. 250).

Ladies and gentlemen I'll raffle this article, twelve members at a shilling a member, any respectable widow lady can have two chances for the same amount, he'll not be an expensive husband he only wears paper collars – why look, do you see that gentleman sitting in the pit with the red coat on? He is one of the defenders of our country – he is one of the brave men who have placed England on its present footing – he is one of those brave men who is ready at any minute to fight bleed or die in the [service] of the country that gave him birth. Well – he was sold for a bob, and yet you think twelve shillings not enough for a second-hand blaggard like you.

❖

No. 51
The Word If

A rather lame little piece, with only one weak joke to make – the bathos of the last line. It is carefully attributed to George Nice, and his departure for America noted below, so perhaps Lawrence included it as a memorial to a friend, rather than for his own future use. It seems somehow appropriate to have been associated with a strongman, however, since it turns upon ideas of size and strength. It may have been spoken by Lawrence during Nice's performance.

> If all the men were one great man
> What a great and mighty man he would be;
> If all the little stones were one great stone
> What a great and mighty stone that would be;
> If all the mountains were one great mountain
> What a great and mighty mountain that would be;
> If all the little rivers were one great river
> What a great and mighty river that would be!
> Then if this great and mighty man was to
> Take that great and mighty stone to the top of
> That great and mighty mountain and throw
> It into that great and mighty river
> What a great and mighty *splash that would be!*
>
> G Nice Liverpool Nov. 1872

G. Nice left Liverpool for America, Wednesday November 13th 1872[80]

❧

No. 52
On Ages

Although this piece, like the last, is attributed to Nice, it is in Lawrence's favoured pattern of the extended comparison or conceit, with his usual mysogynist sting in the tail. It is furnished with an interesting lead-in, which is probably addressed to someone in the audience carrying a child, but might possibly refer to a child performer or to business in the ring involving a horse or merely a prop. The list is a useful component since it can be terminated when the next act is ready, with just the punchline dropped in at the end.

---

80. The strongman George Nice sent Lawrence an earlier entry in the notebook (see pp. 208–9). This dateline falls just after Lawrence left Foottit's Allied Circus, and was beginning in business as a portable theatre proprietor.

What is the age of that – must be very young according to my judgement, and I am considered a good judge of ages. I know almost everybody's age:

A soldier's age is cour-age

A sailor's age is voy-age

A merchant's age is till-age

A gambler's age is crib-age[81]

A lawyer's age is dun-age[82]

A preacher's age is verb-age

A farmer's age is herd-age[83]

A doctor's age is pill-age

A drunkard's age is dam-age

A lover's age is court-age[84]

A policeman's age is lug-age[85]

A cook's age is pot-age[86]

An Irishman's age is bog-age

A Frenchman's age is carn-age[87]

A German's age is saus-age

A tailor's age is cabb-age[88]

But the worst of all ages is marri-age.

G Nice Liverpool Nov. 1872

81. Cribbage is a universally popular card game, also mentioned on p. 177, but 'to crib' is also thieves' cant for 'to steal'.

82. A dun is a debt collector, but dunnage is the light or less valuable parts of a cargo stowed below or around the things that need protection in a ship's hold.

83. 'Herdage' is not a real word; may be in delivery it would slur into 'herbiage'.

84. OED gives 'courtage' as meaning brokerage.

85. To lug is to pull or take hold of roughly – in this case, to carry off into custody.

86. One of the better lines, in that pot and pottage (soup) are both appropriate to the cook.

87. From the Latin root *caro*, *carnis*, meaning flesh, 'carnage' entered English via Old French, but the interesting thing is that while Lawrence and his audience think of the Irish in connection with bogs, the Germans with sausages – both crudely belittling national stereotypes – the French, under Napoleonic rule since the beginning of the century, mean war, death, slaughter. Presumably his audience would have immediately in mind the chaos and mismanagement of the French forces during the Franco-Prussian War, which ended in 1871.

88. Cabbage is slang for the rest of the cloth, paid for by the customer but not used in making up his order, which is appropriated by the tailor as his perquisite.

✢

No. 53
The Word Fast

Nice's final contribution is a brief segment, a wordplay that simply reiterates the contradiction that 'fast' can mean either 'rapid' or 'held in check'. The most interesting thing here is that Lawrence has thought how to integrate it into his act, adding a final stage direction directing himself to an earlier wheeze, 'Watches' (p. 213).

Of all the words that the dictionary contains, the word *fast* is the most contradictory. They say a horse is *fast* when it goes at speed: now it must be *fast* when it is locked in the stable: they say a river is *fast* when it flows swift: now it must be *fast* when it is frozen over: they say a man is *fast* when he lives beyond his means: he must be *fast* when he has no means to live on: they say that I am *fast* when I talk too much: now I must be *fast* when I have nothing to talk about. They say a watch is *fast* when it goes ahead of time: now it must be *fast* when it is in pawn for 15 shillings and you can't get it out

(go to watch wheeze)
G Nice Liverpool Nov. 1872

✢

Fourteen blank leaves are left here before the fragment of Jane Shore (pp. 240–1), which is written on the verso of the fifteenth leaf; it is followed by another blank leaf. The next opening is occupied by a list of materials, cut lengths of wood, from which to build a portable theatre – as we know Lawrence did, in 1873. The rest of the book is occupied not by wheezes but by the lyrics of seven songs (below, pp. 241–50), and finally a sketch – the burlesque dog drama (p. 250).

Our interpretation of this use of the book is that Lawrence wrote out the songs and the sketch starting from the back of the book, during the same period of time that he was filling the book with wheezes from the front; he inserted the fragment of the drama randomly, for some reason, and then, when he no longer expected to be collecting songs, used the pages left over in the back part of the book for planning his new venture. He clearly used the endpapers and inside covers similarly, making rough drafts of letters soliciting work and asking for the extension of a loan.

The brief extract from Jane Shore *is one of the most extraordinary items in the gagbook. It stands apart from the rest of Lawrence's materials written at back and front. It is a dramatic speech, not burlesqued, though presumably its delivery by a clown could have had that effect (see the note on James Boswell of Astley's, p. 188). Perhaps Lawrence interjected this in the midst of his clowning to change or heighten his impact. The cod-tragic recitation that is about shaving rather than suicide (pp. 188–9), would have been designed for that effect. But here there is no deflationary last line; it seems absolutely straight. The audience would need to know what it was all about, in particular having familiarity with the story of Jane Shore. Nicholas Rowe's tragedy of 1714 was a very long-lived stage standby, and there were several other plays and also chapbook versions of the story of Edward IV's mistress who was outlawed by Richard III so that she starved to death, no one daring to help her. Lines very like this appeal, addressed to the king himself, appear in two portable theatre manuscript texts belonging to Joe Hodson, one 'An original drama by J. Procter', the MS dated March 26/96, and the other without any surviving mark of authorship but including a pasted-in section from a playbill giving a synopsis of the five acts and (roughly) these lines in print, headed 'Jane Shore's prayer for bread'. We may deduce that the 'prayer' could have been familiar to Lawrence and his audience both from performance and from the bills of this enduring piece. The layout is suggestive of the performance. Lawrence does something similar in 'Potatoes' (pp. 230–1), where the list is physically dragged out on the page. Here dramatic pauses in the performance are signalled by dropping on to the next line.*

> I starve
>> Dost hear
>>> I perish
> For three whole days I've tasted naught to eat
>> The snow has been mine only bed fellow

Oh give me bread if only a morsel
This hunger gnaws my vitals
I am hungry
Dost know the meaning of the word
Oh King – oh man
If thou wert born of woman
Pity! Pity!
Poor
Jane Shore

♣

*The songs collected at the back of the gagbook all belong to the rich
common stock of nineteenth-century popular music. The first is a
children's song, from the tradition of chapbook verses published
since the previous century and taken over by writers like Isaac
Watts as vehicles for moral lessons. Just such a song for children,
called 'The Robin', was written 'by a lady' 'to an old air' and
published in 1857[89] for the benefit of an orphan, to be sold at
ladies' bazaars; it tells of a poor, cold and starving little bird succoured
by a fortunate child from a middle-class family fireside and happily
returned to his nest and his 'little birdies' and wife. The next step
from patronising anthropomorphism was the reappropriation of
such forms for satirical purposes: there is a hint of 'Tit-willow' from*
The Mikado *(1885) in Lawrence's tale of a cockrobin tied to his
perch, as well as a suspicion of the callous edge that makes
Belloc's* Cautionary Tales *(1907) such a memorable twist on the
tradition.*

Song: Poor Little Too

Little tootle dee doo was a dandy *cock Robin*
Who was tied on his perch with a yard of *blue bobbin*[90]

89. By I. Willis of Bond Street, one of a set
of songs for children, n.d., but received by
the British Library 1 January 1858.

90. A bobbin is the spool on which thread
is wound; hence by transference the
thread itself.

His tail was no bigger than that of a flea
Yet he thought it the handsomest tail that could be
Chorus: *Poor little too, poor little too, poor little too,*
                 Poor little toodle dee do.

Now little Toodle dee doo was so proud of his tail
That to show it the better he hopped on a rail
When a large hungry Thomas cat jumped on a wall
And he swallowed Poor Toodle dee doo tail and all
Chorus: *Poor little too etc*

Now to all you young folks, thus my moral appears
Do not be too fond of putting on airs
But whilst you are thinking of this thing and that
Think of Toodle dee doo and the large Thomas cat
Chorus: *Poor little toodle Dee Doo*

❖

Song: Old Joe's Ghost   Tune: Misteltoe Bough

*The second song is squarely in the form of the penny broadside, which
had been enjoying a publication boom since the 1840s. 'Mistletoe
Bough', a well-known and often-parodied Gothic tale by Thomas
Haynes Bailey set by Henry Bishop in the 1830s,[91] lends not only its
melody but also a characteristic 'bob' refrain, the words fitted to it here
being 'Oh poor old Joe'. A long-ago clown named 'Joe' immediately
suggests a reminiscence of the famous Grimaldi; but the donor of the
piece is also called Joe – Joe Gee, with whom Lawrence worked. Many
other songs in popular circulation used such a simple refrain or burden,
which differs from the more pointed chorus of the full-grown music hall
song (see the next item for an example); and the whole composition is
a traditional kind of humour, in which the subject of a mock-panegyric
is made mythic but also monstrous by gross comparison (cf. the
traditional 'Derby Ram', for example). Alternatively, it might derive
the monstrous imagery from minstrelsy: the huge feet, steam-driven*

91. See Derek Scott, *The Singing
Bourgeois (Milton Keynes: Open

University Press, 1989), p. 36, for the
popularity of this song.

*legs, fearfulness, stupidity, grotesque and surreal events such as his
shadow demolishing a church (an interesting choice of building) might
all be part of the caricature stereotype of the negro found in American
minstrel songs. There is a similar double reverberation in the physical
description of 'Blacksmith's Daughter' (p. 203).*

> About ten thousand years ago,
> There lived a clown, and his name was Joe;
> And many of the people say
> His ghost is living to this very day.
> > Oh poor old Joe!
>
> Old Joe was a clown both young and strong,
> His big toe measured ten feet long,
> Such strength did in his muscles lurk
> His shadow once knocked down a church.
> > Oh poor old Joe!
>
> Old Joe one night he dreamed a dream
> That his legs they went by steam;
> And when he awoke he fell in a swoon,
> For he thought his head was a large balloon.
> > Oh poor old Joe!
>
> *(Very slow)*
> Old Joe one night he went up stairs
> His ghost came to him unawares –
> He jumped out of bed,
> Pulled the clothes over his head,
> And when he woke up he found he was dead.
> > Given by J Gee Feb 23/71 Cheltenham

❖

Song: The Fellow That Looks Like Me

*This is a very different piece. In style it is a music hall song, with
the typical pattern of a framing idea in verse one, plus a variable
number of verses following the thread suggested by the catchphrase*

title, but each telling a self-contained story, strung together by a
chorus suitable for audience participation. This is a satisfying
example of such abbreviated narratives, since there is a funny twist
in the tale of the final stanza that makes a fresh joke – the fellow
that looks like him is very old and ugly. It was eagerly appropriated
into the halls. There is an unpublished, presumably lost, song
recorded[92] as sung by George Lashwood, called 'There's Another
Fellow Looks Like Me', as well as two published versions, both
dating from 1876, well after Lawrence wrote out these words. 'The
Fellow the Image of Me', said to be written by Henry Leslie and
composed by Carlo Minasi, has verses like these but by no means
identical, and has lost the twist in the tale; the cover shows two 'coons'
in blackface clown outfits, one smiling and the other disconcerted by
their identical appearance. No singer is named. The sheet music, from
a lesser-known publisher, arrived at the British Museum copyright
library a week before that of 'The Fellow that Looks Like Me',
claimed by G. W. Hunt, and sung by Henri Clark. This version has a
Concanen cover design, is published by Hopwood and Crew, and is
very different in words and tune. So Hunt's song, apparently out of
the music hall top drawer – it is the only version to make it into the
record books – was obviously not his original idea. Lawrence's rather
better verses, written down five years before, and published in a
variant version with a slightly different title while Clark was working
Hunt's song, demonstrate the shameless plundering by the successful
men of the halls of a fruitful popular tradition.

> In sad despair I wander,
> My heart is filled with woe,
> When on my griefs I ponder
> What to do I do not know;
> For cruel fortune on me frowns
> And my trouble seems to be –
> There's another fellow in this town
> That's just the image of me.

92. Kilgarriff, *Sing Us One of the Old*
Songs, p. 247.

Chorus: Oh wouldn't I like to catch him
             Whoever he might be,
             Oh wouldn't I give him partikler hits
             That fellow that looks like me!

With a lady fair I started
Around the docks to go,
But was stopped in the street
By a man who said,
'Pay this Bill you owe.'
In vain I said I knew him not
But he would not let me free,
Till a crowd came round, so the bill I paid
For that fellow that looks like me.
Chorus

The other day whilst walking
Through a narrow street up town,
I was seized by a man in a rage, who said,
'I've caught you Mr Brown!
You know my daughter you have wrong'd.'
Though his girl I ne'er did see –
He beat me till I was black and blue
For that fellow that looks like me.
Chorus

I went to a ball the other night
And was just enjoying the sport,
When a policeman grabbed me by the arm
Saying, 'You're wanted down at Court!
We've missed you twice but this 'ere time
You don't get off so free.'
So I was arrested and locked up
For that fellow that looks like me.
Chorus

245

I was tried next day, found guilty too,
And about to be taken down,
When another policeman then brought in
The right criminal – Mr Brown.
They let me go and locked up him
Oh he was a fright to see –
The ugliest wretch you ever saw,
Was the fellow that looks like me!

❖

Song: Cockles and Mussels

This is an intriguing text. 'Cockles and Mussels' or 'Molly Malone' is part of the modern mythologising of Irish cultural heritage: it has become 'a sort of unofficial anthem of Dublin city', where a statue of a girl and her barrow was erected in 1999, supposedly to commemorate the 300th anniversary of Molly's death. The legend was industriously fostered during the Dublin millennium celebrations in 1988, but is apparently entirely fictitious: assiduous searches have turned up no version of the song in print before 1883, in Cambridge, Massachusetts. The British version, attributed to the Scottish writer James Yorkston and sung by the minor music hall performer Edmund Forman, was published by Francis Brothers and Day in 1884, with acknowledgements to an Edinburgh publisher. But here we have a version of two of its stanzas donated to Lawrence by Joe Gee in Cheltenham in 1871. Francis and Day printed it as a 'comic' song, and its maudlin pathos was presumably meant to be treated as parodic, as no doubt Lawrence would have done. Its chorus may be derived from a street-vendor's cry, but there is nothing more traditional about it than that. Its various appropriations are part of the devious web of profit and fantasy that makes up the publication and reception of popular song.[93]

93. Quotation and information from http://homepage.eirecom.net/ ~seanmurphy/irishmys/molly.htm, consulted 5 June 2004.

1st

Twas in Dublin sweet City
Where the girls are so pretty
Twas there I first met with sweet Molly Malone
As she drew her wheelbarrow
Through the streets wide and narrow
Crying cockles and mussels alive, alive oh!
    Alive, alive oh, alive, alive oh
    Crying Cockles alive alive oh
2nd
She died with the fever
And nothing could save her
So that was the end of Miss Molly Malone
Now her ghost wheels her barrow
Through streets wide and narrow
Crying cockels and mussels alive, alive oh!
    Alive, alive oh, alive, alive oh,
    Crying cockles and mussels, alive alive oh!
              Joe Gee Feb 20th/71 Cheltenham

♣

Song: Learn to Know Thy Self

*The heading asserts that this is sung, but with its studied female rhymes
and its emphasis on a moral message it seems much more like a recitation,
in the style of countless penny readings. It differs from the common run of
such material, perhaps, in the tone of its sermonising, which seems intent
upon reproving the self-righteous and exempts no one.*

Let each man learn to know himself –
To gain that knowledge let him labour,
To improve those failings in himself
That he condemns so in his neighbour.
How lenient on our faults we view
And conscience's voice adeptly smother;
But oh how harshly we review
The self-same evils in another!

247

And if we meet an erring one
Whose deeds are blameable and thoughtless
Consider, ere you cast the stone,
If you yourselves be pure and faultless.
Oh list to that small voice within
Whose whisperings oft make men confounded,
And trumpet not another's sin –
You'd blush deep if your own were sounded.

Or in self judgement if you find
Your deeds to others are superior,
To you has Providence been kind
As you should be to those inferior.
Example sheds a genial ray
Of light that men are apt to borrow;
First improve yourself, today,
And then improve your friend tomorrow.

Newbald[94] Feb 1871 Cheltenham

♣

Song: **Which Is Which** Tune: Johnny Sands

This is another example of the continuum between oral and printed song culture, the circus ring, the halls and the theatre, illustrating the processes of appropriation and profit. The lyrics Lawrence has written out here appeared in print, with minor variations only, in 1865, as 'The Twin Brothers, a song of mystery', a title suggesting a burlesque of the famous melodrama The Corsican Brothers. *The cover advertises it as being sung by Arthur Sketchley esq.; it was published by the London house of Cramer. No writer or composer is named on the title page, but the music itself has the byline 'written by Henry Leigh'. In broadside fashion, Lawrence has 'tune: Jonny Sands', which is not, however, the same as the printed tune; perhaps in the*

---

94. Newbald cannot be traced, but was presumably part of the Cheltenham company, with Joe Gee.

*ring a familiar folk tune with a pronounced beat would be
more suitable than the other. Arthur Sketchley (aka George Rose) and
Henry S. Leigh were collaborators from the theatrical world of the
time: they wrote a burlesque of* Robinson Crusoe *with* W. S. Gilbert
in 1867.

In form and feature, face and limb
I grew so like my brother,
That folks kept taking me for him
And each one for the other.
It puzzled all our kith and kin
It reached a fearful pitch
For one of us was born a twin
But not a soul knew which

Last line repeated

One day to make the matter worse
Before our names got fixed
As we were being washed by nurse
We got completely mixed
So thus you see, by fate's decree,
Or rather nurse's whim,
My brother John got christened me
And I got christened him.

This fatal likeness ever dogged
My footsteps when at school,
For I was often being flogged
For John turned out a fool.
I put this question fruitlessly
To every one I knew –
What would you do if you was me
To prove that you were you?
This close resemblance turned the tide
Of my domestic life,
For somehow my intended bride
Became my brother's wife.
In fact, year after year, the same
Absurd mistakes went on,

And when I died, instead of me
They buried brother John.

Given by Joe Gee
Tottenham Feb 17th/71

❖

Dog Piece

We know from Frowde's memoirs as well as many bills that circuses cheerfully staged full-scale plays if they thought they could avoid prosecution for it under the licensing laws. This cod version of a melodrama with a canine star is, however, a deliberate burlesque of stage drama, and it mocks acting conventions from the local and portable theatres with which audiences would probably have been familiar, rather than circus performance. The relish with which the clown gets up a homemade version of a popular entertainment is irresistibly suggestive of children playing at their favourite television series; and like those games, it relies on the ingrained familiarity and current popularity of conventions such as the 'tragic walk' and titles like 'The Murderer's Doom'. Beneath the special addition of the dog performer, and the physical comedy that this enables the clown to use in his climactic mimed combat with the stuffed star, lies the age-old scenario of the young reprobate and his miserly guardian familiar in dozens of variations from The London Merchant *to* A School for Scandal. *Reminiscence of stage language, as well as stage action, is central to the humour of the piece. It is therefore a childlike but not unsophisticated little play, invoking a whole range of performance experience with a few 'supposed' scenes, a sound effect, a table, a cartoon bag of sawdust and a carrot.*

Are you fond of acting? Then we will have a play, the same as they do it at the theatres. You shall be my uncle and I will be your nephew; what name shall we call it? No, we will call it *The Cruel Uncle* or *The Murderers Doom*[95] – that will be a capital title. Now you must be an old miser very fond of your gold, and I am a spendthrift and when I ask

---

95. Both are titles of actual dramas, *The Cruel Uncle, or The Usurping Monarch* (unknown author, 1743) and *The Tomb of Sigismond; or, The Murderer's Doom*

you for money you must refuse me with scorn, and I am so enraged at your refusal that I murder you – only in fun.

How shall we manage about the scenes?

Never mind, we will suppose them.

But what shall we do about a wardrobe?

Oh, oh! I had forgot the wardrobe – never mind I'll borrow something. *(Fetches morning gown, an old coat and two old hats and puts them on in the ring. Gives ringmaster bag marked 100)*

Take this hundred pounds. (*aside*) Don't let anybody know it's only sawdust.
Joey bring a table and two chairs.[96]
Now let me see how you can walk the stage.

(Buss. ringmaster)

No, that's not the way, my uncle is an old man of seventy, not seventeen, look here this is the way to do it: 'My gold, my gold, they shall not rob me of my gold, I would sooner part with life than my darling gold, who's there! Thieves! You shall not have my gold, no no I will pile it in ashes round my grave spare my hard earned gold' – there, that's the way to do it.

(Ringmaster imitates)

That's it! Now, you sit at the table as though you was counting your gold, and I'll come in.

(unknown author, 1823). The titles, rather than the content, are played with here.

96. It is not clear whether this is a stage direction or an instruction given by the lead clown to an assistant, for whom 'Joey' would be a generic name. The effect is the same in either case.

(Ringmaster takes chair nearest to entrance.
Enter clown – tragic walk.)

There he sits, counting his ill-gotten wealth whilst I am starving for food. I am almost ashamed to ask it – he has given me so often and I have spent it in dissipation. No matter! my wants have made me desperate! I must make the trial – should he refuse, it will cost him his life! His life! No, I could not kill so good, so kind so splendid an uncle! No, I must not think of that. Uncle – dear Uncle –

You here again what want you? Money, I suppose – I have none.

Oh do not say that dear Uncle! My wants have compelled me to ask charity from your hands, I beg of you do not refuse me for the sake of my wife and children.

Where am I to get money from to supply your extravagances? Would you send me to the workhouse?

Oh uncle hear me, on my knees I ask you, 'tis not for myself I sue, but for my wife and children, they are starving, they have not tasted food this three months. Spare me a trifle, say one small part of the 300 pounds from that bag of sawdust. I know I have been a bold bad man, have committed many crimes but remember uncle, 'tis never too late to mend.[97]

Begone! I will not give you one farthing.

Is it so! Farewell uncle, keep your ill-gotten wealth, for so it has been, and may the joy you feel in counting it, be poisoned by the thought of how you gained it. Farewell (*Part aside*) and the next time we meet you shall lay a bleeding corpse at my feet! (*aside*) Now for a sensational rush out. (*Buss. – extravagant exit.*)

97. The title of Charles Reade's very
successful prison novel and drama of 1864.

I am glad he is gone for I was almost afraid of him. Well, after the fatigues of the day I feel quite overcome. I'll set me down and rest a while.

(sits in chair nearest entrance and falls asleep. Clown enters with caution, a lighted candle stuck in the spout of a tin teapot)

By a secret door I have entered unobserved – no one saw me, no, there was no one about – and see my uncle sleeping over his ill-gotten wealth, it must, it shall be mine. Should he awake, this shall strike his heart.

(pulls a carrot from under his coat. Buss.: goes to table and convinces self that the old man is asleep; just as clown raises the carrot to strike dog barks without, clown is frightened drops the candle which goes out. Ring dark. Clown gets behind table; the old man rises in alarm, and says **I thought I heard footsteps, the dog seem'd to warn me of danger, it must be fancy I'll to sleep again.** *Sits in the other chair and sleeps, the clown comes from behind the table and says)*

So – all is quiet! Now to complete my work of robbery and murder.

(seizes the back of chair)

Now uncle your last hour has come – this to your heart!

(as the clown stabs the chair the old man runs out, crying **help, murder, murder,** *the clown takes the opposite side of the ring and exclaims)*

The house is alarmed, where shall I fly for concealment? By that door – it is my only chance!

(As the clown crosses the ring to go out of the door by which his uncle went, he is met by the dummy dog who seizes him by the throat. A terrific struggle with dog and clown all over the ring and scuffle out at ring doors) (The barking of a dog is kept up from the time the clown stabs the chair till the dog comes in the ring)

✣

The Rhino

This song, the final substantive item in the notebook, appears to be copied in a different hand. In form and sentiments, however, it is of a piece with Lawrence's other songs. Exhibiting conventional tropes suggestive of the broadside and/or the drawing-room song, its most interesting feature is its chorus, which looks like a drinking song or possibly a parody of the traditional Tyneside dance number 'The Keel Row'. It shows the clown relying to the very end on the bathetic transformation of romantic sentiments to the bluntly material: 'rhino' is slang for (ready) money, and goes back to the seventeenth century.

I've wandered for weeks all about this famous City
In search of employment, but none can I find –
The wealthy and rich for the poor have no pity,
To want and starvation they are both deaf and blind.
When I had plenty I'd friends all around me,
Who smiled and caressed me wherever I went;
If I called at their house I'd an easy chair found me
It's not the case now my money's all spent.

Chorus
There's nothing like the Rhino, the Rhino, the Rhino!
It makes a man feel fine O, of that there's no doubt
The dearest friend that I know, is Rhino, the Rhino
Then take advice of mine O, and never be without.

When I had plenty I oft was invited
By pals and acquaintances with them to dine,
Who vowed with my company they were delighted,
Oft swore lasting friendship and pledged me in wine.
The publicans smiled as they saw me approaching
Because they well knew I was good for a round,
And said they'd a barrel that just wanted broaching
And whispered, 'That's him lads, he'll soon melt a pound.'
Chorus

At length my bank broke and a pauper it made me,
My friends turned their backs on me when I drew near,
The cash I had lost then they swore they had paid me,
They feasted on wine whilst I could not get beer,
The publicans frowned who were once glad to greet me
And called me a fool for the cash I had spent;
Those I had befriended did with coolness treat me
And told me my folly at ease to repent.
Chorus

Gone are the times when I dressed in the fashion,
Decayed is the broad cloth I once used to wear;
Gone is the carriage I once cut a dash in,
My fine suit of black is worn and threadbare.
But this piece of knowledge experience has taught me –
Things never are bad but they might be much worse.
Believing in friends to this sad plight has brought me:
In future I'll carry my friends in my purse.
Chorus

Bibliography

❖

Anderson, Patricia *When Passion Reigned: Sex and the Victorians* (New York: BasicBooks, 1995).

Assael, Brenda 'The Circus and Respectable Society in Victorian Britain' (PhD thesis, University of Toronto, 1998).

Bosworth, Willan G. *Clowning Through* (London: Heath Cranton, 1937).

Bradby, D. et al., *Performance and Politics in Popular Drama* (Cambridge University Press, 1980).

Bratton, J. S. 'Theatres of War: The Crimea on the London Stage 1854–5' in D. Bradby et al., *Performance and Politics in Popular Drama* (Cambridge University Press, 1980), pp. 119–38.

Bratton, J. S. and Jane Traies *Astley's Amphitheatre* (Cambridge: Chadwyck-Healey, 1980).

Cameron, David Kerr *The English Fair* (Stroud: Sutton Publishing, 1998).

Carmelli, Yoram S. 'Performing the "Real" and "Impossible" in the British Travelling Circus', *Semiotica* 80 – 3/4 (1990), pp. 193–220.

— 'Performance and Family in the World of British Circus', *Semiotica* 85 – 3/4 (1991), pp. 257–89.

Carroll, Lewis *Through the Looking-Glass and What Alice Found There* (1872).

Crane, Harrey *Playbill: A History of the Theatre in the West Country* (Plymouth: Macdonald and Evans, 1980), pp. 117–19.

Curtis, Jnr, L. Perry *Apes and Angels: The Irishman in Victorian Caricature* (Washington & London: Smithsonian Institution Press, 1997).

Dickens, Charles *Memoirs of Joseph Grimaldi*, ed. Richard Findlater (London: Macgibbon and Kee, 1968).

— *Nicholas Nickleby* (1839; Harmondsworth: Penguin Books, 1986).

Disher, Maurice Willson *Clowns and Pantomimes* (London: Constable, 1925).

Earl, John 'The Rotunda: Variety Stage and Socialist Platform,' *Theatre Notebook* 58 (2), (2004), pp. 71–90.

Elder, T. C. *Dan Leno Hys Booke, written by himself: a volume of frivolities.* (London: Greening, 1899).

Featherstone, Ann '"Goose Fair is with us once more" – The journals of Sydney Race, A Nottingham lad', *Nineteenth Century Theatre* 28 (Winter 2000), pp. 161–95.

Findlater, Richard *Joe Grimaldi, His Life and Theatre*, 2nd ed. (Cambridge University Press, 1978).

Fitzroy, David *Charles Keith: The Roving English Clown* (privately printed), 1998.

Forbes, Derek *Illustrated Playbills: A Study with a Reprint of A Descriptive Catalogue of Theatrical Wood Engravings* (1865), (London: The Society for Theatre Research, 2002).

Foster, Frank in collaboration with Willan G. Bosworth *Clowning Through* (London: Heath Cranton, 1937).

French, David *The British Way in Warfare 1688–2000* (London: Unwin Hyman, 1990).

Frost, Thomas *Circus Life and Circus Celebrities* (London: Chatto & Windus, 1881).

Haggar, Walter 'Recollections', *Dock Leaves* (1953), pp. 8–22.

Handelman, Don 'Symbolic Types, The body, And circus', *Semiotica* 85 – 3/4 (1991), pp. 205–25.

Hippisley-Coxe, Antony 'The Lesser-Known Circuses of London', *Theatre Notebook* 13 (3), (Spring 1959), pp. 89–100.

— *A Seat at the Circus* (Connecticut: Archon Books, 1980).

— 'Equestrian Drama and The circus', in D. Bradby et al., *Performance and Politics in Popular Drama* (Cambridge University Press, 1980), pp. 109–18.

Hotten, John Camden *A Dictionary of Modern Slang, Cant, and Vulgar Words* (London: John Camden Hotten, 1859).

Hugill, Beryl *Bring on The Clowns* (London: David & Charles, 1980).

Humphris, Edith and Douglas Sladen *Adam Lindsay Gordon and His Friends* (London: Constable, 1912).

Keith, Charles *Circus Life and Amusements* (Derby: Bewley & Roe, 1879).

Kershaw, Caroline 'Dan Leno: New Evidence on Early Performances and Style', *Nineteenth Century Theatre* 22 (1994), pp. 30–55.

Kilgarriff, Michael *Sing Us One of the Old Songs: A Guide to Popular Song 1860–1920* (Oxford University Press, 1998).

Kwint, Marius 'Astley's Amphitheatre and the Early Circus in Britain, 1768–1830' (PhD thesis, Oxford University, 1995).

Leacroft, Helen and Richard *The Theatre in Leicestershire* (Leicester: Leicestershire Libraries and Information Service, 1986).

Le White, Jack and Peter Ford *Rings and Curtains: Family and Personal Memoirs* (London: Quartet Books, 1992).

Little, W. Kenneth 'The Rhetoric of Romance and the Simulation of Tradition in Circus Clown Performance', *Semiotica* 85 – 3/4 (1991), pp. 227–55.

Macrcady, William Charles *The Journal of William Charles Macrcady, 1832–1851*, abr. and ed. J. C. Trewun (London: Longman, 1967).

Mayhew, Henry *Mayhew's London. Being Selections from London Labour and the London Poor by Henry Mayhew*, ed. Peter Quennell (1851; London: Spring Books, 1969).

Meeres, Frank *A History of Norwich* (Chichester: Phillimore, 1998), p. 106.

Meizel, Martin *Realizations* (Princeton University Press, 1983).

Mellor, Geoff J. *Bradford & District Theatres and Music Halls* (Bradford Local Studies Library).

Osterley, Herman *Shakespeare's Jest Book* (London: John Russell Smith, 1866).

Partlett, David *The Oxford Book of Card Games* (Oxford University Press, 1990).

Partridge, Eric *A Dictionary of the Underworld* (Ware: Wordsworth Editions, 1989).

— *The Penguin Dictionary of Historical Slang*, abr. Jacqueline Simpson (Harmondsworth: Penguin Books, 1972).

Paskman, Dailey *'Gentlemen, be seated!'* (New York: Potter, 1976).

Paterson, Peter *Glimpses of Real Life as Seen in the Theatrical World and in Bohemia: Being the Confessions of Peter Paterson, a Strolling Comedian* (Edinburgh: William P. Nimmo, 1864).

Postlewait, Thomas 'Microhistory and the Writing of Theatre History Today' (unpublished paper for the Historiography Working Group: IFTR/FIRT: Worcester, England, June 2003).

Rattenbury, Arnold *Clowning: An Exhibition Designed and Catalogued by Nottingham Festival 1977 by Arnold Rattenbury* (Nottingham Castle Museum/City of Nottingham Leisure Serivces, 1977).

Remy, Tristan *Clown Scenes*, tr. Bernard Sahlins (Chicago: Ivan R. Dee, 1997).

Rosenfeld, Sybil 'Muster Richardson – "The Great Showman"' in *Western Popular Theatre: The Proceedings of a Symposium Sponsored by the Manchester University Department of Drama*, ed. David Mayer and Kenneth Richards (London: Methuen, 1977), pp. 110–21.

Sanger, 'Lord' George *Seventy Years a Showman* (1908; London: J. M. Dent, 1969).

Saxon, A. H. *The Life and Art of Andrew Ducrow and the Romantic Age of the English Circus* (Connecticut: Archon Books, 1978).

Scott, Derek *The Singing Bourgeois* (Milton Keynes: Open University Press, 1989).

Scott, Harold *The Early Doors: Origins of the Music Hall* (London: Nicholson & Watson, 1946).

Speaight, George *A History of the Circus* (London: Tantivy Press, 1980).

— 'Some Comic Circus Entrees,' *Theatre Notebook* 32 (1978), pp. 24–7.

Stoddart, Helen *Rings of Desire: Circus History and Representation.* (Manchester University Press, 2000).

Stroud, Nell *Josser: The Secret Life of a Circus Girl* (London: Virago, 1999).

Taylor, George *Players and Performances in the Victorian Theatre* (Manchester University Press, 1989).

Teasdale, Harvey *The Life and Adventures of Harvey Teasdale the Converted Clown and Man Monkey, Written by himself* (Sheffield, 1870).

Toulmin, Vanessa *Pleasurelands: All the Fun of the Fair* (Sheffield: National Fairground Archive/The Projection Box, 2003).

Towsen, John H. *Clowns* (New York: Hawthorn Books, 1976).

Traies, Jane *Fairbooths and Fit-ups* (Cambridge: Chadwyck-Healey, 1980).

Turner, John 'Hengler's Circus and Gloucestershire', *Gloucester History*, no. 3 (1989).

— *Historical Hengler's Circus*, 5 vols. (Liverpool: Lingdales Press, 1989).

— 'Frowde the Proud – The Clown Evangelist', *Gloucestershire History* (1994), pp. 9–14.

— *Victorian Arena: The Performers. A Dictionary of British Circus Biography*, 2 vols. (Formby: Lingdales Press, 1995), I.

— *Victorian Arena: The Performers. A Dictionary of British Circus Biography*, 2 vols. (Formby: Lingdales Press, 2000), II.

— 'Pablo Fanque, Black Circus Proprietor' in *Black Victorians, Black Victoriana*, ed. Gretchen Holbrook Gerzina (New Brunswick: Rutgers University Press, 2003), pp. 20–38.

Wallett, W. F. *The Public Life of W. F. Wallett, the Queen's Jester: An Autobiography Of Forty Years' Professional Experience & Travels in the United Kingdom, the United States of America (inc. California), Canada, South America, Mexico, the West Indies, etc.*, ed. John Luntley (London & Derby: Bemrose & Sons, 1884).

Wallis, Alfred *Some Reminiscences of Old Derby. No.17* (bound volume of Newspaper Cuttings, Derby Local Studies Library).

Wild, Samuel *The Original, Complete and Only Authentic Story of Old Wild's*, ed. 'Trim' (1888; London: Society for Theatre Research, 1989).

Wiles, David *Shakespeare's Clown* (Cambridge University Press, 1987).

— *A Short History of Western Performance Space* (Cambridge University Press, 2003).

Wilson, A. N. *The Victorians* (London: Arrow, 2003).

❖

Index

❖

Bedford, Paul 141, 142, 143
Beeton, Mrs
  Everyday Cookery 227 n.68
Belfast
  Alhambra Music Hall 207
Belloc, Hilaire
  Cautionary Tales (1907) 241
Belper 15
Bentley, Richard 34
Bibb, Mr and Mrs 143
Birmingham 29, 63, 79, 80, 81,
    122 n.191
  Bull Ring 64
Bishop, Henry 242
Blackdimond, North Wales 14
blackface minstrelsy, *see also* songs,
    minstrel 150, 152, 244
  Christie minstrels 201 n.45
Blackpool 24
Blanchard 6
Blanchard, L. 207
Blight's Dogs and Monkeys Show 14
Blizard, Mr (architect) 23, 26, 127
Boswell, James (Shakespearean clown)
    188, 240
Bourne, Harry 123
Boxing booth 116
Boyle, Ann *see* Nunn, Mr and Mrs
Boyle, Captain 140
Bradbury, Robert 6
Bradford 22, 23 n.33, 99, 100, 138, 140
  Bermondsey Hotel 140 n.239
  London Music Hall 140 n.239
  Oddfellows' Hall, Thornton Road
    140 n.235
  Sun Inn, Ivegate 138
Bridges, Mr and Mrs Anthony O'Neil
    141
Bridges, Selim (equestrian) 67, 69
Brighton 71, 74, 78
Bristow, James 100
Broadfoot, William 47, 63–7, 101, 103
Broadsides 150, 152
Broom, Johnny 78
Buckley's Performing Birds 18
Buckstone, John Baldwin 77,
    119 n.189
Burnett's 18

Cambridge 116
Cambridge, Massachusetts 246
Canada
  Fenian activity in 207
capital punishment 169
  Parliamentary Select Committee on
    169 n.13
card games *see names of individual
    games*
Carey, Henry 167
Carl Manges' Royal Pavilion Portable
    Theatre 32
Carpenter, J. 208
Carroll, Lewis
  'The Walrus and the Carpenter'
    179 n.24
Cassidy, Jim 97, 99
Catnach 130 n.209, 152
Chamberlain, Rev. G. 137
Charity Organisation Society
    231 n.78
Chart (Chartre), Miss (equestrienne)
    47, 60
Cheltenham 23, 26, 62, 105, 109,
    126 n.199, 131, 153, 243, 246,
    247, 248
  Claren Street 127
  Clarence Boarding House
    127 n.201
  The Fleece 128
  St Matthew's Church 127 n.201
  Cheltenham Looker-On 127 n.203,
    130 n.209, 131 n.211
Chester 14, 109, 118, 132, 135, 136,
    137 n.225
  Minshull and Hughes, Eastgate
    Row 136
  The Roodee 118
Chester-le-Street 96
(John) Chittock's Dog and Monkey
    Circus 14
cholera 73, 76
Chorley 25 n.42
Cibber, Colley 205
circus 153
  see also animals, horses, *individual
    circus companies, individual
    towns*